MANAGING LARGE SYSTEMS
ORGANIZATIONS FOR THE FUTURE

LEONARD R. SAYLES
MARGARET K. CHANDLER
Graduate School of Business
Columbia University

HARPER & ROW, PUBLISHERS
New York, Evanston, San Francisco, London

Those who carry on great public schemes must be proof against the most fatiguing delays, the most mortifying disappointments, the most shocking insults, and worst of all the presumptuous judgments of the ignorant upon their designs.

—Edmund Burke

In advanced nations, the great organizations—of government, of industry, of education, of research, of communications . . . become the units of social energy.

—Arthur M. Schlesinger, Jr.

MANAGING LARGE SYSTEMS: Organizations for the Future
Copyright © 1971 by Leonard R. Sayles and Margaret K. Chandler

STANDARD BOOK NUMBER: 06-013811-4

LIBRARY OF CONGRESS CATALOG CARD NUMBER: 77-158542

To James E. Webb
Dedicated public executive and management scholar

CONTENTS

FOREWORD

James E. Webb

In 1961, when I agreed to serve as Administrator of the National Aeronautics and Space Administration, I little suspected that the emerging potential of rocket technology, added to our know-how in aeronautics, would almost immediately set in motion through NASA an organized effort involving over eighty nations, more than four hundred thousand people, twenty thousand industrial units, and two hundred universities. The previously limited capabilities of vehicles and systems operated on land, on the ocean, or in the air, gave way to concepts based on certain unlimited capabilities of rocket launched and controlled systems operated in space. I joined with key leaders in government, industry, distinguished institutions and academies to strive toward bringing practically every scientific and engineering discipline into a massive team effort that would within a decade accomplish such spectacular results as landing men on the moon and sending spacecraft to Mars and Venus.

☐ We participated in building administrative patterns that would test to the limit the best of available theory and practice in almost every area of management and of executive leadership.

☐ President John F. Kennedy told me that he felt that the NASA Administrator should be not a scientist or an engineer but someone familiar with the development and implementation of high-level national and international policy. To him, the opening of the limitless regions of space to man and machines meant pioneering on a new frontier—a "New Ocean" on which we must learn to sail.

☐ Congress was pressing for successes to erase the image of "falling behind the Russians" in space, an image which had been improving since Sputnik. Some scientists wanted to use rockets in reaching outward into space. Others were deeply concerned about the costs, risks, and value of sending men out beyond the earth's atmosphere. There was great excitement. Would the use of rockets enable us to discover life elsewhere in the solar system?

James E. Webb served as the Administrator of the National Aeronautics and Space Administration from 1961 to 1968. He was formerly Undersecretary of the Treasury, Undersecretary of State, and Director of the Bureau of the Budget. He has also held executive posts in industry and currently serves as a director of several large corporations. He was active in founding the National Academy of Public Administration and has sought to stimulate the study of management in universities and in government.

☐ In basic terms, scientists felt that the rocket would increase their knowledge of the universe. Engineers saw a tremendous challenge in the advance in technology required for efficient use of rockets. Military leaders feared that the rocket would shift the technological balance of power and permanently affect our nation's military posture. Thoughtful diplomats saw the prestige of the United States and the hoped-for emergence of stabilizing forces in international relations challenged by our poor showing in space. It was evident that many of the concepts associated with national sovereignty would have to give way to an advancing technology that knew no national boundaries.

☐ Leonard Sayles and Margaret Chandler have been able to identify and describe the extraordinarily important and elusive managerial requirements imposed by the nature of large-scale endeavors. They document the extent to which leadership must go to assure the highest degree of personal involvement and commitment both to the goals of the effort and to continuing effective working relationships with their colleagues.

☐ If the findings documented in *Managing Large Systems* had been available in 1961 to the senior management group in NASA—Dr. Hugh Dryden, Dr. Robert Seamans and myself —I am sure we could have used them to great advantage.

☐ Some time ago I stated the requirements placed on our executives in these words:

. . . Because of its extent and scale, the large endeavor is particularly subject to unpredictable difficulties and unanticipated opportunities. The main task of leadership is one of continually organizing and reorganizing, directing and redirecting, diverse human and material resources and complex activities under conditions that always contain elements of uncertainty. The process of management in the large-scale endeavor becomes that of fusing at many levels a large number of forces, some countervailing, into a cohesive but essentially unstable whole and keeping it in motion in a desired direction.

☐ Executives within such a large-scale endeavor thus have to work under unusual circumstances and in unusual ways. They cannot function in accord with the simplified scheme of traditional enterprises. Take, for example, such traditional principles as "well defined areas of authority and responsibility," "unity of command," "one man, one boss," "unity of direction," "one objective, one plan," "compensation commensurate with contribution," "centralized operations," the "Scalar" unbroken line of command, "a place for everything and everyone, and everything and everyone in its place," or "stability of tenure, no unnecessary turnover."

Such principles might work well for the static organization, but more is needed for the dynamism required in a successful large-scale endeavor. The executive trained only in such traditional principles, able to operate only in accord with them and uncomfortable in their absence, would be of little use and could expect little satisfaction in a large complex endeavor. So too would the executive who has to be psychologically coddled in the fashion that the participative school of management advocates.

☐ In the large-scale endeavor the man himself must also be unusual; he must be knowledgeable in sound management doctrine and practice, but able to do a job without an exact definition of what it is or how it should be done; a man who can work effectively when lines of command crisscross and move in several directions rather than straight up and down; one who can adjust to, and be himself, several bosses at the same time; one who can work effectively in an unstable environment and can live with uncertainty and a high degree of personal insecurity; one willing to work for less of a monetary reward than he could insist on elsewhere; one who can blend public and private interests in organized participation to the benefit of both.

☐ More than anything else the executives within a large-scale endeavor must be able, one by one and all together, to see and to understand the totality of the job that the endeavor is designed to do. Each must see and understand the relationship of his evolving and changing individual assignment, and of the functions and people involved in that assignment, to the whole job and its requirements. This requires more than knowing his place and his responsibilities within the organization itself or knowing the organization "upside down." It requires an awareness of the relationship between the total job as it exists at that time and his own particular job within the total framework, including the elements of the environment that are so much a part of the total.*

☐ This important and elusive management requirement is little understood. Few of our national leaders have a clear understanding of the complex nature of the care, feeding, and effective utilization of large-scale efforts such as NASA. Administrators dependent on political support cannot count on their understanding the very complex nature of an organization that can press forward with massive investments in advanced areas of development and progress toward national goals. The absolute need for an administrative framework within which large numbers of professional workers put aside their personal aims and invest almost unlimited energy in relating their skilled know-how to others who are highly skilled in other fields, is hard to state in precise terms. This

* James E. Webb, *Space Age Management,* New York, McGraw-Hill, 1969, pp. 135–137.

need is particularly acute in such new and difficult areas as high-performance aircraft and spacecraft. It is equally acute in efforts directed toward solving urban and environmental problems.

☐ In *Managing Large Systems,* Dr. Sayles and Dr. Chandler lay the groundwork for a large measure of improvement in the understanding needed by those who must plan, obtain support for, and manage future large public and private organized efforts. They have described pioneering research which required their personal involvement in many NASA decisions on a real time basis. It is my earnest hope that their findings will encourage other scholars to respond to this challenge.

☐ In my last conversation with him, about two weeks before his death, President Kennedy expressed appreciation for what NASA had accomplished and then said, "I don't know how you do it." A large measure of NASA's success came from the fact that many of our political leaders were confident that NASA's administrators both in Washington and in the field centers knew best how to get the work done. They had much confidence also in the role of the industrial and university units that played such a vital role.

☐ A tremendous personal effort was made by the men and women within NASA to overcome all obstacles and deliver what was needed and to press forward to the highest possible levels of accomplishment. Sayles and Chandler have recorded the management decisions and processes that produced this result and have described the response of highly trained professional personnel.

☐ *Managing Large Systems* provides fresh insight into situations where, even with the best of systems engineering and carefully planned organizational structure, an almost unbelievable amount of energy must be invested in making the systems work—to interpersonal bargaining and "buy-off" sessions when the outcome of a major launch is at issue. The nature of much of NASA's confidence-building activity is carefully set down. Sayles and Chandler devoted four years to detailed observation of the participants, the organizational patterns, and the substance of the work-flow. They were given great freedom to pursue their work. They were free to publish their findings. They were the beneficiaries of NASA's policy of opening its records to responsible scholars and inviting them to participate in intimate high-level sessions.

☐ The nature of large technology programs is complex. At NASA the name of the game is uncertainty, and a great deal of time and effort is devoted to influencing highly trained professionals to work as a team for larger goals. Technological programs are implemented through complex social networks.

☐ There is a tendency to discount the relevance of management experiences in science and technology to the social and political problems of our nation or the economic problems of business. One of the most important contributions of this pioneering study is that it lessens, if not eliminates, this distinction.

☐ Dr. Sayles and Dr. Chandler took the leadership in implementing this major research project. Rather than endeavoring to confirm one tenet or another of some current theories, they devoted several years to pursuing a basic anthropological-type study on the nature of these new organizations that were established to achieve difficult goals in an uncertain, turbulent environment. Their findings represent a very new view of management and organization which should have a significant impact both on students of management and on future generations of administrators.

PREFACE

Most Americans, not just executives and students of organization, have grown accustomed to both hearing and saying that their world is becoming more complex, more interdependent, more challenging (and more frustrating) almost daily. To paraphrase a popular title, it is not "future shock" but everyday shock to which we refer. And yet there is always the possibility that a most functional human capability, accommodation and adaptation, weakens our ability to perceive change and differences. And reference to change then becomes just another part of conventional wisdom.

☐ Certainly in the prescriptions one reads and hears for "good" management and "sound" organization, it often appears that authors are still talking about the simple production shop that attracted Frederick Taylor or one of Max Weber's government bureaus. But modern organizations are indeed strikingly different from these primitive structures, and it is not difficult to believe that they require significant innovations both in styles of management and in organization structure.

☐ One of the most profoundly complex and successful of our contemporary organizations is the National Aeronautics and Space Administration. Prior to the moon landing, its total system included thousands of public and private organizations and hundreds of thousands of employees, many of whom were highly trained professionals encompassing diverse disciplines and together facing an awesome task.

☐ As social scientists we were profoundly grateful for the opportunity provided by the then Administrator of NASA, Mr. James Webb, to have totally free and unencumbered access to the entire organization, including attendance at a wide variety of both top- and bottom-level meetings in Washington, at various NASA Centers, and opportunities to visit and observe ongoing operations at contractor sites. The extraordinary openness of NASA, its welcoming of such research, is by no means a typical research experience. In part, we are certain, it reflects Mr. Webb's own interest in developing the field of professional management and his conception of public service and responsibility. Mr. Webb's unstinting support and encouragement allowed us to interview just about anyone in the system, and we did talk with more than a thousand managers and technical personnel, as well as observe them coping with critical problems and painful choices.

☐ In addition, we have had the opportunity to compare the administrative process we observed within NASA with a number of Japanese and British programs. We have also sought to relate our findings to other published research on the management of complex systems.

☐ Throughout, our emphasis has been on the actual behavior of managers and professionals engaged in problem solving, decision-making, and negotiations. As students of organization we are aware of the dearth of studies that concentrate on *how* managerial work is done, in contrast to the plethora of management publications emphasizing *what* managers *should do.* Thus, we have sought to examine the planning process, integration and control systems, and project management by identifying the recurring patterns of interaction and human behavior associated with the effective performance of these managerial functions in a truly complex organizational system.

☐ For both business and the public arena, for economic and urban affairs, there is increasing concentration on the "policy sciences." Regrettably, these often emphasize the decisions themselves rather than the organizational process through which effective decisions are reached. Surely, as we move more toward larger and more complex organizational systems that encompass business-government interfaces, there needs to be more attention given to the management side of such systems. While it is easy to say that management is a profession, the field of management consistently takes a back seat to the more easily quantified or more academically respectable professions. In the process, the solutions to our urban ills and new economic challenges are sought in engineering (and the newer computer sciences), political science, economics, and law. While we would not have the temerity to ignore these, we hope that this work serves to facilitate the professionalization of management, a critical and oft neglected component in policy analysis.

☐ Therefore, the objective of this volume is to review and reconstruct the traditional management functions in the context of complex systems: planning, organizing, staffing, directing, controlling. . . . To do so we have also sought to bring together the formerly separate strands of management and management science (including computer-based information systems) and to interweave both with organizational behavior.

☐ Our study required four years of intensive field work. Rather than developing questionnaires in our offices which would be administered by assistants or graduate students, we acted as our own field staff. Working as anthropologists, we evolved concepts inductively from our observations rather than deductively from established doctrine.

□ Our colleague, Professor James Kuhn, carried out most of the work with university-based scientists and the NASA science program. He wrote the original drafts of Chapters 3 and 11, and we are indebted to him for his superb field work, enormous energy, and unique insights into the organizational problems surrounding the integration of science and scientists into ongoing organizational processes. Professor Robert Guest of Dartmouth was most helpful in undertaking a case study for us at the Marshall Space Flight Center that validated many of Kuhn's findings.

□ A major share of the field research was conducted under the auspices of the National Academy of Sciences, and John S. Coleman, the Academy's Executive Officer, was consistently helpful and exemplified uncommonly skillful administration of science. Dr. Guyford H. Stever, President of Carnegie-Mellon University, served as Chairman of the Academy-appointed advisory committee for our study, and they were most helpful at the early stages of our research.

□ The Ford Foundation generously provided a grant to cover the costs of the comparative international research. While these studies are still continuing, preliminary findings on the impact of culture on the management of complex systems are incorporated into the text, particularly in Chapter 6. Mrs. Mariam Chamberlain of the Ford Foundation has given generously of her time and wisdom in helping launch this phase of our research program.

□ Any of our readers who has undertaken to learn about contemporary organizations by living within them for a period knows the extent of our debt to managers within NASA, in aerospace contractor firms, in universities, and in government agencies and private companies located overseas. It is modest and inadequate acknowledgment to simply state the magnitude of our debt and the sincerity of our appreciation. As representatives of all of those we cannot thank personally, we express our gratitude to Francis Smith, NASA's Assistant Administrator for University Affairs, and Harry Finger, now Assistant Secretary for Research and Technology, Housing and Urban Development. Ronald Phillips, at NASA Headquarters, was a patient, sophisticated guide in helping us see some of the intricacies of the federal government.

□ Our knowledge of the public arena was broadened immensely by the opportunity to view the operations of the criminal justice system through the eyes of Ernest Friesen,

Jr., who established and became the first director of the Institute for Court Management. In a similar fashion, Dr. Alfred Freedman, Chairman of the Department of Psychiatry, New York Medical College, provided a wealth of experience in the operation of community mental health programs.

□ Professor George Strauss of the University of California, Berkeley, assumed the heavy burden of reading and criticizing an early draft of our manuscript, and we hope at least a small number of his characteristically high standards were applied to the later drafts.

□ Mrs. Jean Raymond in Washington and Mrs. Nancy Pearce at Cape Kennedy coordinated many of our research appointments and eliminated much of the drudgery of field work.

□ A Preface ought to allow for more personal insights than the body of the text. In concluding the book we were concerned that the reader and the student might too easily forget a critical element. The body of our material deals with administrative problems and conflicts. Social scientists seek to ferret these out as a means of comprehending a system, because conflict highlights those basic parameters which may well be hidden in more perfected routines. Further, the mark of a truly effective organization is its ability to surmount problems and difficulties; anyone can exist in a utopia (well, almost anybody). NASA has had profoundly challenging problems; the very nature of its awesome objectives assured that—and it was further assured by the ability of the world to monitor its progress, since these were measurable objectives. We would not want the reader to forget that NASA has been successful, indeed very successful, in overcoming the problems inherent in the scale and challenge of its assignments. Because of that success and managerial competence, which *Fortune* magazine prophesized may be NASA's greatest contribution to a better world, we are most grateful of all for the unique privilege accorded us to study and observe first-hand the U.S. space program.*

Leonard R. Sayles
Margaret K. Chandler

* Tom Alexander, "The Unexpected Payoff of Project Apollo," *Fortune*, June 1969, p. 114.

THE NEW ORGANIZATION:
FROM HERE TO TRANQUILITY

ONE

Highly developed, modern, technologically based societies look to the future. Change, progress, and planning are integral parts of our entire way of life and crucial to our managerial processes. This book emphasizes the future, a future that will be characterized by large engineering systems matched by, and reflected in, large organizational systems. As we shall see, such systems will involve both management problems and opportunities for human expression that dwarf what we encounter in the more routinized production organizations that are the prototypes for nearly all contemporary management theory and practice.

□ But this is not a book of speculations and forecasts, and the authors are not "futurists" (in part because we are painfully aware of the historical box score on prediction and prophecy). Our society already has created a number of large organizational systems to accomplish unusually challenging goals. TVA, the Manhattan Project, and NASA are among several that come easily to mind; there are many more. We intend, then, to look at actual institutions, not hypothetical ones. Our purpose is to examine the distinctive management and organizational challenges associated with large systems.[1]

NEW SOCIAL PROBLEMS, NEW FORMS OF ORGANIZATION

□ An increasing number of responsible observers view the coming decade as one that will require our society to come to terms with an imposing array of problems. Rebuilding the decayed "cores" of our cities, improving medical care, controlling pollution, increasing popular sensitivity to ecological balance, and developing more convenient and safer ground and air transportation are but a few of the objectives, staggering in terms of cost and effort, now on the horizon.

[1] As readers of the Preface will be aware, much of our analysis has been derived from an intensive three-year exploration of NASA, particularly the non-Apollo portions, supplemented by field work in other aerospace organizations in the United States, Western Europe and Japan and in several other types of large projects, including community mental health and atomic energy.

☐ There is a corresponding tendency to view the solutions to these problems in rather simplistic, primarily financial, terms—for example, in terms of shifting resources from private (selfish) consumption to public (selfless) capital or developing greater citizen awareness of the awesomeness of these problems and the costs of further neglect.

☐ Yet, if we take the time to look at any one or all of the actual or potential new programs in these areas, we find that they share a number of characteristics which would suggest that implementation is going to involve a good deal more than willing it so by votes or dollars, or even a selfless consensus that revises national priorities (although we are not suggesting that those factors are irrelevant). First, all these objectives imply the collaboration of a relatively large number of organizations, and it would appear that these will be a mixture of public and private institutions. An obvious characteristic of modern society is ever increasing interdependency; little can be changed without affecting a wide array of institutions, and many new developments depend upon close, collaborative, and integrated activities that criss-cross organizational boundaries and the dividing line between the public and private sectors. For example, improving safety in air transportation involves the development of new avionics and air transport equipment, perhaps by government research centers working with private industry. This equipment will have to be produced by private companies, certified by the Federal Aviation Agency, accepted by commercial airlines, and fitted into the existing airport and navigation-communication systems, which are regulated by local authorities and by national and international agencies.

☐ While we shall not be at great pains to document the point, it would appear that an increasing number of purely private ventures, because of their size, their capital requirements, and their technological uncertainties, require collaborative "federations" as well. When the Columbia Broadcasting System recently sought to exploit a new technique for taping television programs (a technique that can be viewer controlled), it joined forces with U.S. and foreign electronics and film manufacturers as well as with other internationally based mass-media producers and distributors.

☐ If one looks at urban redevelopment, exactly the same network appears. New technology, privately or publicly sponsored, must be coordinated with the requirements of builders and developers, the massive array of government agencies, tenants, and landlords, and the financial institutions that will risk the capital. But our point is more than the multiplicity of involved organizations; it is the need for some common direction, some real federation or confederation that can act in concert.

□ Partly because of the American penchant for organization, there is a temptation to ignore the possibility of confederation and to believe that every new social problem must be handled by a totally new social organization. To be sure, it is always easier to start afresh than to modify existing programs, but the result is a high cost in obsolete but persisting organizations and needless social complexity.[2]

Uncertain Technology: Uncertain Management

□ A second element common to many large programs is uncertain technology. Whether we are talking about new construction methods, electronic devices, spacecraft, or pollution-control methods, there are numerous uncertainties that derive from inadequate knowledge of the basic technology or its specific implementation. Further, these programs are often *one-of-a-kind efforts:* building a science-oriented spacecraft, developing new collision-avoidance and blind-landing aircraft control devices, or what-have-you. At most there may be a very short "production run"; as a result, there is no opportunity to develop finely tuned routines amenable to the strictures of scientific management. Worse yet, many, if not most, of the problems have no clear-cut solutions. Largely because of the number of organizational units involved, as well as the uncertainties and risks, "the problems and processes involved can be typified as 'messy'; solutions must be 'invented' on the spot that are not simply derived from scientific and engineering principles."[3]

□ Traditionally, ours is an optimistic culture. Although faith in our omnipotence has been shaken by profound social unrest, American technological pragmatism is unchallenged. Confidence in the expertness with which we can move from research through development to implementation, even

[2] Parenthetically, one can observe the same phenomenon within business organizations. A new problem encourages the creation of a new department or the hiring of a new expert rather than an effort to modify existing managerial jobs to include the instability that has been identified.

[3] George Kozmetsky, "Education as an Information System" in *The Management of Information and Knowledge,* Committee on Science and Astronautics U.S. House of Representatives, Washington, D.C., Government Printing Office, 1970, p. 96.

when the organizational and engineering obstacles are staggering, has resulted in a growing demand that this engineering-management "know how" be redirected toward solving the growing problem of American urban life.

☐ Such understandable enthusiasm and confidence, both in the transferability of technology and in our ability to solve any problem "we put our minds and backs to," need some tempering. First, there is an impressive and growing list of failures in large-scale advanced-technology programs. Witness the observation of Senator Proxmire, who, after reviewing Budget Bureau data, concluded:

. . . In the procurement of some 2 dozen major weapons systems costing tens of billions of dollars during the nineteen-fifties and sixties, the performance standards of the electronic systems of these weapons seldom meet the specifications established for them. . . . Of 11 major weapons systems begun during the nineteen-sixties, only two electronic components performed up to expected standard. . . . A majority performed at a level of 25 per cent or less than the standards and specifications set for them.[4]

☐ Many of these failures involved military programs for new planes, tanks, helicopters, missiles, rifles, and the like; but there has also been an impressive number of failures in nonmilitary projects in recent years—for example, in perfecting high-speed trains, in the fabrication of high-pressure nuclear vessels, in the manufacture of "heavy water," and in advanced electronics and construction projects.

☐ A second point, perhaps closely related to the first, is that we probably know less than we think we do about the management process by which new technology is converted into operating systems. It is all too easy to assume that American know-how plus large doses of impersonal rationality will almost mechanically produce results. Thus there is cynicism concerning the recent triumphs in space. A national news magazine argued,

The [Apollo] moonshot, in short, was a triumph of reason and technology, and it came at a time when large numbers of young people had turned in rebellion against both. Technology seemed too methodical, reason too stultifying of human spontaneity. . .[5]

[4] *National Priorities,* Washington, D.C., Public Affairs Press, 1969, pp. 126–127.

[5] *Newsweek,* December 29, 1969, p. 18.

☐ This statement is ironic indeed. It implies that (1) we know very well how to manage such large programs, (2) it is not very difficult anyhow, and (3) engineering and science bear little relevance to the social and political spheres of our society. We are suggesting, of course, that all three implications are wrong.

The Trend Toward Bigness and "Federal" Organizations

☐ The trend toward bigness is not, as some would believe, simply an extension of man's greed and folly or history's inexorable repetition of the dinosaur syndrome. It is related to the older trends of economies of scale (bigger chemical plants are more efficient than smaller ones) and growth of world markets. But size is also a product of some relatively new trends, like those outlined above. Newer technologies may require the collaboration of many organizations because of the enormity of the problems that must be solved. The development of nuclear energy, viable commercial communication satellites, and space flight are all beyond the capacities of any single industrial organization or government bureau.

☐ Our traditional predisposition to fear goliaths is easily aroused, but there are indications that the organizations of the future will be structured quite differently from the stereotype corporation of today. For many the idealized frontier and agrarian spirit are suffocated by a rigid hierarchy, in which commands flow down and reports up while the individual is confined in a narrow vertical channel. The large organizations of the future cannot be constructed in such a fashion; there will be too many diverse and far-flung subunits that owe only modest loyalty to the core. NASA, the European atomic energy "community," and COMSAT (the consortium that constructs and operates international communication satellites) already demonstrate a new federalism in which the parts have some independence and are perhaps more demanding. The core of such endeavors is made up of the one or several sponsors or clients, closely surrounded by their major contractors, followed at a somewhat greater distance by subcontractors and still farther by advisors, actual or potential beneficiaries, auditors, licensors or controllers, and many others.

☐ A major paradox suggested by the NASA data is that effectiveness in development programs requires a high order of responsible autonomy and the opportunity to innovate and even to change plans. But large-scale projects with the demanding quality and performance requirements of a space program also require unbelievably precise integration and coordination among the parts. While these "parts" (experiments, launch vehicles, spacecraft and their subsystems) are designed and fabricated in a number of separately organized and directed institutions, with perhaps incompatible objectives, they must intermesh perfectly. Thus a wide array of intellectual and economic commitments must be simultaneously focused on a very explicit task without destroying the motivations that release energy and commitment.

☐ One result of this paradox is the role of personal contact in a highly technical milieu—the amount of human interaction and exchange required and the extent to which impersonal methods of communication fail to substitute for direct confrontation.

☐ Our system of government almost guarantees organizational complexity because of the overlapping jurisdictions of local (community, county, precinct, school-district, ward) state, and federal agencies. Introduce a new medical program, engage in urban redevelopment or massive flood-control and water-power (TVA) programs and one comes to grips with not only these "publics" but the countless private and semiprivate organizations that have, or seek, the right to be heard. The *New York Times* noted, for example, that "300 different local, state, Federal and private groups . . . try to deal with social problems in the Milwaukee area."[6] NASA, at its peak in the mid-1960s, sought contributions from 20,000 different organizations!

☐ While there may be a number of permanent operations in such projects, much of the work is temporary. People get shifted around and plans get changed in an environment quite different from the tiresome monotony bemoaned by so many in traditional institutions. Projects, task forces, and temporary "teams" also mean that individuals have multiple organizational "homes." A scientist may be part of a university, responsible for the design and testing of an experiment to be flown by a NASA spacecraft, serving as a consultant to an industrial contractor that builds equipment for the agency, and a member of an advisory board that helps shape future science policy for NASA and other government agencies.

[6] March 24, 1968, p. 28.

Management in "Federal" Organizations

☐ And then there is the matter of authority, the control of one individual by another, the power to reward and punish. As we have already noted, "federal" organizations are populated by highly trained, self-sufficient, and reasonably contentious professionals and technicians who demand the right to be heard. Many of the critical contributions must be made by outsiders. Individual managers must learn the subtle skills involved in control at a distance, in penetrating outside organizations to assess what is happening and in influencing them so as to gain timely responsiveness. These "federal" organizations train their administrators to shift back and forth from structural constraints—assuring conformity without administrative intervention—to direct leadership. Short-run improvisations overlay long-run strategies. In fact, improvisation and spontaneity, the presumed absence of which in modern technology is so decried, turn out to be critical managerial skills.

☐ Even planning is a rather different function in these large developmental systems where uncertainties predominate. Traditionally, managers are taught to identify their ultimate ends and purposes, set objectives that will help attain these ends, and then develop operational plans. Unfortunately, this comforting and logical sequence gets upset in the real world of large systems. Clear objectives often disguise conflicting purposes reflecting the divergencies among the temporarily allied groups in the federation. Existing operational techniques often seek objectives that they can implement, rather than the other way around. Planning turns out to be a dynamic, iterative process. This inevitably disperses authority, since a small group of expert, high-level "planners" cannot define strategy.

☐ In traditional management theory administrators are expected to collect and weigh facts and probabilities, make an optimal decision and see that it is carried out. In large-scale development projects, a clear sequence of action is not possible because of their *extended duration,* the many technical unknowns, the changing balance of power among interest groups, the continual discovery of new "facts," and constantly changing constraints and pressures. Thus an administrative system must be designed that allows recommitment, reassessment, and redirection without permitting the other extremes of never-ending "improvements" or perpetual excuses for missing budgets and schedules.

INTEGRATING THE TOTAL SYSTEM

☐ One conclusion is clear: The communications requirements in these projects are overwhelming compared to
those of more traditional manufacturing processes. The impact of a newly identified problem or discovery or the search
for the source of an unexplained difficulty demands that a
number of people in a variety of organizations be involved
almost simultaneously. Programmed and computerized information and retrieval systems can handle only routine
situations and are most useful in freeing the human participants to interact on more problematic levels.

☐ Another aspect of the myth of our technical invincibility
concerns the ease and directness with which these large
programs move from new ideas and concepts to the development of hardware and its usage. It is assumed that the
problems are simply and directly solved by rational analysis
when, in fact, a great deal of interplay and negotiation may
be necessary.

☐ Regularization, routinization, and systematization are at
the heart of traditional management practice. In fact, it is the
effort to regularize—to stabilize—which distinguishes the
manager's art from that of other professionals.[7] In large, one-
of-a-kind efforts there can be no perfection of routine.

☐ In addition, there are always the organizational upheavals
associated with shifting from conception to design to development to testing and early operations. This cycle not
only changes the numbers and orientation of people that
must be attracted, absorbed, and released, but also the mix
of managerial, professional, technical, and service personnel.

The Not-So-Clean Interface

☐ Many have argued that one of the distinctive aspects of
the management of these large-scale endeavors is the
formal attention paid to their *system* characteristics. Unlike
their predecessors, the managers and engineers in advanced technology are concerned with "systems"; they concentrate on the interfaces, the interrelationships among the
components. Yet engineering systems too turn out to be
straightforward design problems only in the most superficial
sense. Nuclear power projects, for example, are held back
by a failure to consider environmental pollution safeguards.

[7] See Eliot Chapple and Leonard Sayles, *The Measure of Management,*
New York, Macmillan, 1961.

Space experiments have overwhelmed the computational facilities available to process data. New high-speed trains are less successful than they might be because of antiquated ticketing procedures, and jumbo jets have baggage-handling problems.

☐ One reason for this failure to solve the "systems' " problems is that the interrelationships among components turn out to be much more complicated than the usual simple flow diagrams of systems engineering imply. Increasingly, the interfaces become blurred as technology progresses. In nuclear power plants there are no neat dividing lines among the functions of fueling, heating, and power generation. Until recently there was a clear division of labor and function between the launch vehicle and the spacecraft, or payload, in NASA's activities, and the development of each could be assigned to a given organizational unit. Future developments, such as the space shuttle, suggest that the two will meld or blend into each other. It will no longer be possible for each "side" to write specifications that meet at some common interface and for each development group to assume that the other system is fixed or constant.

☐ This may be a prime justification for the difference between the way NASA handles contractors and some earlier DoD (Defense Department) relationships. Traditionally the government defines the specifications, gives them to a carefully selected prime contractor, and makes sure he lives up to his contract. NASA, on the other hand, will get involved with both the contractor and his subcontractors in what is often an evolving engineering design and an evolving division of labor. At times, NASA centers may furnish technical expertise or new contractors may be added.

☐ Put another way, traditional contract monitoring can be conceived as a legal or an accounting problem. Questions like "Who is responsible for what?" and "Did we get what we paid for?" get answered in legal or accounting terms. As we shall see, the whole concept of responsibility changes where interfaces are not clear-cut and designs keep evolving. Thus, when NASA speaks of developing internal technical expertise so as to get actively involved in the on-going stream of work, it is responding to this inability to make a clear-cut division of labor between various work-flow stages, between the planners and the doers, and between the doers and the monitors:

In NASA we have found that we must be able to speak and understand the language of those on whom we rely, to know as much about the problems they are dealing with as they do, to check and supplement their work in our own laboratories, to step in when required with the necessary specialists, and, in some cases, help untangle snarled situations.[8]

Unanticipated Crises and Standoffs

☐ Modern development programs have life histories filled with unanticipated crises, unpredicted barriers and impediments. What appear to be reasonable designs, given prior knowledge and experience, turn out to have neglected some small, crucial factor, and some subpart, say a new valve, fails to work. This in turn means that the subsystem may have to be redesigned to "work around" the problem, which in turn affects other subsystems and the larger system. A small technical problem thus pyramids within an interdependent, integrated system.

In NASA's biosatellite program, the artificial bladder designed to handle the waste products of a monkey passenger turned out to be inadequate for the task. A "2 bladder" replacement system cost half a million dollars and created enormous design problems.

NASA found that perfecting small switches and transistors that would not fail was enormously costly and time consuming, even though such components were based on known technologies.

☐ At times, the problem may involve an external factor that was either ignored or taken as given. In India, the planners of a new paper mill assumed a given supply of raw material (bamboo) only to find after completion of the plant that a once-in-a-decade destructive "flowering of the bamboo" eliminated the needed raw material.[9] A strike of French peasants once caused the severing of a key telephone cable transmitting tracking or control information for a space experiment. Similarly, a sudden illness of a sailor can immobilize part of a tracking network. The demise of a key supporter of urban redevelopment can change difficult administrative problems into almost impossible ones.
☐ Just as difficult, perhaps worse, are those technical problems we would call *standoffs*. In the large-scale systems we are describing, the solution to any problem often requires

[8] James Webb, address at Harvard University, September 30, 1968.

[9] Albert Hirschman, *Development Projects Observed,* Washington, D.C., Brookings Institution, 1967, pp. 9–10.

the cooperation of a number of organizations, each of which is reluctant to make the first move. For example, urban redevelopment provides many instances in which new, creative solutions to housing problems were held up by antiquated zoning ordinances or building codes. These could not be changed easily without a successful demonstration project that would prove them unnecessary, and no demonstration projects could be implemented without a change in the rules. Jeanne Lowe describes the difficulties encountered by an architectural planner, Mrs. C. W. Smith, in transforming southwest Washington, D.C.:

Another obstacle was that five different sets of legal specifications for "light and air" had to be considered and reconciled. The Federal Housing Administration had one set under its Minimum Property Requirements; the District redevelopment agency had another, as did several city departments. Another problem was locating underground sewer lines in this pre-Civil War area. No District bureau had the necessary information. Yet, until Mrs. Smith knew where sewer connections could be made, she could not start placing buildings. She finally convinced the redevelopment agency to make a survey for her. There was also the urgent matter of a new elevated expressway that would cut through the area close to the first apartment house. The Highway Department's plans called for the road to be so high that it would block the view from the bottom three floors.

. . . District regulations proved more and more exasperating. One bureau wanted to make sure that the opening in the latticework on the outside walls of the apartment house would not be big enough to admit the District's ever-present starlings. The Department of Health, afraid of mosquito-breeding pools, would not approve the lily pond unless the developers agreed to stock it with a special kind of mosquito-eating fish. Restrictions on building heights threatened to force a choice between constructing the ground floor on stilts and building one less floor of rooms than was allowed by law and the official plan.[10]

☐ The *New York Times* noted a number of problems surrounding a proposed swing-wing arrangement for the SST that might be solved by the adoption of what is called a *boundary-layer control* on the wing. Boeing was reluctant to consider this solution for fear that it would make certification by the Federal Aviation Authority more difficult. The FAA in turn was reluctant to establish clear-cut certification require-

[10] Jeanne R. Lowe, *Cities in a Race with Time,* New York, Random House, 1967, pp. 181–182.

ments because of lack of experience with BLC-equipped aircraft.[11]

☐ Thus, given these complex interdependencies, the executive is faced with the demanding task of getting a number of individuals and groups *simultaneously* to change their positions.

Long Lead Times

☐ The new technology imposes long lead times, simply because large, complex endeavors take a long time to implement. "Long" can mean many things in terms of objective program duration, but we are concerned here with the problems it causes for the manager. Several are apparent immediately.

☐ Techniques must be found to assess progress and organization effectiveness during the period when no tangible results are forthcoming. While all sorts of milestones, the attaining of which indicates organizational effectiveness, can be constructed, there are frequently doubts among the top management people that these really represent equivalent progress toward the final goal.

☐ And, of course, where there are external sponsors who provide funds or political support, there is the need to provide them with some demonstration of what is being accomplished. Care must be exercised that the accumulation of these contrived performance data does not distort the operating system or swerve it from its major goal. Numerous instances of good progress reports combined with long-run failures to meet cost, schedule, or performance criteria are well known in the R & D industry.

☐ On the opposite side, techniques must be found to provide employees with a sense of accomplishment. This is particularly a problem for scientific personnel whose careers depend upon the publication of papers and experimental data, and hence on completion of the project. Good scientists may shy away from space research which involves 5- to 10-year commitments before academic rewards are likely or may quit in discouragement when program cancellations or shifts in emphasis wipe out a project in which they have invested a good deal of time.

☐ Long lead times also complicate planning. Obsolescence is a continuing threat; the objectives or methods acceptable when the mission was planned may be obsolete by the time the project is nearing completion. Newer technologies or

[11] *New York Times,* May 3, 1968, p. 58.

new data may make the chosen design wasteful or even useless.

A significant element in an experimental package to be landed on the lunar surface, one that required several years to develop, was threatened with obsolescence by data secured from other experiments during the period in which the first experiment was under development.

☐ Again, there is an opposite side of the coin. Recognizing this obsolescence factor, scientists participating in a project may demand changes in the presumably final plans that will allow the most up-to-date experiments to be conducted. There is a tendency for every schedule slippage to be compounded as the professionals in the program seek to use this delay to justify improving the sophistication of their contribution. This "creeping sophistication" further delays the project, increases costs, and complicates enormously the whole development process. There will always be constant pressure for changed plans to convert older designs into what is currently pushing the state of the art.

☐ The analogy in nonscientific programs is much the same. The parameters that were considered when a dam or renewal project was planned are likely to have changed by the time it is completed. The demand for hydroelectric power or the population distribution in the city will have shifted. Thus there is a search for an adequate compromise between the need for frozen plans (to minimize costly changes) and the desire for flexible planning (in a sense a contradiction in terms).

☐ It is somewhat surprising that, given the ever growing store of knowledge, know-how, and engineering capacity, the lead time on major projects seems to be constantly increasing, not decreasing. The atomic bomb was detonated successfully just six short years after Hahn reported to a generation of startled physicists that he had split the uranium atom. NASA's Orbiting Astronomical Observatory had been in development for eight years before the package actually went aloft, and the Apollo Telescope Mount will fly in a minimum of eight years from the time the program was conceived and "sold."

☐ One can, of course, note that the United States mounted an all-out effort in the Manhattan Project to convert theoretical knowledge into practicable bombs. But the people actually involved are often going "all-out" during the entire life span of any program, and eight years represents a very sizable chunk of a working career. Further, the intrinsic rewards that come from mission success must be postponed over and over again. The turnover of key people may be high; if this happens, the momentum that is based on what these people carry in their heads is dissipated.

THE LONG AND THE SHORT OF IT

□ Perhaps the psychological adjustment problem is somewhat more profound than we have just implied. Our research-oriented, technologically based, progress-oriented society produces a strange paradox. In a relatively short span of years, five to ten, there can be major transformations based on new technology.[12] Yet the introduction of even modest technical or procedural changes within a given organization can be painfully slow and involve endless frustrations. Even patently desirable changes may be held back by petty jealousies, interest-group competition, and individual learning curves that seem to rise slowly, if at all.

□ Psychologically, in our age, one must learn to adapt to what can only appear as rapid, profound changes while we still struggle, seemingly endlessly, to accomplish what can only be described as minor improvements. Starting from a modest base nine years ago, we have put men on the moon, yet fuel-cell technology, which has been under development for many years, still poses many unsolved problems. The same discrepancy is observable in the social world; we struggle to obtain modest improvements in human relations at the same time we are buffeted by enormous transformations in family life, sexual mores, and communications.

Interdisciplinary Effort vs. Professionalism

□ By definition, large programs are mission- or problem-oriented and require interdisciplinary efforts, yet most professionals have been trained in the context of increasing

[12] The rapidity with which the United States moved into manned space flight in 1961 is sharply contrasted with the rather primitive assumptions and proposals of the late 1950s in the excellent historical study of Project Mercury, *This New Ocean* (Washington, D.C., National Aeronautics and Space Administration, 1966). Of course, the quickness with which resources and talents were mobilized was in large measure due to the substantial background of talent and knowledge in such diverse fields as aero-medicine, missile trajectories, and techniques for dissipating aerodynamic heating. Nevertheless, there is evidence of a remarkable leap in capability if one compares the Army and Air Force proposals of 1958 and 1959 with what was achieved a few short years later.

specialization and expect to pursue their careers in the same context. Specialization can be justified in that new knowledge of certain kinds is more easily generated and transmitted in the context of a single discipline; this is the history and the organization of our universities and our professional associations. The melding and interweaving of professionals and professional knowledge required by complex endeavors challenges the manager to find ways of uprooting the professional yet allowing him to maintain his ties to his field of expertise.

□ The biologist is asked to conceive of the impact of a hard vacuum on genetics and to work with aerospace engineers on joint endeavors. The project manager is asked to move for six months to a distant location to be closer to a critical development team and to shift both his organizational identity and his family's home every several years. Specialists are asked to give up their specialities in favor of joining multidisciplinary teams and to learn from those whom they would normally ignore or consider beneath their dignity. University-based electrical engineers are asked to learn to work with geologists or chemists with whom they usually share only the common membership of a faculty club. Companies must abandon comfortable product lines to produce experimental equipment.

Permanence vs. Flexibility

□ Such programs as we shall be considering highlight the inevitable tension between mission and program needs and institutional needs, between a narrow disciplinary approach and a broader mission approach, and between the temporary and the more permanent organizational and social group arrangements.

□ The human need for continuity and regularity is both strong and persistent. Mankind has sought permanent homes in all his worlds: the world of work, of intellect, of physical and family life. What we call vested-interest groups, bureaucracies that resist change, territoriality, the discipline orientation of our universities, and even our monogamous family structure are all, in part, testimony to this pervasive human requirement.

□ Complex endeavors impinge upon and conflict with this search for permanence and regularity, since they require some giving up of autonomy and of well-established procedures and thought patterns in favor of new, and often temporary, combinations. They are a further extension of the

profound trend that began with urbanization and industriali-
zation. These developments shook the secure and psychologically comfortable world in which all the areas of human
interaction were, if not part of a single network, at least
highly congruent and complementary. The traditional vil-
lage, the extended family, and agrarian "technology"
swaddled human beings—sometimes to the point of cultural
asphyxiation—in a tight, predictable network of thought and
action, of behavior and sentiment.

MAMMOTH PROGRAMS: THE PROMISE AND THE DESPAIR

□ The obvious point made by this lengthy recounting of the
characteristics of these new *polyorganizations* designed to
implement complex endeavors is that they can hardly be
operated largely by the wizardry of computers or within the
confines of neat, engineering plans implemented by dutiful
technicians. In fact, these complex technical endeavors
come more and more to resemble large-scale political-
business systems. They require not less but more human
ingenuity, improvisation, and negotiation than old-style business and government organizations. As we shall see, human
intervention, confrontation, and compromise are indispens-
able to their governance.

□ Very large programs with highly ambitious social and
technical objectives can, as has been said, be a magnet for
courageous, imaginative, energetic administrators and technical personnel. Such programs provide a focus and an
incentive for the best efforts a society can produce. Just as a
city is a productive cauldron that forces and reinforces the
interaction of new ideas and creative people, the large
program, by intermixing and supporting risk and ambition,
can shorten by generations the evolution of new knowledge
and new institutions.

□ To the uninformed eye, these new *multiorganizations*
usually appear in one of two deceptive forms. The urban-
redevelopment programs appear to be all politics, a morass
of jealous and competitive interest groups. The AEC and the
space program, on the other hand, appear to be the epitome
of the rational, computer-like system where people and
machines are united by their common allegiance to both a
goal and a technology that brooks no political nonsense.

□ Both views reflect a defect in vision, a myopia that sees
only the public image and not the private reality. The outsider, perhaps because of the emphasis given to computers
and the public-relations releases that show scientists and

engineers linked in a common effort, tends to forget or minimize managerial inputs. Dedication and common objectives would appear to eliminate the need for much managerial effort. Nothing, of course, is farther from reality.

☐ Students of business-government relations have always relished the distinction between the rational predictability of the business world and the politicized world of government. (The word "politics" in private bureaucracies usually refers to *informal* maneuvering.) But large development organizations, with their federal structures and highly professionalized retinues of staff, advisors, and workers operating in a context of many technical unknowns and stalemates generated by the need to evolve a consensus among uniquely motivated groups, have a profound political life. The challenges to management are immense in these hybrid economic-political bureaucracies, and the "rules of the game" turn out to be rather different from the prescriptions of either scientific management or old-style politics.

☐ Joint endeavors, consortia, and contractor relationships all require a new style of interorganizational relationship that is as differentiated and involved as intraorganizational behavior patterns. The purchaser of a nuclear power plant anticipates an involved series of negotiations and prolonged relationships with government (AEC) officials, key contractors, and perhaps expert consulting firms. Increasingly, university science experts and community groups concerned with ecological balance are becoming involved in such projects. A large proportion of the work of the program takes place at the boundaries of the constituent organizations. Thus, the "environment" and the organization are not neatly bounded; what is "inside" and what is "outside" becomes more a matter of semantics than anything else. With complex business and community endeavors becoming more the rule than the exception, we must find ways of dealing with the organization that do not assume a complex internal life and a stereotyped external life.

☐ Up to now the student of organization, for the most part, has resembled the early "free enterprise" economist, viewing the world in terms of highly discrete, independent units suspended in some murky environment. That environment consisted of a number of different forces—government, consumers, suppliers, labor markets, sources of new technology, trade unions—which both posed threats and offered opportunities. But as Drucker has foreseen, the world of the future will be one in which highly differentiated, specialized organizations are bound to and must "use" one another, and where the lateral relationships that tie them together are as important as, if not more important than, the traditional pyramidal relationships.[13] These are the "systems" problems that will engage our interest in this volume.

CONCLUSION

□ It is easy to assert that the onrush of technology is further widening the gap between the ease with which we solve hardware problems and the difficulty with which we cope with social and political dilemmas. This is the old and trite distinction between malleable inanimate objects and recalcitrant human beings. Ironically, the truth may lie in the opposite direction. Our research suggests that organizing and managing large-scale technical problems may involve some of the same, or similar, "political" problems that have traditionally been associated with the public sector. Advanced technology requires the collaboration of diverse profession and organizations, often with ambiguous or highly interdependent jurisdictions. In such situations, many of our highly touted rational management techniques break down; and new, nonengineering approaches are necessary for the solution of these "systems" problems. It is these new approaches that will be relevant for a wide variety of management challenges in the 1970s.

[13] Peter Drucker, *The Age of Discontinuity,* New York, Harper & Row, 1969. See particularly Chapter 1.

THE PLANNING FUNCTION
FOR NEW TECHNOLOGIES

TWO

When modern management methods are discussed (or envied by those who believe they lack them), the chances are good that planning will be mentioned first. Nothing epitomizes more the application of rational methods to the world of human affairs than planning. The organization, like the individual, rising above the encumbrances and obfuscations of the present to help shape the future, is extolled and idealized.

□ Unfortunately most discussions of the paraphernalia of planning (the committees, forecasts, budgets, and experts) have little to say about the organizational process by which contending parties evolve a consensus within some ongoing framework that allows for major shifts in emphasis and structure. Since the large systems which are our special concern here usually encompass programs with specified life spans, and thus the stops and starts of a somewhat predictable cycle, planning is somewhat more discernible, at least to the naked eyes of the researcher. While these large systems and programs clearly have more profound planning problems (and more complex planning techniques), many of the concepts evolved in this research have application to a wide variety of business and government organizations.

THE EVOLUTION OF NEW PROGRAMS

□ Science usually evolves by the crystallization of theory, the meticulous testing of hypotheses and concepts derived from that theory, the further refinement of theory, and finally the application of these concepts to human needs. Large-scale development programs appear to go in the opposite direction. For social, economic, or political reasons, an *objective* is established; it may be to build an atomic bomb, land men on the moon, or drill through the earth's mantle. Concepts, designs, and tests of the concepts are determined and, finally, an operational *method* is implemented.

□ A third element is the *purpose:* the ends for which the objective is being sought, the usefulness to society. In science this can be, or so it is argued, very simply stated: The purpose is to advance knowledge, to seek truth, to increase understanding. In most major development programs there is ample room for ambiguity in defining purpose.

☐ For example, the space program can be conceived of as a contribution to national power or prestige, as a source of economic or scientific progress, as a source of new technology, and perhaps in other terms too, either more crass or more altruistic. Of course, in very large programs that have a major impact on people and organizations, it is useful to have multiple purposes and hence enough flexibility to shift the emphasis as political and organizational forces shift.

☐ A multiplicity of purposes also reflects the need to attract and hold the loyalty of diverse groups who must collaborate in these large, dispersed programs. A good example is provided by the famous "Mohole" project, which sought to develop new technology that would allow an anchored drilling ship to penetrate the earth's mantle.

The AMSOC scientists [the original group of sponsoring scientists who generated support for the effort to drill a hole through the earth's mantle] were concerned with maximizing the scientific returns from the drilling. The contractor understandably sought to confine the project as nearly as possible to a straightforward engineering task. Meanwhile, [the President's Office of Science and Technology] was concerned over the international and prestige aspects of success or failure of the project, particularly if there was indeed a race on [with the Russians]. The [National] Academy leadership was concerned to preserve the prestige of science, free from controversy. . . . The National Science Foundation . . . sought to sustain the impetus of an important project in earth sciences, but at the same time to support orderly progress in all other fields of science it was sponsoring.[1]

☐ The full impact of major new technological development efforts may not be known for a decade; most predictions and forecasts as to the more enduring effects of new technology tend to be wrong.[2] This raises serious questions about some

[1] *Report to the Subcommittee on Science, Research and Development,* Committee on Science and Astronautics, U.S. House of Representatives, 91st Cong., 1st sess., April 25, 1969, Washington, D.C., Government Printing Office, 1969 p. 168.

[2] Retrospective analyses of the impact of major new technological programs are not particularly reassuring when it comes to the ability of even informed participants to predict the ultimate consequences of their efforts, even in the rather limited areas of the impact of new technologies on a company's production and marketing efforts. See Donald Schon, *Technology and Change,* New York, Delacorte Press, 1967.

of the underlying assumptions of cost effectiveness at very early planning stages, particularly when the uncertainties resulting from multiple purposes and shifting emphases are considered. Further debate and acrimony are maximized when one seeks a clear definition of ends; these are the most controversial, the most shifting, of sands.[3]

☐ Even when purposes are clearly stated, they may be less operational than they appear. In business, the traditional nebulous goals of "growth and profitability" provide a great deal of room for maneuvering by various interest groups seeking to justify their objectives. Even in the more scientific aspects of the space program one finds elements of this:

In 1965 the NAS Space Science Board established priorities for those explorations that would reveal most about the origins of life and the solar system. This still left ambiguous the definition of missions to the moon, Mars, and Venus. How many and which ones should be manned, and what was the relative value of intensive exploration of the moon versus a one-shot landing on Mars or a fly-by?

Objectives as a Catalyst

☐ But politically and psychologically,

One of the lessons of the present spectacular voyage to the moon is that the American mind and the American political system seem to need great challenges and clear goals to work at their best. . . .[4]

☐ While both purposes and plans need to have a great deal of flexibility to allow for changes in sentiment, new information, and unforeseen problems and opportunities, objectives need to be relatively fixed and highly specific. They become the emotional *symbols,* the universally visible *target* that attracts and holds political support. They can also become the *catalyst* that mobilizes resources and encourages whole new technologies by capturing the imagination, the commitment, and the dedication of both those who will support the program and those who will actually do the work. Apollo and

[3] *Earth Resources Satellite System,* Committee on Science and Astronautics, U.S. House of Representatives, Washington, D.C., Government Printing Office, 1968, concludes that cost-effectiveness studies would not be useful during the early developmental stages of an earth-resources satellite system. By implication, it might be useful at the time an operational system was to be installed.

[4] James Reston, *New York Times,* July 18, 1969, p. 30.

Mohole were two such programs. There were a wide variety of ultimate purposes, some of them conflicting, but the objectives of the program were clearly stated.

☐ This very clarity, as we shall see, may be deceiving. It encourages Congress to demand comparably well-designed advance planning as to operational method, costs, and schedules. Yet defining the target moves one rather a short distance in terms of defining the problems of attaining the target.

☐ However, a target does facilitate the development effort and prevent a good deal of floundering about. For example, in NASA, as the Apollo Program moved toward a climax lacking any such central objective, NASA centers wasted a good deal of effort submitting stillborn proposals:

We find the other Centers that may have backed one of our proposals [for a new project] are likely to back out when they get to Washington. If we only had some clue as to how the Agency was likely to move we would be able to make more sensible proposals.[5]

Interdisciplinary Effort

☐ A well-chosen, appealing objective can also facilitate the breaking down of barriers among and between disciplines, functions, and institutions. There is no need to belabor the well-documented processes of increasing parochialism within professional groups. At least some groups may be stimulated to pay more attention to interdisciplinary problems under the spell of a mutually accepted common objective. In a few instances there may be a permanent institutional impact when new hybrid disciplines and new patterns of coordination are created, as has happened in the fields of urban affairs, ecology, and the space sciences.[6]

☐ As we shall see later, such mutual adaptation and acceptance of common objectives also requires the opportunity

---

[5] This and other anonymous statements were recorded in interviews with center managers and other personnel at various levels.

[6] It is interesting to observe that, with very few exceptions, NASA was *not* able to accomplish this melding or mutual cooperation between social and physical scientists. James Webb, in particular, through a number of imaginative devices, sought to stimulate multidisciplinary endeavors focused on the space program in U.S. universities. However, while space science laboratories, for example, were created, with adjoining offices populated by sociologists and engineers, there is little evidence that they interacted creatively.

for frequent and easy interaction; it is not simply a function of the existence of common goals. But given these organizational facilitations, a common goal can be most productive:

. . . The needs of designers for systematic surveys of various areas and for research in support of development must be recognized and promoted by frequent and close contact between designers and research workers. The selection of some common advanced technical development as the goal of both groups has proved to be an excellent means of promoting cooperation and channelling research into directions permitting early application, without sacrificing the values inherent in the personal enthusiasm, initiative, and freedom of the research worker.[7]

□ As we noted earlier, a clearly stated target also inhibits sniping by critics. It is difficult to go halfway to the moon, and a half-finished dam has little utility.[8] Proponents of Apollo have noted the degree to which the program is "locked up"; it is impossible to change very much without destroying the whole.

□ But large, unambiguous objectives also have their shortcomings. In a more rational world, it would probably make sense to allow the end goals to emerge gradually as a result of the "confluence" of a number of more modest activities. As one or more of these new methods or technologies "proved" themselves, one would take advantage of certain synergisms to combine them into large efforts. As long as possible, alternatives would be left open for massive shifts in the light of new knowledge and new public needs.

□ A disadvantage of having "one big objective" is that it deters such continuous planning. NASA, for obvious reasons, was reluctant to commit itself to new goals until the moon landing was accomplished. Only in 1970 was centralized long-range planning institutionalized.[9] However, perhaps such singlemindedness is necessary to cope with technological problems of the scope of a manned moon landing or a Manhattan Project. Only after the major breakthroughs have occurred can the comparative luxury of dynamic planning be allowed.

[7] Dr. Hugh Dryden, 37th Wilbur Wright Lecture, London, England, April, 1949.

[8] See Albert Hirschman, *Developmental Projects Observed,* Washington, D.C., Brookings Institution, 1967.

[9] Werner von Braun was shifted from the position of a center director to head up this new top management planning group in Washington.

OPERATIONAL PLANS—MEANS

☐ How do large programs move from establishing objectives to the specific plans which involve choices of technology and organizations to do the development work? We
shall see that while the kind of politics and bargaining that
goes on may differ from that associated with establishing
objectives, it also is not a simple rational process, with each
step following automatically. Any substantial new effort always has implications for numerous ongoing programs, particularly R & D programs; and some kind of organizing effort
is necessary to build linkages between the new development
project and these existing programs and their institutional
bases.

☐ One generally thinks of planning as a process that *precedes* negotiations for contractual services. Through the
planning process one specifies exactly what one wants and
then one proceeds to enter into negotiations with contractors who will perform the work in question. However, in
R & D contracting, planning and negotiating cannot be
separated. In recognition of this fact, R & D managers have
devised systems such as *phased project planning,* in which
serial negotiations become an integral part of planning—
hopefully serving as a means of achieving the clearest
possible definitions and tests of concepts and designs.

Planning Myths and Organizational Reality

☐ Planning is often described as an abstract process involving the rational definition of objectives, the determination of
technical and economic feasibility, and the review of management, cost, scheduling, and technical considerations. An
older view presupposes a small number of well-informed top
managers with very similar outlooks, easily concurring on
objectives to be sought by the total organization, which is
largely composed of modestly educated subordinates whose
job is to follow clear directions from the top. However, it is
difficult to conceive of an organization staffed, at least in
part, by professional and technical personnel in which there
are not a number of competing, attractive ideas, nascent
developments, and open lines of inquiry seeking support.
Further, although various organizations interact during the
planning process, the usual treatment of planning indicates
little about this aspect of the process—who takes part, when,
and how.

☐ Some commentators treat this whole side of the planning
process as undesirable, labeling it advocacy and contrasting

it unfavorably with "pure and noble" technical considerations.[10] But are technical and organizational factors separable? Technical concepts must have an organizational
reality. Someone has to be actively promoting a given concept or a given line of development, and this more general
activity precedes the start of any specific planning effort.

□ At one point three alternative missions were under active
consideration within NASA:

Mission A will make use of hardware or development plans
already associated with the competency of Center A and will
therefore be advocated by this group.

Mission B will serve to extend the competency of Center B into
an area that appears to represent a major growth axis for the
future, guaranteeing employment for existing resources or even
an expansion of resources at B.

Trajectory C in Mission C will favor one type of scientific inquiry; Trajectory D will favor another or will be oriented more
toward engineering considerations. Science and engineering interests will have their various institutional homes.

□ The decision-making sequence in the planning process
can become complicated, as in the following example:

1. Program A wanted Program B to agree to share the development costs of a common piece of hardware that was a major cost
item in both programs.

2. Program B would not agree since they felt their own program
needs demanded a more elaborate and more versatile piece of
equipment.

3. After A lost this battle, and since they could not acquire the
original hardware without B's acquiescence, they modified their
objectives to take advantage of the more versatile equipment.

4. When A's new plans were reviewed by an outside group of
experts who advise NASA on the scientific worthiness of their
projected flights (in comparison to costs), they were rejected on
the grounds of needless complexity.[11]

□ So that the record may be clear, we intend this discussion
of the planning process to emphasize what we feel are legitimate managerial concerns and inputs. The view that plan-

[10] C. Danhof, Government Contracting, Washington, D.C., Brookings Institution, 1968, p. 127.

[11] The administrative problems of incorporating outside scientists into
the planning process are discussed further in Chapter 4.

ning is an Olympian process, removed from the lively elements of the day-to-day organizational world, is both a naive and a potentially harmful view. Similarly, excessive emphasis on highly elaborate quantitative planning techniques is questionable: One must always consider the motives of the contributors and their data.

☐ Another limitation of rationality is that in very large programs with long lead times incremental decisions must be made before the results of prior decisions are known. Step 4 depends upon what happens in Step 3, but it may be necessary to begin 4 without knowing the results of 3. Yet, given the requirements of the Congressional appropriation process, at least in government programs there is a need for incremental approval. Long-lead-time projects with enormous interdependency among the parts must justify *next* year's budget on the basis of what has been accomplished *this* year. Since Step 3 has yet to justify the investment in Step 4, justification becomes a challenge to the persuasive skills of those managers charged with Congressional liaison.

☐ Alternative technologies can either pose a threat or promise a reward to any organization with a distinctive competency. Each seeks to promote those technologies and development pathways that are consistent with its unique institutional interests. Even within the development process, alternative tactics will favor one group over another. In NASA, the type of rocket and trajectory chosen favors some experiments over others.

☐ Some new technologies are highly upsetting to existing routines and perceptions. For example, dieselization of U.S. steelmaking was resisted by companies long after the economics of shifting technology were shown to be overwhelmingly favorable. Given the greater uncertainties associated with the kind of complex technologies we have been discussing, it is hardly surprising to find imperfect coupling at the application stage.

☐ It is naive to believe that these organizational considerations can all be ignored in the interests of something called pure planning. There are too many unknowns, there is too much uncertain projection and too much at stake to cast aside institutional loyalties, existing commitments, and previously held ideas as to what is feasible and desirable.[12]

---

[12] Of course such interactions are more observable in a more loosely defined Apollo Application Program than in the more tightly defined Apollo Program. Obviously the earlier stages of any program allow for more of this give-and-take than do the later stages.

Other Institutional Considerations

☐ The choice of specific plans and their institutional "homes" involves a number of what we have called *institutional considerations* for top management. Encouraging an organization to continue in its present technical direction has obvious advantages in terms of useful experience. The disadvantages include:

1. increased dependency on that organization as perhaps the sole source for that technology,

2. increased risk that prolonged developmental trends within a given organization will encourage group entrenchments and parochialisms, and

3. the danger that activities that can be misperceived as simple extensions or extrapolations of existing efforts will not receive the same "fresh" innovative treatment they would receive in a less well-prepared environment.

These problems can apply to both the sponsor and his contractors, and they encourage the search for new organizational homes for particular aspects of a program.

☐ Such questions continue to plague the administrator during the life of the program. Since, as we have stressed repeatedly, plans never work out as projected, there will be many points at which a decision will have to be made as to whether projects favoring certain institutions should be allowed to continue or should be terminated.

☐ Science itself and the personality of some scientists causes these linkages to extend almost indefinitely into the future. Now that we've learned to do A, we can do B; and having to do B requires that we develop a new competency, C, which just demands that we use it to get to D, from which we learn things that can help us reach E, and so on. Cutting off these natural extensions too early means losing a number of unanticipated secondary benefits. Letting them extend too far may mean that one gets committed too deeply in an area that may not really warrant continued or extensive funding at that time.

In the Apollo Program, the need for strict biological quarantines for men and materials returning from the moon had not been fully appreciated at the outset. The development and funding of a whole new set of procedures, facilities, and personnel (the Lunar Receiving Laboratory) was an additional requirement imposed on the Apollo Program rather late in the game.

In turn, this unanticipated problem led to the development of some extraordinary new facilities which provided some new opportunities that had not been anticipated. For example, a facility with a very low level of background radiation (better, by a factor of 20, than any existing facility) was developed for some of the testing procedures on lunar samples; it also had other potentially fruitful uses.

☐ As a given field develops, the organizational underpinnings of various concepts and designs increase greatly in magnitude. On the negative side, these are described as "vested interests." On the positive side, they often serve to provide the enthusiasm and thrust needed to follow a given line of investigation to the end. To obtain the best efforts of these various groups—to counteract the development of "locked-in" relationships—managers have had to revise traditional concepts of planning and negotiating. Some kinds of planning are almost completely dependent on data generated via negotiations. In government R & D work, for example, cost estimates ultimately depend upon information supplied by contractors vying for assignments.

☐ In R & D phased procurement planning, the sponsor is unable to specify initially exactly what he wants to buy from the contractor. Thus the planning process represents a gradual evolution that includes the results of the creative efforts of all those engaged in the various sequential negotiations. Managers in the sponsoring organization need considerable skill to properly initiate this process. A sponsor's requests for proposals require some structure but not too much. Too much structure discourages technical innovation and gives the contractor's personnel a sense of being left only the routine work. Too little structure creates a sense of uncertainty, which in turn creates a *dependency* reaction. Lacking sufficient guidelines, the contractor may try to "second-guess" the sponsor, rather than innovate. He may begin an organizational study of the sponsor's shop—a study aimed at determining the preferences of various key managers. As one informant noted, "If you leave project definition open, the contractor is apt to try to learn what Manager A's and Manager B's hot buttons are and to pick a winner that way. What are your pet ideas? That's what we'll do."

Contractor Participation in the Planning Process

☐ It is a mistake to view the contractor as an essentially passive contributor to the planning process. Quite the reverse, he is apt to be extremely active. He tries to invent opportunities, to convince the planners of the rightness of a certain course. He does not just enter negotiations, he initiates them.[13]

☐ In order to obtain a hardware contract, the contractor has to participate in the planning phase, and in order to participate in the planning phase effectively, he must be sensitive to the needs of the sponsor and the sponsor's view of the future. The contractor's concept must not only be a good one, it also must be capable of generating an adequate and vigorous base of support in the sponsor's organization.

☐ Support in breadth may be achieved by including elements reflecting the interests of the various program offices in the sponsor's organization. Support in depth may be obtained by allying with the most likely candidate for the lead group in the sponsor's house. Such institutional interests play a legitimate role in planning, for they serve to generate the kind of enthusiasm that ensures the successful completion of a project.

One contractor development group secured *internal support* for its preliminary investigations by promising to contract back to various engineering groups within the same company significant portions of the work. Thus the budget provided by these "sponsor" groups trickled back into their own departments and served to support work in which they were interested.

☐ As more than one contractor is involved in this process of securing organizational support, a number of different kinds of alliances will be developed with interest groups in the sponsor's house, and the competition among these can serve to counteract the possibility that extraneous political factors will determine the course of the planning effort. Here is an example from our field notes:

In the case of the space station, element 1 in the sponsor's organization regards the station as a logical follow-on for its own rocket program and wants the project so that it can make use of its current capability. It has no interest in an artificial gravity station that would not employ this capability. Element 2 is in-

13 The negotiating process in any organization may be divided into a series of major steps: (1) giving and seeking information—mapping power relations, feeling out zones of agreement (at this stage there is much interpersonal interaction); (2) the tactical phase—persuasion, rationalization, consolidation of one's position; and (3) making agreements, and settling on terms, sometimes with the assistance of third parties. See Carl Stevens, *Strategy and Collective Bargaining Negotiation,* New York, McGraw-Hill, 1963.

terested in an artificial gravity station so that it can develop its own unique contribution to the field.

Then there are other points of view to be considered. If the basic design is to appeal to the sponsor's *manned group,* the station must include man. If it is to appeal to the *planetary group,* it must be capable of reaching the planets. If it is to appeal to the *flight group,* it must have superb flight characteristics. Those concerned about this aspect of performance fear that any emphasis on special features may detract from flight capability, and negative reactions on their part must be avoided.

☐ It is understandable that the sponsor's personnel do not like to admit the details of this process (it does not have the proper ring of rationality), although it is a perfectly legitimate way of operating and merely illustrates the fact that planning and the interorganizational negotiation process cannot be separated.

PHASED PROJECT PLANNING AND THE NEGOTIATION PROCESS

☐ Current NASA and DoD planning practices emphasize a phased process which in the early stages involves giving simultaneous encouragement to parallel efforts. *Phased project planning,* as it is called, is a technique for reducing the impact of narrow political factors. Such factors tend to play a greater role when final commitments must be made before the true outlines of the program are discernible. Unfortunately, specification of parallel contractor-sponsor group efforts is easier than its actual realization.

☐ For example, with regard to the orbiting space station, three NASA centers and allied contractors were engaged in parallel, competing Phase A concept design efforts.[14] In the subsequent Phase B definition stage such competition may involve two center-contractor combinations. Needless to say, monitoring these efforts to ensure that they are truly parallel is no small task. Control obviously is much simpler if the sponsor-group factor is held constant and only the contractor component is allowed to vary. On the other hand, the sponsor may consider it worthwhile to be able to test the quality not only of its contractors' efforts, but also of its own various in-house components. While this system is conceptually simple, *its administration is exceedingly difficult.*

☐ Because R & D work involves a great deal of uncertainty, committing resources at an early stage can cause problems.

[14] See Table 1, p. 33.

Initial concept and definition studies are necessary to determine objectives and their feasibility, as well as the potential cost, management, and scheduling dimensions of the project. If these exploratory studies are not made, a contractor may be engaged to start costly development work on an enterprise doomed to failure. Expenses mount rapidly in such cases, and stopping a failing effort is never easy. For these reasons a system has been adopted that permits step-by-step negotiation and provides a series of go-no go decision points. The sponsor can halt the enterprise at four points during the process. The work of contractors also can be evaluated at the various stages. Moreover, special talents can be tapped. A "think tank" organization that lacks all-round capability can be brought in at an initial knowledge-building stage such as the concept-definition stage.

☐ The process of continual negotiation in the face of uncertainty has a parallel in the union-management collective-bargaining field. One-shot bargaining has proved to be inadequate in the treatment of complex problems relating to technological change. In such cases devices such as continuing-study committees have been introduced (though not always successfully) to permit the gradual development of understanding and the considered exploration of alternatives.

☐ The phased project system provides for flexibility and permits repeated testing of proposed concepts and systems designs. Parallel efforts can be conducted, and because contractor organizations can enter at various stages in the process, the sponsor need not support all these efforts. During the Voyager (Mars) Lander project, for example, McDonnell Douglas and Martin received contracts for the Phase B definition stage. Two other companies did not receive such awards but continued on their own in the hope of obtaining a Phase C systems-design contract.

Costs of the Phased Project Planning System

☐ Phased project planning, although it permits the sponsoring organization to retain flexibility and to keep its options open, obviously adds to the costs of contract negotiations. When one generates one's own competitive process, the additional negotiations place an added burden on administrative time and energy.

☐ As we have noted, the phased system is conceptually simple but administratively complex. In the absence of strong administrative leadership, it can be more of a delusion than a reality. In the days when DoD first introduced the system, it found that contractors and project managers would pay little more than lip service to Phases 1 and 2. Development work would be conducted from the very start. A project manager would say, "We're in Stage 1," when actually he was building a prototype. In other cases several phases would be worked on simultaneously, with the same contractor serving in all of them.

☐ Even after the phased process becomes an accepted part of organizational life, strict adherence to its requirements is difficult to achieve. One sponsor's key contracts official estimated that in his organization there was some deviation from the four-phase design in over 90 percent of the projects: "In practice we combine Phases A and B or B and C or we go from B to D, skipping C. The Project Manager doesn't want to wait. He says if he has to go four years at one year per phase, he will be working with an obsolete technology."

☐ In reality, even those who would rigidly adhere to the process find that there are no automatic route markers ticking off the points at which one leaves one phase and enters another. Skilled judgment is needed to make this decision. As one informant noted, "You need guys who are bright enough to know. If you don't have them, the whole process breaks down."

☐ The nature of sponsor involvement in this sequential process also raises serious policy and procedural questions. If the sponsor participates in the various stages too fully in the course of his "monitoring efforts," the existence of real intercontractor competition can be challenged. Thus, if a sponsor evaluates the work of Contractor A and suggests various improvements and then does the same for a competitor, Contractor B, the eventual loser can charge that his ideas were transmitted to the winner or that the winner got the edge as a result of the sponsor's assistance.

☐ To assure a fully competitive relationship, the sponsor would have to let each contractor independently evolve his own best design. However, insistence on preserving competition deprives the process of potentially valuable inputs from the sponsor's staff. Sponsor role definition is another case in which the contractual aspects of phased project planning diminish the initial appeal of the concept.[15]

[15] Fairchild Hiller raised the issue described in these paragraphs when it challenged NASA's selection of General Electric to build two Application Technology Satellites. See *Business Week,* July 11, 1970, p. 18. Shortly after, the selection decision was reversed and Fairchild received the award.

Table 1 Phased Project Planning

Objectives: 1. To create an option-preserving sequential decision process, with four major management-decision points.
2. To progressively refine project requirements to produce a detailed work statement that will permit the use of contracts containing appropriate forms of incentives.

Project Stages	Objectives	Parties Involved	
		In-House	Contractor
1. Planning and Definition			
Phase A—Preliminary Analysis	Analysis of alternate overall project approaches and concepts	Primarily an in-house effort	Support role for university and industry study contractors (FP or CPFF contract); need not be capable of Phase B, C, or D.
Phase B—Definition	Selection of one of several project approaches for further definition and eventual development, if this seems advisable; effort may be cut off here	An analysis role	Study contractors develop information (FP or CPFF contract); not a competition for Phase D contract.
Phase C—Design	Definition in detail of the project approach selected in Phase B	Integration and validation of contractor data	Major portion of work is contractor conducted (CPFF or incentive contract); generally two or more prime contractors selected; only firms capable of performing through Phase C are eligible since Phase C provides competition for Phase D.
2. Project Implementation			
Phase D—Development/ Operations	Final hardware design, development, fabrication, testing, and operation	Monitoring and review functions	Major portion of work is contractor conducted; restricted to Phase C contractors, except in unusual cases; one prime contractor (incentive contract).

Note: FP = fixed-price contract   CPFF = cost-plus-fixed-fee contract

Can Organizational Reality Cope with Phased Project Planning?

☐ Despite its flaws, phased project planning has the merit of introducing into R & D work a stepwise, layered process that permits the continuation of a fluid situation and the retention of options. Intermeshing planning and negotiating means that these two processes are not frozen into a structured sequence. In advanced technologies the planner knows what his goals are and that they are technically feasible, but there generally are several different and yet to be explored ways of achieving these goals. Therefore, it is impossible for a planner to specify exactly what shall be produced. Realistically speaking, planning cannot precede negotiating.

☐ However, negotiating can precede planning. In the simplest case, a sponsor could select a single contractor and instruct him to proceed through Phases A, B, C, and D, considering alternatives and picking the best in each instance. As a matter of fact, this type of procedure actually is followed in other countries. The Japanese regard prior commitment as essential to inducing the best possible performance. The man or company not assured of a future with an enterprise owes it no loyalty. If he makes a discovery in Phase 1 but feels that he may soon be ejected from the project, he cannot be blamed for not revealing this information. Under this system of logic, a group of, say, three or four contractors may be selected who then participate to about the same extent in the work at all stages of the project. Of course, all systems have their costs, and "equal sharing" (among contractors) can be a burden to a large, production-oriented contractor who is not enthusiastic about participating in the first and not-so-profitable concept-formation stage.

☐ Some Japanese describe this system as *cooperative competition,* since the situation is controlled and predictable. The number of companies permitted to enter work in a certain advanced field is limited to prevent "excessive competition." Referring to one particular technology, a manager remarked: "We have tried and tried to get this business, but it is limited to just those four companies. Sometimes we get work in [an allied field] but it is less than [one of the four] loses in penalties for being late." Thus the committed group is surrounded by jealous excluded competitors who serve to underline the desirability of its status.

☐ American project managers whom we interviewed sometimes noted the advantages of keeping the same project group together throughout the life of a given effort. One project manager, discussing a highly successful effort, remarked: "We made our project group responsible from beginning to end, for designing, testing, operations, everything. We told them until this spacecraft flies, you and it are never going to be separated. By the time the group went down to the Cape to fly the craft, each one knew all of its idiosyncrasies." Thus, by committing a group to an entire project from start to finish, one commits the members to achieving its success. However, the project cited above worked entirely with known systems, and thus there were no difficult choices in the early stages.

□ The argument for developing parallel efforts stems from the need to explore competing concepts and approaches rather fully. Inducing competition is one way to prevent either the project's in-house people or the contractors from taking on the role of advocate for a technology in which they have a substantial prior investment. Followed literally, this system would involve parallel efforts at every stage but final production. Those best able to function in each stage would be chosen as members of a revolving group of contractors, with the whole process somewhat like a game of musical chairs.

□ However the problem of transmitting the efforts of members of a completed phase to a group of entirely different organizations involved in the next phase may make this highly impractical. In practice, budgetary pressures and the lack of able and willing competitors intervene to modify this design. The British, for example, have similar procedures derived from the famous *Downey Report,* but cost-conscious parliamentarians are likely to be unsympathetic to the idea of supporting two contractors beyond the feasibility studies of Stage 1.

□ In the case of small, applications-oriented projects that can choose among only a few major contractors, phased project planning is in many ways a luxury design which has only limited application. On the other hand, directors of a sponsor's large projects facing similarly large vested interests on the contractor side can obtain some measure of control by employing these procedures, for they at least serve to underline the sponsor's desire for the best in concept testing, systems design, and so on, as well as his willingness to monitor the work closely in order to achieve these ends.

□ Those who intermesh planning and negotiating via the phased planning process and those who precede planning with negotiations in contrary strategies such as cooperative competition share a similar goal—the induction of excellence of performance in new technologies. Proponents of these two strategies simply take different routes to this goal and respond to different types of incentives to stimulate the desire to perform successfully. Phased project planning seems to be the more complex of the two strategies from an administrative standpoint, but as one American manager in a sponsor's house noted, "We hold out that carrot, and it's very tempting, the next stage. So we feel they will do their best." Acceptance of one or the other procedure may be less a matter of abstract principle and more a matter of the relative size of programs, the nature of the prior relations among the parties involved, and the expectations of each party. One thing is clear: No system is followed literally; all of them have to bend to the demands of organizational life.

Phased Planning vs. Total Package Procurement

□ Given the inherent uncertainties of these programs, it is ironic that both Congressmen and public-spirited citizens still seek rigid, early contracts that appear to tie the contractor down to some fixed price in some current "total package procurement" procedure. While this approach is often associated with former Secretary of Defense McNamara, until recently it still was favored in DoD.

When a highly advanced military helicopter to be built by Lockheed Aircraft Company was stillborn, the cause was said to be a "total package contract that locked in a commitment from research and development to production. Lockheed was committed from the drawing board to the finished product, and it had to make assumptions about technology long before it got into production.[16]

This kind of package may be legally appealing, but it is inconsistent with the technological process.[17]

[16] *Newsweek Magazine,* quoting the Army's Chief of Research, Lt. Gen. Betts, June 2, 1969, p. 71.

[17] Extreme examples of the military following through on inflexible, unrealistic plans are provided by the experience of French and German general staffs during the early part of World War I. These experiences are described graphically by Barbara Tuchman in her *Guns of August* (New York, Macmillan, 1962).

☐ It is not difficult to cite many other examples of profound shifts in "well-planned" programs caused by changes in some factor that was assumed to be "given." Early space shots were held up by the requirement of sterilization and by propulsion systems that either did not materialize or were less powerful than anticipated.

INDIVIDUAL PRESSURES AND INITIATIVES

☐ It would be naive to ignore individuals in any description of the planning process. Where the unknowns are substantial, where professional expertise is widely distributed, and where innovation and creativity can occur in many places, an intelligent system allows for individual initiative, particularly at low organizational levels.

"At the time the Apollo Program's major outlines were being determined, a critical decision was the method of making the lunar landing: the quickest, cheapest, safest route to the moon."[18] Earth-orbit rendezvous had a number of high-level adherents, but a center scientist, Dr. John Houbolt, having become convinced that a lunar-orbit route was preferable, began "leapfrogging the chain of command" to proselytize space-agency officials.[19]

On a smaller scale, a university scientist's idea for a new camera was "sold" by his energetic persuasion of an aerospace company which, with the assistance of the professor, was able to convince a NASA center to make this system a key element in a new applications satellite. It is said that one of the responsibilities of a center director is to "sell" the better ideas of his staff to Washington.

☐ Individual initiatives are not always functional. There probably is some tendency to restrict a legitimate amount of hardware commonality as a result of these initiatives. Ideally, a scientist would like a spacecraft to be designed just for his experiment so that the craft itself, its trajectory, and the propulsion system would be ideally suited to his work. As second best he wants a spacecraft and propulsion system selected for scientific reasons, not one suited to application work (engineering) or perhaps the manned program. In the same way there are pressures not to develop common tape

[18] *New York Times,* January 26, 1969, p. 50.

[19] *Ibid.* It is interesting to note that this critical decision took two years to make.

recorders or common circuitry that would compromise individual needs for some larger interest.

□ Realistic planning presupposes that key line managers, who in turn will be responsible for implementation and the expending of resources, play a vital role. It is not unusual to see a "planning advisory body" composed of the heads of major departments and programs, designed to work with the chief executive or administrative officer and his staff to "add up" the total organizational implications of various alternatives. Planning, then, emerges from the interchange and negotiations among these line heads, guided and constrained by those who are trained to "see" interrelationships and trade-offs.

SUMMARY AND CONCLUSION

□ We have sought to disabuse the reader of a number of common misconceptions about planning, particularly its presumed separation from on-going organizational processes and the operational validity of rigid projections and interpolations. Planning inevitably is part and parcel of the institutional needs of the various groups whose ideas and consensus are required, and plans necessarily undergo continuous modification in the light of unanticipated realities. Both the iterative and negotiating aspects of planning, however, can be sources of strength for an enterprise on the forefront of new technology or dealing with multiple (and political) imponderables. Organizational adaptability and flexibility, perhaps stemming from changing structural forms (which discourage the formation of rigid norms and perceptions), become a necessary counterpart to this type of dynamic planning process. Most important, the administrator needs to comprehend the substantial gap that separates mechanical and abstract planning and procurement techniques from the realities of an organic world of constantly changing relationships.

□ Modern planning theory often emphasizes logic and probability theory. Managers are encouraged to evaluate all the consequences of a number of alternative possibilities, remove inconsistencies, and factor in the appropriate probability estimates to arrive at a desirable timetable of objectives and their subgoals.

□ One difficulty of applying this type of depersonalized rationalism to advanced technologies is the number of imponderables. Sometimes planning assumes that one moves sequentially from improved competency (new hardware, new technology, and the rest) to certain predetermined objectives (such as improved communications methods or more astrophysical knowledge). In fact, this is likely to be an iterative process. If and when a new technology is proven out, previously unanticipated uses will develop. For example, NASA's success with developing synchronous satellites has suggested a whole series of navigational, meteorological, and communications applications that were not conceivable previously.

☐ The reverse is also true. As new actual or potential users of the new technology come into existence, previous development plans may have to be modified to take into account the special requirements of the new application, particularly when there are major new users whose budgets may help justify a financially somewhat shaky development effort.

| Alternative Technologies | ⟶ | Development Process | ⟵ | Potential Applications |

The development process of major European satellite programs has been interrupted as user requirements changed. In one case the decision of an intra-European telephone service to consider becoming one of several customers for a newly proposed satellite imposed the requirement for major new designs. In another case, U.S. technological changes in what was to be a compatible military communication satellite forced the Europeans to change their specifications.

☐ There is nothing special about these examples; they simply reinforce a rather well-worn observation that advanced technologies really are tightly knit systems that extend from design and development through to application. Changes ramify quickly and profoundly through the system.

☐ We have stressed the difficulty of moving from objectives to ends or purposes. It may be relatively simple to get diverse groups to concur on a common objective: a major technological or scientific breakthrough, an urban-redevelopment program, a new watershed or waterway reclamation. But hidden behind the consensus can be, and usually are, diverse and conflicting interests that represent the distinctive goals of the contributing or affected groups within both client and contractor institutions. Some will be seeking an opportunity to perfect some new technique or to gain entry to a new field, while others will be seeking to upset or to rearrange the balance of power or status in a community or even a nation. It would be naive to expect a common goal to eliminate these divisive forces.[20]

☐ In urban redevelopment commercial, financial, and political interests, racial and ethnic groupings, advocates of open housing, of racial balance, of urban and suburban balance seek to utilize the massive reconstruction program to serve their special needs, which may extend from short-term real-estate profits to a fresh and wholesome conception of civic responsibility.

☐ Such diverse interests underline the need for unambiguous objectives. There are many good psychological reasons why, in planning, policy objectives should be reasonably well-defined. They motivate people and satisfy politicians; they facilitate commitment and discourage *plunderers,* those who seek for their own ends the financial resources or the power now controlled by the program itself. On the other hand, both the human purposes being served and the plans by which the objectives are to be accomplished require a certain amount of flexibility. New knowledge typically has many unintended consequences, both positive and negative, and it would be shortsighted to assume that the original purposes, particularly in long-lead-time programs, should always take priority over those that reveal themselves during the program's evolution. For instance, communications, rather than one of the other predicted major uses, conceivably could become the primary use of space technology. The use of atomic energy in pollution-free techniques for energizing "agro-industrial complexes" (producing salt-free water and fertilizer) may be more important in the years ahead than the present electric-power and weapons applications. Surely urban redevelopment too will have many unanticipated consequences.

☐ Similarly, implementation plans have to be flexible to adapt to unforeseen and unforeseeable political and engineering barriers. In NASA's post-Apollo planning there have been a wide variety of improvisations on the plans for earth-orbiting laboratories ("skylabs") and telescopes ("ATM" 's). The amount of funding available, the data already obtained by earlier experiments, the relative availability of different types of launch vehicles (with their very different power

---

[20] As organization theorists have pointed out, the commitment of these diverse groups to the common objective is not cost free. Various "side payments"—jobs, status, prerequisites, income, etc.—must be made to gain their acquiescence. For a discussion of the theory of side payments, see Richard Cyert and James March, *A Behavioral Theory of the Firm,* Englewood Cliffs, New Jersey, Prentice-Hall, 1963.

capabilities), and the applications conceived for the data to be obtained—all are variable and affect the specific mission profiles and hardware requirements.[21]

☐ It is comforting to believe that intellectual effort progresses sequentially, but organizational planning resists this nicety.

In one large organization concerned with advanced technology, top management recently enunciated the following dictum: "We've been too hardware-oriented and haven't concerned ourselves with application. In the future we're going to start with applications and move our planning from there." Interestingly, the remainder of the discussion was devoted to possible uses of *existing* hardware and expertise. When one executive noted that a particular application could be well served without one of the organization's more important technologies, his suggestion was vetoed on the grounds that every application must make use of this particular technology.

☐ The objectives of a project (the immediate catalyst; the definition of the mission), the operational plans (the methods and capabilities required to achieve the mission), and the purposes (the applications, or uses, or ends) must be continuously reconsidered. Even changes that appear in operational plans, by providing unanticipated barriers or opportunities, can affect both the objectives and the purposes. The availability of a capability or a methodology encourages the search for both missions (objectives) and applications whereby the development of the capability can be justified or amortized. Similarly, top management can hardly afford to ignore institutional or even personal strengths.

☐ While we stress flexibility and dynamic adjustment as crucial elements of planning, it would be misleading to understate the structural contribution of planning. After all, this is the process through which the basic political-power dimensions are determined. In sharp distinction to the lateral work-flow process in which day-to-day problems are resolved, planning seeks to make explicit "who is going to get what" and "who is going to have to defer to whom." It seeks, in other words, to set a balance of power in allocating resources, in selecting courses of action and identifying beneficiaries, both potential and actual. In many well-func-

---

[21] We do not underestimate the painful human consequences of this type of flexibility. Scientists are understandably dismayed when their carefully contrived experiments are modified or sometimes scrubbed.

tioning organizations, an observer might be hard-pressed to identify this underlying distribution of power. Individuals and groups enthusiastically contribute their skills and knowledge as needed to facilitate the movement of projects through to completion. Periodically, however, basic decisions must be made that inevitably involve hard choices among competing alternatives. The manifest content of planning discussions concerns projects and programs; the latent content involves the power and position of the constituent groups and organizations. Policy and power are almost synonymous, and for the participants there may be no distinction.[22]

☐ To conclude, planning is not synonymous with forecasting, not by any stretch of the imagination. Rather, it is a dynamic process by which both inside and outside interests arrive at a new balance of power—reflected in new structure and new policy—designed to establish the parameters of executive decision-making for some period of years, but not forever.

☐ A recent commentary by Ada Louise Huxtable, the New York Times' wise observer of urban planning and misplanning, echoes our observations. In assessing favorably a new comprehensive plan for New York City's future, she said:

First, the textbook scientistic-Utopian planning of long-range policies based on statistical extrapolations and translated into massive rebuilding schemes has proved such a conspicuous failure in the last 25 years that doctrinaire planning, and its adherents, are in considerable disrepute and disarray. The impressive theories and presentations that seem so intellectually compelling go up in smoke when faced with the human and political equation.

Therefore, the [new] plan deals with the processes; with the forces of growth and decay and the inconstant human factors that underlie the city's serious disorders—things that cannot be pinned down on charts or graphs. It is designed for the greatest flexibility.[23]

[22] For a further discussion of this and other planning factors in the evolution of international projects, see Chapter 6.

[23] New York Times, November 16, 1969.

SCIENTISTS IN PLANNING

THREE

As we have already described in the preceding chapter, planning is more an organizational process than an intellectual-technical exercise, since it establishes the balance of power among competing interest groups. One of the more challenging aspects of this process is the integration of expert-specialist advice on highly technical subjects with managerial-generalist considerations. Perhaps the most difficult way to accomplish this advisory function is to seek to integrate the counsel of "outsider" professionals with "insider" professionals.

□ This is part of the larger concern with integrating into larger organizational frameworks professionals who, whether they are "insiders" or "outsiders," have allegiances and goals that tend to set them apart from other employees and managers. Their ambiguous status often is associated with expectations of autonomy and recognition that tax the ingenuity of the administrator. Unlike the contractors and other satellites of the sponsoring agency, advisors or consultants from professional fields tend to work as individuals, although they may speak in the name of "science" or of a particular discipline.

□ Of course, where, as in NASA's case, the sponsoring organization is also an arm of government, a public agency, there is a reciprocal need to gain support of outside groups who have independent political power or have established relationships with legislatures. Private organizations also may seek to involve outsiders who will become their defenders or proponents when and if their future plans are challenged by ecologists or urbanists or regulatory authorities.

□ Even without these political stratagems, the sponsor would need to work with outside advisors in many technical areas. At least in scientific areas, the appeal of a university post is almost irresistible, but this has not deterred scientists from accepting consultantships and even part-time jobs with a variety of nonuniversity organizations.[1]

---

[1] In the future one can anticipate seeing still more complicated arrangements in this area of multiple job-holding (what is called "moonlighting" among nonprofessionals). For example, the former head of the President's

☐ The general problem confronting managers is to obtain a mutually agreeable commitment to the organization from the outside scientists. The commitment must not be so binding as to threaten in-house personnel or disrupt the regular, on-going organizational activities. Nor should it be so binding upon the outsider that it undermines the credibility of his scientific independence or makes impossible the fulfillment of his other responsibilities.

MULTIPLE USES OF OUTSIDERS

☐ Managers use outside scientists to perform several different roles at the same time. Most frequently, they act as advisors, recommending strategies for coping with possible and probable developments as well as suggesting priorities and tactics for exploiting immediate opportunities. They may also supply technical information, consultants' reports, and scientific explanations from research experiments conducted inside or outside the organization.

☐ Besides employing the outsiders as advisors and experimenters, managers also use them to stimulate and encourage the in-house staff. They meet with staff scientists in seminars or consultations to criticize their work and findings, to exchange the latest scientific data, and to identify salient problems for further investigation.

☐ Scientists of independent reputation may lend their prestige and expertise to an organization to legitimize its program or authenticate its work. In the case of a business firm, they may assure stockholders or top management that a company investment in a new technology is as promising as

---

Scientific Advisory Committee, Dr. Donald Hornig, accepted a full professorship in Chemistry at the University of Rochester and also, simultaneously, a high executive post with the Eastman Kodak Company.

☐ The UN has established the International Centre for Theoretical Physics in Trieste, Italy, whose staff is expected to spend two-thirds of the calendar year attached to institutions in their home countries—often a developing country—and one-third gaining intellectual refreshment and stimulation in the Centre. NASA established a Lunar Science Institute in Texas to allow its affiliated members to work with the facilities of the Manned Spacecraft Center (MSC) in Houston while temporarily being affiliated with the Institute and maintaining their academic positions. A former chief scientist at MSC Houston continued as a professor of geophysics at MIT in Cambridge, and the director of the UN Centre in Trieste holds a professorship at Imperial College in London! Another NASA center, the Langley Research Center, operates jointly with the University of Virginia an "in between" institution, VARC, which shares facilities and personnel.

the management has declared, or present scientific briefs to bankers or security brokers in support of a company decision to introduce a technically advanced product or service. A government agency such as NASA always finds beneficial the favorable testimony of notable scientists before Congressional committees, and close identification of outstanding men of science with an agency's program helps to gain public support, or at least to ward off attacks.

□ The multiple function performed by the outsiders creates ambiguities about their position. As a high-level advisor, for example, a scientist working with top management may help determine the goals of the organization. At some future time, or even in some instances simultaneously, such scientists may be competitors for contracts.

□ In NASA's case, given the small number of qualified specialists in the exotic space-science fields, it is not surprising that some of the same researchers who advise also seek to become NASA-funded experimenters. They could then be designing experiments to fly on missions they have recommended.[2]

SCIENTISTS AS ADVISORS: THE ADVICE-GIVING PROCESS

□ Influencing planning and policy formation is not simply a matter of giving expert testimony. As the nonscientist is often surprised to discover, there frequently is no unanimity within the scientific community even on relatively technical questions. What to the layman may appear to be a simple scientific question that can be answered by a simple "yes" or "no" usually turns out to be a rather complicated problem. For one thing, most difficult scientific questions cannot

[2] Most NASA spacecraft carry a variety of experiments which are paid for by the agency but constructed by investigators who work for universities, private companies, and other governmental agencies (as well as for NASA itself). These experimenters receive back the data, assuming a successful mission, analyze it, and are able to publish the findings in scholarly journals.

□ The federal government has been concerned with the conflict-of-interest question here. For example, in the early 1960s the Ramo-Woolridge Corporation had to divest itself of that part of its organization which advised the Air Force in order to continue to supply aerospace equipment. This resulted in the creation of the nonprofit Aerospace Corporation, which has continued to be a high-level advisor ("think tank") of the Air Force.

□ Such conflicts of interest are not unique to government. Private industry, for example, utilizes accounting firms as auditors and advisors, and these same firms sell a variety of other services, such as information systems and management consulting, to the same clients.

be answered categorically; there are always a number of "chancy" factors, trade-offs, and uncertainties. The particular biases, educational background, personality (e.g., his willingness to take risks, his conservatism), and interest of the advisor also will play a key role in how he responds to the problem.

□ Thus some organizational method must be devised either to sift and weigh the differences among the experts or, where major national policy is at stake, to evolve a consensus among experts. In addition, advice is not neutral; it affects the status and interest of "insiders" who have their own expert opinions and programmatic concerns. To be effective, advice must come at the right time in the organization's decision-making sequence and must often penetrate to the tactical level. Otherwise strategic choices will be vitiated and degraded as technical managers make on-the-job implementation decisions.

Evaluating Differences Among Experts: A Managerial Dilemma

□ How does the organization handle good-faith differences in expert judgment? A striking example of this problem involving private industry concerns the efforts of electric utilities to harness nuclear energy.[3]

□ After first investigating the promise of nuclear power and deciding in the early 1950s that it was worth a large-scale effort to realize it, the managers of one company selected an advisory committee of outstanding nuclear physicists from leading universities. The committee was to recommend the best kind of fuels and reactor systems for an initial investment. Unfortunately, and quite by chance, the managers selected physicists who had worked primarily with plutonium during World War II and had investigated its use in breeder reactors. The elegance of a system that would produce more fuel than it consumed and their familiarity with plutonium technology inclined them to favor a plutonium-breeder reactor. Further, almost all nuclear scientists at that time were agreed that in the long run breeder reactors would certainly become the chief producers of nuclear power. However, breeder experience was limited to a few small laboratory models, many scientific and technical

---

[3] Several years ago, our colleague Professor James Kuhn undertook a systematic study of the use of high-level professionals in the development of the nuclear-power industry. The following were some of his conclusions. (For a more complete analysis of his data, see James Kuhn, *Scientific and Managerial Manpower in Nuclear Industry,* Columbia Univ. Press, New York, 1967.) This chapter largely reflects his work.

problems remained to be solved, and hard data were scarce; consequently, the assumptions the physicists made about costs, feasibility, operational life, and time needed for development were exceedingly shaky. Despite their qualifications, the consultants recommended the construction of a full-scale commercial breeder reactor.

□ In following the recommendation, the managers found that they had committed their company to advancing the state of the art far beyond their ability. Development proceeded very slowly as costs rose far beyond all expectations. In the eight years that it took to bring the breeder reactor to a beginning level of operation, other companies had developed simpler, less costly reactor systems.

□ A second utility company entered the nuclear-power field a few years later, in the mid-1950s. It did not have to turn to the universities and government-research laboratories for its advisors, but could choose from among those nuclear experts who had been hired by electrical-equipment manufacturers, few of whom were interested in the long-term experimentation and research that the breeder concept now obviously entailed. The young physicists to whom the company turned for advice had worked at Oak Ridge. There they had become familiar with the theory and characteristics of the enriched-uranium, slow-converter reactor. This kind of reactor appeared to them to offer the best chance of short-term development, and in fact it proved to be a relatively easier concept to translate into a workable system than had the breeder-reactor concept.

□ The advisors, however, could not resist pursuing research opportunities that arose to experiment and to seek exotic solutions to the scientific and engineering problems that arose during the development of the reactor. At Oak Ridge they had been encouraged in such pursuits. Finding a cladding for the fuel elements in the utility-reactor core proved exceedingly difficult. Since the original material, an alloy of zirconium, proved unsatisfactory, the advisors recommended experimentation with a number of other metals. This proved to be so time consuming that the development of the reactor was seriously delayed. A company manager in charge finally decided to dismiss the advisors and to proceed on his own. He explained:

They wanted to explore all possible leads and go off in every direction. I looked at the cost schedule and decided I had to veto their work. They were learning a lot but at our expense. On my own, I chose between the two most promising cladding metals. The cheapest was stainless steel. We knew a lot about it and so I took it without any more research. It turned out all right, too.

Structuring the Advice-Giving Process as a Solution

□ An organization dealing with advanced technology can hardly afford to dismiss the advice of the high-level professional because there are limitations or biases inherent in his recommendations. While top management may be tempted to ignore scientific judgment altogether when they learn that what were accepted as solid facts and reasonably perfect knowledge are, in fact, informed opinions, they probably cannot enjoy this luxury. Thus the administrative question is how the advice-giving process can be structured to minimize the possibility of unbalanced technical decisions. Observation of a number of organizations utilizing outside advisors suggests three strategies:

1. Use only "balanced" advisors who are able to deal simultaneously with a number of conflicting or contradictory parameters, values, and points of view. (Needless to say, such people are scarce.)

2. Balance off what will be individual biases or limitations in experience by building a "pre-mixed" advisory group or groups with diverse experience, backgrounds, and vested interests.

3. Provide multiple stages so that a decision results from a series of advisory judgments and implementation choices.

□ From one point of view, alternative 3 will always play some part in technical organizations. For example, as technical programs move from the idea to the implementation stage, modifications reflecting design, development, and fabrication "realities" will be introduced. Of necessity, these will serve to adjust the balance among competing approaches and technologies as we concluded in our description of phased planning in the previous chapter.

□ In the sections to follow, we shall look at the role of these advisors both in shaping the major strategic decisions, the basic direction of the sponsoring institution, and in contributing to tactical decisions. All our examples will be drawn from NASA, and the process by which experiments are selected to fly on science-oriented spacecraft.

THE ROLE AND POWER OF OUTSIDE ADVISORS

□ Given the level of public trust required by a government agency and the costliness of executive decisions, an agency such as NASA must seek to obtain the very best counsel and to justify its more difficult choices among attractive, competing alternatives. Obviously many of these choices are not simply scientific in nature; they are profoundly political—and even economic and social, although they may have an important scientific component.

☐ NASA has sought both to develop and to work with externally based "trusted sources of information," who would be above reproach both as to their professional ability and as to their willingness to employ this knowledge and skill impartially and unselfishly.

☐ While the sponsoring organization is concerned with the impartiality and quality of the advice it is receiving, the advice-giver is concerned with maintaining his independence, impartiality, and legitimacy. While there are always a number of stories circulating concerning the professional who is owned "body and soul" by some organization, most reputable professionals in all fields are concerned with maintaining both the appearance and the reality of their independence. A major reason for maintaining an academic affiliation is that it allows for continuity of income and status regardless of the acceptability of one's counsel to clients.

☐ Particularly in a very large endeavor such as NASA, with overwhelming national significance and political overtones, academically oriented scientists may feel the need for additional institutional "supports" to guarantee their own public image as objective judges. Insofar as they are members or appointees of the National Academy of Sciences or the President's Science Advisory Committee, each of which may be asked to give counsel to an agency like the space program, that support is obviously provided.[4] Such memberships protect the scientist from even unconsciously identifying too much with the sponsoring institution or from being identified too much with it by his peers.

☐ Thus, in NASA's case, panels of the National Academy of Sciences have sought to identify priorities in lunar exploration for the Apollo Program and to assess the cost-effectiveness of earth-oriented satellites in relationship to their usefulness in locating natural resources, predicting the size of the world grain crop, detecting agricultural disease and water pollution, and improving navigation and communication. NASA has also sought to structure its own advisory boards, in particular an Astronomical Missions Board composed of the outstanding U.S. astronomers who could speak for the astronomical community in shaping future science-

[4] The Space Sciences Board (SSB) of the National Academy of Sciences is NASA's highest-level advisory body.

oriented spacecraft flight programs. It was hoped that such boards would facilitate NASA's chances of obtaining a long-term, continuing, responsible commitment from the scientific community to a program of scientific exploration of space.

◻ Scientists and other professionals frequently find it difficult to draw any hard-and-fast line between what they view as the needs of their discipline and the objectives of the agency which they are advising. This is hardly different from the case of the university professor who feels there is no distinction between what he needs (in the way of assistants, equipment, space, travel funds, time free from teaching, new courses, and so on) and the needs of the university. He views the advancement of his career as synonymous with the advancement of the institution.

◻ Thus NASA advisors have at various times sought:

1. to convert parts of the NASA organization into independent nonprofit corporations under the direct authority and control of the scientists and their universities;[5]

2. to bargain with NASA for a variety of new earth-based laboratories that would only indirectly serve the space program but would directly benefit a particular field of science;[6] and

3. to shift the balance in the total NASA program from engineering and technology (as represented in a large share of the Apollo Program) to more basic scientific research.

Scientists have been most vocal in their complaints that science plays a poor second fiddle. For example, they argue that although the manned lunar landing of Apollo almost grudgingly tacked on a few science experiments, these were not conducted with the care that produces important results

[5] The model for such a proposal was in part Associated Universities, Inc., a consortium of universities who operate some of the key facilities of the Atomic Energy Commission. NASA consistently has sought to distinguish its operations—which require highly coordinated action among the various research and development laboratories, and launching, tracking, and monitoring facilities—from the more fragmented and decentralized activities of the AEC.

[6] Again, the argument can always be made that any field is a unity and that space research depends a great deal upon ground-based research such as that provided by reactors or telescopes. In funding telescopes, some scientists claimed, NASA would be complementing its satellite-based astronomical research. As we noted in Chapter 2, it is very difficult to distinguish legitimate extensions of any R & D effort from those which move the organization outside its "appropriate" jurisdiction. Scientists in private industry can be constrained by profit considerations; in government the political danger of poaching on other agencies' jurisdictions can be the source of comparable restraint.

because engineering considerations predominated. One key scientist even complained that the equipment provided for lowering experiments from lunar module to the moon's surface was too crude to carry adequate weights safely. Others complained that the astronauts' program gave science only a minor role, citing as an example the inadequate attention paid by the first Apollo crew to precisely cataloging the location and alignment of each lunar rock collected.[7]

☐ Scientists, given the prestige of their work and the deference paid to them as university professors, gifted researchers, and honored advisors, have a Ptolemaic view of the world and are unused to filling secondary roles. In NASA, for many obvious reasons, the development and evolution of a new technology, of new engineering, of man's capability to operate in space, frequently took precedence over scientific inquiry. However, the assumption that science will be one of the major users and beneficiaries of this new national competency has always been implicit in the program. There were also scientific aspects to existing programs—significant experiments were conducted both in the manned and unmanned activities. The difficulty is simply that the scientists were not used to having their interests considered subsidiary rather than primary.

☐ NASA consistently sought to resist proposals that would involve a major structural change in the role and authority of their "advisors." Nevertheless, the interdependencies and ambiguities are so substantial in advanced technologies, that it is not surprising to find professional advice evolving a dynamic of its own in the planning process.

Advisor-Insider Relationships

☐ A self-respecting advisor wants his advice to count. He knows that he is not the line authority and that the last word is not his, but there are still a variety of techniques by which he can be more or less influential. One obvious technique is

[7] At least some of the criticisms leveled at the Apollo Program were grossly unfair. The uncertainties, danger, and national prestige involved in the first manned landing dictated a very secondary role for science. Any scientific return was a welcome bonus; the primary consideration had to be the safety of the crew and the completion of the mission. The delicate maneuvers necessary to land the lunar module dictated that an experienced pilot, not a geologist, handle the controls, and the subsequent landing problems of Apollo 12 confirmed the wisdom of this decision. Nevertheless, Apollo 12 did mark the beginning of a significant scientific program on the moon with the implanting of a number of experiments (the Apollo Lunar Surface Experiments Package) and a more systematic exploration of the lunar surface by the astronauts.

meeting with the topmost level of the organization. Scientific advisors seek to meet with the administrative head of the sponsoring agency and even with heads of relevant Congressional committees and key figures in the Executive Office of the President. Particularly in the years since World War II, the top echelons of the American scientific community have discovered many ways of exercising political influence.

☐ Within the organization there are also techniques for increasing one's influence. Advisors learn the meaning of time. Being brought into the situation after many key constraints have been established obviously limits the impact of one's counsel. The earlier in the planning process a man is consulted, the greater the likelihood that his counsel will make some difference.

☐ Advisors also discover that they depend upon lower-level, inside technical personnel to give them a variety of options and trade-offs in order to assess the full range of possibilities. At the same time, these boards and panels must be willing to immerse themselves in "gritty" details concerning, for example, spacecraft configuration, the costs and performance characteristics of various launch vehicles, and the relative competencies of various field centers. The more thoroughly familiar they become with the technological and budget constraints, the more time they spend reading documents, examining schedules, and proposals, the more effectively they can present their own views and influence the sponsor.

A Case Example

☐ It may be instructive to look in more detail at the types of questions which these high-level boards endeavor to answer or the kind of counsel they give. As we shall see, scientific, engineering, and career variables often become intertwined:

In response to a severe budget cut, NASA top management proposed to one of their high-level boards that a major project, one which involved orbiting telescopic observations of solar flares and other solar phenomena, be delayed.[8]

The target year for completion, under the new schedule, would be 1971 rather than 1969, as originally planned. The arguments in favor of a delay were persuasively presented to a mission board,

---

[8] The project has been still further delayed at this writing.

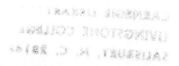

but the drawbacks were serious and obvious. The observation time available to the experimenters in 1971 would be only two weeks unless costly modifications were made. While two weeks might have been sufficient in 1969, a year of solar maximum, the chances of observing a solar flare during a two-week period in 1971 were so remote that the experiments would probably be a failure. The delayed mission could have been extended by automating the spacecraft, but no funds were on hand for such a step and none appeared to be forthcoming. Further, an automated spacecraft mode would not allow recovery of exposed film, making three of the four experiments impossible to carry out.

The mission board was most disturbed by the suggested delay and consequent changes. The investigators had worked on their experiments for nearly five years. To see them delayed another two years, with scant chance of success, was to contemplate disaster. The alternative, NASA program managers replied, was to abandon altogether the experiments that depended upon a 1969 flight to catch the solar maximum; instead, NASA might restructure the spacecraft to carry other experiments that would not require peak solar activity. Both choices were unattractive. The professional careers of nearly a dozen outstanding scientists were involved; all were men whose long-term contribution to space science could probably be significant, and several were members of the mission board as well.

The project had already been delayed a number of years, having been upgraded from a simpler mission using small rockets. Overly optimistic lower-level NASA officials had convinced the principal investigators that the simple experiments could be made more sophisticated and tied in with a larger rocket system. The upgrading promised more rewarding results, though at the price of a more extended period of preparation. The promising scientific returns that had originally enticed the scientists into the NASA program seemed continually to recede into the future.

☐ But the goal of these panels and boards is not primarily to exercise authority within the organization. Influence is only a means for advancing the various objectives of science, useful only insofar as it provides opportunities for the members and their professional colleagues to conduct exciting space experiments or helps their graduate students learn the exacting demands of an experimental science, all of which should contribute to a better understanding of the nature of our universe. Therefore, the members of the mission board must not allow themselves to become so entangled with internal maneuvering and administration that they neglect their wider, external responsibilities.

SCIENTISTS AS EXPERIMENTERS:
SPACECRAFT EXPERIMENT SELECTION

☐ The political scientist and the historian are in a better position to assess the process by which momentous, one-of-a-kind decisions—the commitment to build the atom bomb, to land men on the moon, to build an SST—are made. These are the unpatterned policy choices. We shall seek to understand a more modest decision, but one in which there are still a variety of conflicting pressures, both internal and external to the organization, and where the decision can be strengthened or vitiated over time as implementation proceeds.

☐ Throughout its history, NASA has sought to implement a basic science program, largely by means of flying carefully designed experiments on specially designed spacecraft, aircraft, and balloons through the outer reaches of the earth's atmosphere, to the moon, some of the planets, and toward the sun. The Apollo Program itself has always had a scientific as well as an engineering objective. (However, we shall not seek to describe any of these, except where the examples illustrate organizational processes.)

☐ In the making of these costly and coercive science-based decisions, high-quality scientific advice is obviously a major requirement. Thus NASA established a prestigious Space Science Steering Committee (SSSC) composed of distinguished outside scientists to advise its inside scientific personnel.[9] Their specific assignment was to review proposals by would-be principal investigators (experimenters) who responded to formal announcements of "flight opportunities." These would arise out of previous decisions on the part of NASA's top management to sponsor an unmanned spacecraft that might probe the Van Allen belts surrounding the earth, fly by Venus, or land on the moon. Prospective applicants would typically be university-based scientists or scientists working in industry or at a NASA research center. Those selected would receive funds from NASA to build and test their experiment and to analyze the resulting data.

Decision Criteria

☐ Such committees have no easy assignment. They are in the same difficult position as a foundation board, a laboratory director, or anyone else who must choose among a

[9] In recent years a major share of NASA's basic science work was funded and managed by a division called the Office of Space Science and Applications.

number of competent, imaginative proposals from well-trained professionals competing for limited resources. However, NASA's selections involve the additional complication that these experiments are very expensive (often costing millions of dollars). Further, because most experiments share common "housing," power, and the extreme rigors of launch and space flight, they require an extraordinary ability on the part of the researcher to cooperate with NASA engineers and administrative procedures. The public and Congressional scrutiny can also be intimidating; a scientist can rest assured that the failure of a hundred-million-dollar spacecraft will be fully covered by the world's newspapers. Below are some examples of the reasonable yet conflicting criteria that must be reconciled by the SSSC and NASA itself in making decisions in this pressureful milieu.

□ The steering committee has sometimes had to choose between a minor, though soundly conceived, experiment proposed by a leading university scientist and an imaginative but questionable experiment submitted by an unknown investigator. The leading scientist may have flown experiments before and be well-acquainted with the requirements of space technology and its tight constraints. He may even be a member of the selection committee who has disqualified himself from judging experiments in this case. He may also be an ardent supporter of the space program in the science community and in the public forum. It is difficult for the committee to disregard the scientific worth of the experimenter in judging the value of the experiment. In such a case, it may be neither wise nor proper to do so, for much more than simply scientific results are at stake.

□ The issue of how much consideration should be given to the experimenter arises in other ways too. An experiment may have been chosen for an earlier flight that failed for some reason which had nothing to do with the experimenter —the rocket misfired, the power panels did not operate, or an antenna stuck. Or his experiment may have been taken off the spacecraft at the last moment because it weighed too much. Should his later and succeeding proposals be given priority to make up for the losses to him in time, effort, and foregone research opportunities? If so, just how much priority should he receive? Should his experiment displace another, judged to be a bit more scientifically valuable, or should it be assigned first place only among experiments of equal worth?

□ By what standard should the committee judge three similar experiments, one from a university scientist, one from a scientist employed at a NASA research center, and one from a scientist in an industrial firm? If the mission originated at the NASA center, the NASA scientist may have known about the flight opportunity earlier and have had more time to prepare his proposal than the university scientist, and the industry scientist may have had more assistance in readying his proposals. On the other hand, the committee members, mostly university scientists themselves, may find more scientific worth in experiments that contribute to graduate education in the space sciences and that support the work and add to the prestige of space science departments in the universities. Some observers of the NASA selection process detect a tendency to favor university experimenters for other than immediate scientific reasons.[10]

☐ NASA managers would probably not express themselves in the same way, but neither would they be likely to take the comment as a criticism of their advisory process. It is, indeed, designed to help protect the interests of university scientists, thus encouraging more of them to participate in space science. A manager at headquarters patiently explained, "We know there is a 'faculty club' approach to a lot of the selection. If a great scientist brings up a flimsy proposal, you can be pretty sure that it will go sailing through. You see, we feel lucky that he has even proposed to deal with us." Preference given to university researchers could also serve to blunt the fears of the scientific community that "insiders" (i.e., NASA employees) would be favored as experimenters over "outsiders."

☐ Though the advisory process may have a built-in bias toward university experimentation, no one has accused NASA or the advisors of sponsoring poor research or approving obviously incompetent work or shoddy equipment. What bias there is shows up in the hard-to-decide cases, where reasonable men might very well disagree but where men of common experience and shared values might also very well agree.

Downstream Decisions

☐ As we noted in the preceding chapter, planning, or policy-making, is usually conceived as a discrete, "upstream" type of decision-making. Policy-makers decide what is to be

[10] Dr. Alvin Weinberg, Director of the AEC's Oak Ridge National Laboratory and an observer of scientific advisory boards, has commented that "the whole structure and cast of thinking is geared to the problem of university science . . . it would not be a great exaggeration to describe the advisory apparatus . . . as a lobby for the . . . universities." Alvin Weinberg, quoted in Daniel S. Greenberg, "The Politics of Pure Science," *The Saturday Review*, November 4, 1967, p. 66.

done, and their commands are executed by lower-level administrators. The fact that many downstream decisions really contribute to policy-making can be seen most clearly in these large systems. Here, because of the assured quantity of unanticipated problems, there is a great deal of room for negotiation, maneuvering, and decision-making that either strengthens or diverts the original plans. The decision process is not sequential, but iterative.

☐ In the special case of science experiments, we can view the intricate organizational process by which the standards and needs of scientists get amalgamated with those of engineers and where research objectives and managerial requirements must be intermeshed.

☐ Naive outside advisors are likely to complain that those organizational levels charged with the formal responsibility for selecting experiments only begin the process. It is finished by others who, although they lack the authority to make these decisions, in fact change or dilute them. Experienced and sophisticated advisors will recognize that they must, by the very nature of the technology, negotiate with inside project-engineering managers about rather detailed issues. Ironically, the latter are likely to accuse the scientific advisors of sometimes failing to give them adequate guidance on priorities, of being too vague, or of side-stepping tough choices.

☐ Typically, the advisory committee or subcommittees may winnow a dozen experiments from a hundred proposals received. They then rate those selected into three or four categories according to their probable scientific appeal or contribution. Project managers at a NASA field center are asked to evaluate the proposed experiments on the basis of weight, size, power demands, "bit rate" in transmission, maturity of design, and general compatibility and to try to fit together the largest number of class-one experiments. If one or more of the highly ranked experiments cannot be made to fit, they work on down the list until a package for the spacecraft or satellite is completed. They also make an estimate of costs. An experiment rated high on scientific value may be rated low on its engineering characteristics; for this reason scientific priorities can be greatly modified.

☐ Combining the present two-step procedure would allow consideration of the closely related scientific and engineering aspects of an experiment at the same time. The gains and losses resulting from trade-offs between the requirements of science and engineering could then be more explicitly considered by the formal, responsible advisors, with less chance of a misunderstanding or a slip-up on priorities for experiments. On the other hand, combining the procedures would involve some difficulties. The scientific advisors would have to become intimately acquainted with the complex technological problems of space flight, and the project managers and engineers would have to become expertly familiar with the various scientific disciplines and appreciative of the various scientific purposes served by the experiments.

□ Men with experience and expertise in these two related disciplines are not plentiful. Unless a scientist has already flown several experiments on a number of different rockets and learned firsthand the demanding technological requirements, he is not in a good position to understand the priorities of the engineers. Likewise, until engineers have worked closely on scientific projects and understand the larger purposes that the experiments serve, they may all too easily downgrade the instruments or unwittingly reverse scientific priorities.

□ Even should enough experienced advisors be available, NASA might not try to change the present two-step selection procedure. The existing ambiguities and the blurring of responsibility serve a number of interests and perhaps introduce a useful flexibility in a process that must accommodate frequent change. This functional requirement exists also in many other aspects of the management of complex endeavors.

Putting Together the Final Package:
Negotiations Between Outside Scientists and Inside Engineers

□ The outside scientific advisors implicitly negotiate with the project engineers over the size and capabilities of the experimental package and the priorities of the different instruments that make it up. A spacecraft may have room for no more than five experiments at the most, but the advisors may designate seven as class one, knowing that some later will be disqualified for engineering or technical reasons. If they have a particularly difficult choice to make, they may recommend both, hoping either that the project manager and his engineers can fit in both experiments or that they will find other, sufficient grounds for selecting one or the other. Or, after the experiments for a mission have been selected a new, exciting proposal may come in; the advisors may recommend its addition to the package, having learned from experience that engineers can often rearrange loads or redesign spacecraft to find room for the extra weight or supply extra power. They also suspect that engineers provide conservative specifications for the first estimates of design features. The scientific advisors, then, pad their requests. In their negotiations with the scientists, the engineers protect themselves by not disclosing all the available capability initially and then giving up the contingency capability to the winning bidder. This bidder may be the experimenter who can muster the most support from the advisory committee and put the most pressure on headquarters managers; or it may be the investigator who runs into unexpected, serious technical problems and finally must ask for more weight, power, or some other spacecraft capability than he had anticipated.

□ A manager in an experiments office of a research center described his response to the recommendations of the advisory committee as follows:

I was naïve the first time I drew up specifications and put down the limit of what we thought we could put on in weight and other capabilities. I've never done that since. Headquarters told me to put on an extra experiment, and we had a devil of a time solving the complications it caused. The package was complete, with no room or weight allowance left. But the scientists at the university needed this low-energy particle detector on the flight to correlate measurements in space with ones to be made simultaneously on earth. They put a lot of pressure on headquarters.

Well, we were told we just had to make room. We decided to redesign the whole package, splitting it into two parts. Though we had to put in additional fibers and heavier shielding to keep noise from one experiment from interfering with another, we were finally able to save 30 pounds for the 37-pound instrument. The investigator then told us that he would have to have another two pounds. I had to let him have it, for he'd already demonstrated his ability to get the scientific and headquarters pull that he needed. We squeezed one pound out of shielding for the encoder, made a few other changes, and got close to the required weight. Finally, my back was to the wall. If the experiment flew at its full weight we'd have to dump at least a pound of peroxide [used in thrusters to stabilize and orient the craft in space]. That requires a high-level decision since we were now changing the overall capabilities of the mission. Believe me, since this experience I've learned my lesson; I build in some padding. Or a better word would be "contingency." We need a contingency capability reserved for the unforeseen in all our calculation. It always gets used up; of that you can be sure.

☐ An investigator in whom the project engineers do not have confidence will have to bid higher than one upon whom they can rely.

When we are asked to evaluate the experiments for a package, we look at weight, size, power requirements, and so forth. But we also consider carefully who will do the work and who the principal investigator will be; these factors are important in determining the rating we put on an experiment. You know you can rely on some more than others. That information is not in any book, you just learn it from experience. Some investigators do exactly what they say and you don't have to guard yourself, but for others you have to double everything they offer. You know all their weight and time schedules are too low.

☐ A project manager at another field center noted that the scientific advisors do not accept the engineering estimates of costs and capability at face value, by any means.

They do not always believe we are correct in our evaluation. They may feel we are raising costs or causing difficulties that are not really necessary. They accept our word partly on the basis of who is pushing the experiment. If our evaluation is more or less in line with theirs, the decision stands. If the investigator has friends on the committee or at headquarters, though, we may be pushed hard to change our figures or make adjustments in our evaluation which would improve the rating of a particular experiment.

☐ The scientific advisors do not, however, add experiments at whim or evade making clear-cut priorities because of friendship ties, as the harassed project engineers often invidiously imply. Unexpected discoveries, improved data and techniques, late submission of an utterly different but scientifically exciting experiment, are sufficient reasons for either recommending an additional experiment for a mission or keeping priorities tentative and changeable.
☐ Sometimes the advisors will judge a newly proposed experiment promising enough to justify bumping another experiment from the flight if technological constraints are too narrow to allow both to fly. Removal of an investigator's experiment is a serious move, however, that can cause much hard feeling. The investigator may have spent anywhere from two to six years of his professional life preparing his experiment; to deny him the promised opportunity raises serious questions of ethics and equity as well as of science. Understandably, the advisors tend to pressure the engineers

to add to the payload and capabilities rather than face the difficulties of making subtractions from the roster of experiments.

ITERATION IN PLANNING

□ How and why advice and planning are continuous activities in the context of advanced technology and the role of informed negotiation can best be seen in the context of an actual case. We have included some of the technical background to allow the reader to get a feeling for the issues that provide the framework for these decision-making efforts.

Scientific advisors are reluctant to set fixed priorities on experiments when lead times are long. Flexibility is often needed to accommodate unpredictable changes. In one mission with a lead time of six years or longer, the Space Sciences Steering Committee established a general priority of experiments, subject to change if some of the investigators who had proposed exceedingly sophisticated instruments could not meet the scheduled deadlines. Three years later, the findings of Scientist A, involved in a wholly separate and different space probe, suggested that the number three experiment was obsolete. Scientist A's findings indicated that the phenomenon for which number three was to test probably did not exist. Since the investigator had already spent nearly $5 million in developing his instrument, and since A's findings were not entirely conclusive, the advisors did not immediately disturb the priorities, though they discussed the matter at some length.

A short time later they learned that the payload would be cut back 38 pounds, over 10 percent of the total. Tests had shown that the spacecraft was not strong enough to withstand the stress to which it might be subjected. Other preliminary missions provided data that indicated an environment for the spacecraft substantially different from the one that had been assumed. Consequently, reinforcing struts were being added, using up weight that had been allotted to the experiments. The advisors could no longer avoid a review of the priorities for the array of experiments.

If experiment number three was taken off, two other smaller instruments for detecting solar wind and atmospheric particles would lose some of their value. Experiment number one was easily separable into at least three parts, and some scientists suggested that the last part might be dropped with a saving of anywhere from 3 to 14 pounds, depending on how it was divided. All agreed that experiment number two should keep its position because its data would provide the best clues about phenomena scientists would want to investigate on later missions.

The advisory committee then examined the problems of readying a simpler, contingency array of experiments. An already available, simple, proven instrument replacing that for experiment number two could not be used because it transmitted data on an L-band, and the spacecraft for this mission used F-band transmission. For similar reasons all the replacement instruments, even if simpler, would have to be built anew. Another isotopic power source would be needed unless the committee wanted to use one of the three assigned to later missions. Such use would reduce the number of missions and cut one-quarter of the experiments. But to build a new power source would cost at least $2 million, given the speed with which it would have to be built, and work on the rest of the contingency package would divert hardware, test chambers, and manpower from the regular, planned experimental package. The diversion would probably delay the last mission so much it would have to be canceled, since at the time of the review it had not yet been funded.

One scientist complained, "If we had been brought these problems a year ago we might have been able to devise more options. I recognize that the project managers did not know the weight as accurately as they do now. The more details we get, the more stringent our constraints and the more difficult our job." If the scientific advisors do not "do their job," someone will have to make the unpleasant decision whether to insist upon the old priorities or to establish a new list.

☐ Thus, unless the advisors stay on top of the technological as well as the scientific developments and are readily available when critical issues arise, decisions seriously affecting the scientific capability, performance, and worth of a mission will be made by those whose knowledge and appreciation of the purposes to be served differ markedly from those of the experimenters and scientists.

☐ The case above suggests some of the technological and managerial complexities that can disrupt a sequential planning process. There will also be times when a whole project is endangered by one "volatile" experiment. An experiment may be proposed that, if successful, has a high payoff in terms of research results but if it is unsuccessful will cause the failure of all other experiments on the spacecraft. What criteria can be used to decide whether it should be included? The interdependencies and vulnerabilities associated with a tight package of experiments whose instruments must endure the rigors of launching and space travel without any opportunity for on-site inspection and repair puts great pressure on decision-makers.

SCIENTIFIC ADVICE AND ENGINEERING DECISIONS: THE BLURRED INTERFACE

☐ We can begin to understand some of the reasons why the outsider, in some ways, must become an insider if his knowledge and expertise are to be most useful in these complex projects. The outsider must stay "involved" in order to be in a position to make relevant and timely judgments and painful choices without undue "warm-up" time.

☐ Keeping the scientific community informed is also a way of protecting the organization against potential critics who might charge that scientific criteria are undercut when the real choices are made or when the pressure is on. Those "in the loop" are also in a position to provide sensible, informed answers to internal and external critics.

☐ Understandably, program people may resist the extended involvement of outside consultants because it complicates what is already a difficult decision process. It is easier and quicker to deal with one's immediate superiors and associates than to have to face distant boards and advisory groups. The project manager is concerned with completing, within severe time and budget limitations, designs and hardware that will prove "successful." His operational definition of success may be the narrow one of "it worked," quite aside from how fruitful or original or spectacular were the results. If the scientific advisors were in-house consultants whose recommendations recognized the same constraints and objectives that the project people accepted, they would meet with much less resistance.

☐ Criticized by scientists for making decisions in areas where they have little competence, project engineers may, consciously or unconsciously, try to protect themselves simply by failing to recognize that a problem may be of scientific interest. By labeling something a "technical" or "engineering" question, they can justify not involving scientists.

For example, when designing early spacecraft for soft landings on the moon was first discussed, questions of dust contaminations could not be answered. Would there be dust on the surface? If there was, would it coat all surfaces with a covering film, settle only where blown, fall from space, or be repelled by the metal craft? The engineers were primarily concerned with dust stirred from the surface by the retrorockets interfering with the operation of the spacecraft. They defined the problem as an engineering one and designed an experiment that would provide a technical answer—a modified microphone used to detect micro-meteorites in space.

A scientist who later discovered their plans was indignant: "It was plain silly. Dust may reach exposed surfaces in a number of ways, and we need to test for the most likely. It is a matter of considerable [scientific] interest to find out how dust behaves on the moon. A microphone will certainly not detect creepy-crawly dust that slowly moves across and covers a surface. I offered a better device, just as simple as theirs and providing more scientific information about the characteristics of lunar dust. It was a solar cell with an instrument to measure the changes in current as dust interfered with light from the sun."

☐ The failure of one party in an experiment to recognize the interests of the others, the lack of understanding by each party of the other's problems and constraints, and "passing the buck" when priorities have to be established, occur, in part, because many of those working on scientific missions have not yet learned enough about the constraints and limitations involved.

☐ A scientist who had worked on several experiments commented:

You have to get deeply involved to make a contribution. You have to go through the experience to see what is involved. And as we build up a core of people who know this technology and have learned to operate within the NASA organization, we're working out some of the problems better. That doesn't mean that I like what is done always, but as we work with the project people they learn from us, and we both find out there are good reasons for making the decisions we do; a reasonable man—a rational man—might very well have decided them that way.

☐ The complex intermeshing of scientific needs, engineering requirements, budgetary limitations, organizational constraints, and personal goals and values almost ensures that project decisions will involve a complex of trade-offs among many different gains and a variety of losses. Experienced and knowledgeable participants cannot eliminate the need for trade-offs, but they can approach the bargaining with a realistic evaluation of the possible solutions.

PLANNING AND TIME

☐ The critical role of time in the planning process can be observed in the effect it has on selection of experiments. Scientists complain that there is inadequate time between the issuance of invitations to the scientific community and the final date for submission of experiments. Of course, preliminary work can be encouraged by funding a *definition phase* in which scientists are encouraged to define future experiments for possible submission; obviously those who receive funds during this phase are in a much better position to respond to flight openings than those who start from scratch.[11]

☐ When time is short or an experiment is delayed by engineering difficulties, easier or "quicker" experiments often get flown. On the other hand, there is the often-observed tendency for experiments to grow in cost and complexity as a function of the time available—what an engineer calls *gold-plating* occurs.

☐ On the other hand, engineers and production managers can have pressures on them to reduce the gap between flights. This is particularly true where launching crews must be kept intact and well-trained, where component production schedules are costly to slow down, and where storage of hardware leads to some loss in quality.

☐ The relevance of time is most obvious in the difficulty one has in distinguishing tactical from strategic decisions. Tactical decisions as to which experiments should be selected from a number of proposals made by competing scientists in universities, government centers, and industry are very much a function of certain strategic decisions. The latter determine what kinds of missions will be flown with what major objectives. A spacecraft designed to orbit Mars will require a very different range of experiments from an earth orbiter or a lunar probe.

☐ The point in the decision process at which expert counsel is obtained is of the utmost importance:

The early planning by NASA centers for exploration of Mars with Mariner spacecraft demonstrated to university scientists how important it was for them to be on hand to help define the mission. As originally conceived, the 1969 Mariner was to reconnoiter Mars for manned or unmanned landings. The payload was to be planetary experiments and advanced television equipment: No weight was left over for interplanetary-particle and magnetic-

11 Space Science Board, *Lunar Exploration, Strategy for Research 1969–1975,* Washington, D.C., National Academy of Sciences, 1969, p. 35. The SSB also notes that less than two million dollars have typically been made available under the Supporting Research and Technology Program (which is administered by one division of NASA, although the experiments may be selected by another division).

field experiments—solar plasma detectors, cosmic-ray counters, or magnetometers—which would be of singular value during that year of maximum solar activity. The scientists were further distressed when they realized that the mission's demands upon the tracking network and data-receiving facilities, along with those of other planned launchings, would seriously limit NASA's ability to monitor particles and fields experiments on Pioneer spacecraft already launched and from which valuable information would still be coming. The important trade-offs had already been made by the managers themselves before the university physicists had a chance to present their case or press for a full and careful consideration of their interests.

CONCLUSIONS: PERSPECTIVE VS. COMMITMENT

☐ The use of prestigious, talented scientists as advisors in the planning process raises a number of challenging managerial issues. For one thing, it is no easier to obtain clear-cut, relevant advice than it is to take it. The organizational solution to this problem is not to separate the scientific advice from the technical capabilities. Thus means must be found to provide an active interchange between the engineering "implementers" and the scientific advisors. Each must be willing to adapt his conclusions to the specifications and the needs of the other. Planning is then a dynamic process extending over time and involving a great deal of interaction. Decisions are reached by successive approximations as reactions and counterreactions are accumulated, as technical barriers are sighted or overcome, as resubmissions occur, and as modifications are made.

☐ Unforeseen engineering or financial problems that occur in programs run by the scientists themselves are likely to be perceived as part of the inevitable risks associated with advanced research. However, when a government agency or a business is managing these critical supporting elements, the problems can easily be attributed to the organization's indifference to science and its priorities. The feeling is, typically, "If it wasn't for 'them,' we would have the program in good shape." Many times it is easier to blame others than to blame fate, nature, or oneself.

☐ On the other hand, the insider can come to resent the special care and feeding given to prestigious outsiders. To a harried manager who must be responsive to a massive quantity of conflicting day-to-day pressures, it can be the epitome of unrealism to invite an outsider to give advice. He is likely to feel that the outsider knows little or nothing about the wide range of technical, organizational, and political considerations that are part of his day-to-day life. The outsider must convey the impression that he both comprehends the manifold disadvantages under which the insider labors and respects the insider's judgment and experience. Keeping them working together, as they must if the advice is to be meaningful—they cannot be completely isolated from each other—is thus a continuing administrative challenge.

☐ The advisors who are chosen must be willing to get involved in some of the mundane details of the project, both in order to make realistic proposals and to guard against a "degrading" of their proposals as a result of engineering "problem-solving." On the other hand, this involvement must be limited or the outsider (scientist) becomes an insider, with all the commitments, vested interests, loyalties, and concomitant loss of perspective this entails. Thus there is a very delicate balance between the naïveté of the true outsider and the partiality of the insider.

☐ In the more sophisticated programs there is a need for very high-level scientific advice. In fact, more than advice is needed; often managerial inputs and a high level of commitment are also required. Yet, particularly in programs that involve extended development efforts—and hence may run for 5, 6, 7, or more years—such a commitment can be inconsistent with the need for professional challenge and growth in other areas. Realistically, it would appear that such researchers will have to sustain multiple commitments, one to the program itself and others more relevant to their specific discipline.

☐ Advice-giving, of course, is never truly impartial or without conflicts of interest. The number of professionals in any one area of high expertise is sufficiently small that one always finds overlapping interests. As a result one cannot obtain "pure" advice; within each discipline there will be camps and party lines. Any sponsor must weigh carefully the advice it receives. At any one time, unfortunately, there may be no clear consensus upon which to base program planning.

☐ There are probably few, if any, government agencies or private organizations who have struggled with such diligence and originality to incorporate outside professionals in the intricacies of the planning process as the space program.

☐ To the neophyte examining the operations of a far-flung but highly interdependent and vulnerable agency such as NASA, it may come as a surprise that outsiders with the political instincts and "clout" of key members of America's scientific establishment are encouraged to gain this intimate familiarity with the agency's affairs. Rather than being held at arm's length, they are encouraged to learn a good deal about internal technical and organizational matters. In a sense they are more than advisors, they are representatives of a critical segment of the "public," of a "constituency" who, it is hoped, will aid in legitimizing and endorsing that aspect of the agency's program relating to science. They come to resemble trustees, or a nascent board of directors, as much as consultants. This may suggest a trend that will come to affect private as well as public agencies in our highly interdependent world in which varied public interests diffuse and infuse the actions of nearly all institutions.

The Scientist—Manager or Managed?

☐ The United States has a monolithic space program, but in other countries, such as Japan, England, and Canada, the program is more apt to be a diversified effort. Especially interesting is the presence in these latter countries of separate and distinct scientific efforts directed by the Ministry of Education. The scientist, in such cases, is not a mere adjunct to a major national engineering effort. He has his own budget and his own space program. Of course, such a development is quite natural in a smaller country which has little or no reason to launch a massive moon-landing program. For such nations the program cannot be justified unless it produces some direct and fairly immediate benefits, either to the scientist in his research or to the economy. Scientists were apt to jump in early and to take the lead in the initiation of the space program in such countries. Thus the first moves in Japan were made by a group of professors in one of the research institutes of the University of Tokyo.
☐ Inevitably scientists, working through the research and educational ministries of their governments, have acquired companions in the space effort. Other ministries—construction, the post office, meteorology, transport—developed their own programs, generally focusing on applications. As the effort multiplied, organizationally speaking, there were the inevitable attempts to coordinate and control. Ministries, organized to concern themselves with "Technology" or "Science and Technology," have moved to rationalize these widespread efforts. The Japanese space program was unified when the National Development Agency was created in 1970.
☐ The scientist, in his relations with NASA, has always faced a massive bureaucracy, with its own unique goals and programs. He has never known a better kind of relationship

from his own standpoint. But with the smaller scientific and applications-type space programs, this is not true. The initial steps may allow scientific investigators a very free hand—a hand which becomes less free as time goes on and those who control the purse strings begin to assert their demands. ☐ In either case the scientific group finds itself obliged to deal with the bureaucrats. And as an early leader in the space program in one of the smaller countries noted, "Professors and government people do not mix well. We are so free and they have their red tape." Apparently this relationship presents much the same kinds of problems the world over.

SPONSOR AND SATELLITE:
THE PRICE OF DEPENDENCY

FOUR

Mission-oriented advanced technological systems have been obliged to concern themselves with alternative patterns of conducting relationships with other organizations in order to cope with one of their basic problems: exercising control and gaining cooperation in a work environment which calls for a finely tuned effort that can be neither specified contractually nor achieved through traditional supervisory methods. In their search for means to accomplish this task, they have had to treat as variables certain factors, particularly contextual factors (i.e., those having to do with the context, or setting, within which relationships are developed), that others often take as "givens." *Dependency,* for example, is a contextual variable that has a basic effect on the manner in which control can be exercised and on the extent of cooperation that can be anticipated in a relationship.[1]

□ *Contextual designs* for achieving managerial control can be contrasted with strategies, drawn from conditioning theory, which are based on the assumption that certain stimuli will predictably lead to certain responses. An example of the latter would be incentive systems, such as the *cost-plus-award-fee* approach, to encourage high-quality work in organizations participating in a sponsor's project. Such *conditioning-theory measures* operate at what might be called the "surface" of the work relationship and are assumed to function equally well in any context.

□ As we shall see, incentives appropriate for an organization seeking work competitively and almost completely independent of the sponsor are totally inappropriate when applied to one that is almost completely dependent. Dissatisfaction with conditioning-theory measures has led managers in sponsoring agencies to conclude that the underlying contextual design, involving variables such as dependency, cannot be ignored as a potent means of control. Controlling outside organizations through these factors involves determining their orientation, commitment, and responsiveness,

---

[1] For a discussion of the relationship between dependence and certain structural factors, see D. S. Pugh *et al.,* "The Context of Organization Structures," *Administrative Science Quarterly, 14,* March, 1969, 91–114.

whereas the conditioning approach concentrates on pre-programming actual decisions.

□ From a structural point of view the complex endeavor represents a new type of federalism.[2] However, the federation cannot be a loose alliance, and key cooperating organizations cannot be distracted by numerous other commitments. A mission orientation introduces special constraints. This orientation clearly is not consistent with a literal interpretation of the "independent contractor" concept. Sponsor and satellite must be able to act in concert to be immediately responsive to a program's needs. A certain degree of separation from external pressures that might prematurely abort potentially significant advances is also required.

□ Thus, the development group needs a working arrangement that will insulate it from its environment, and a monopoly or near-monopoly of certain relationships is one way of achieving this goal. To get on with the job, the sponsoring agency is almost forced to make itself the central figure in a closely knit group of organizations, insulated from external pressures—from the environment—and therefore dependent upon the sponsor. To secure this relationship, the sponsor is obliged to provide unusual guarantees as protection against risk, such as compensation for losses that may be incurred as a satellite organization tests various engineering approaches that show promise but eventually prove unfeasible.

□ It may be surprising to see *dependency* elevated to the status of a significant relationship in complex systems, but we have witnessed, in endeavors like the space program, the development of an unprecedented style of close, intense, protracted relationships among officially "independent" participants such as major sponsoring agencies and contractors. Management of this style of relationship is of special significance because it is by no means limited to advanced technologies. In the future we can expect a much greater use of mission-oriented aggregations composed of a sponsoring agency and a diverse group of satellites who have banded together to achieve a major social or economic goal.

DEPENDENCY AND INTERDEPENDENCE

□ It is important to contrast dependency and interdependence. The term *interdependence* refers to the *system* of interorganizational exchanges or transactions. Organiza-

---

[2] For a general analysis of this concept, see Carl J. Friedrich, *Trends of Federalism in Theory and Practice,* New York, Praeger, 1968, pp. 2–27.

tions are interdependent when there is interaction between their inputs and/or their outputs. An organization that participates in many joint programs would be high on a scale measuring interdependency.[3]

☐ *Dependency,* on the other hand, refers to the *status* of a participant in a joint endeavor. Status is determined by the number and type of sources from which a participant receives support, broadly defined to include a variety of resources in addition to financing. A sponsor and his satellites form an *interdependent* group. But some satellites are more *dependent* on the sponsor than others, because they receive a larger portion of their total support from him. A 100-percent-dependent organization is a member of only one sponsor's family and receives all his support from this one source. Reversing the tables, a sponsor may be 100-percent dependent on a satellite with regard to a given function. These dependency statuses are not stable, for both sponsor and satellites are continually working to improve their position with regard to this variable. Nor are these relationships necessarily reciprocal. A sponsor may be highly dependent on key advisors who for their part have a high degree of independence stemming from their preeminent position in a given field.

HIERARCHICAL AND EGALITARIAN STRUCTURES

☐ Dependency, then, is conceptually a rather simple notion. The extent of a satellite organization's dependence on a given sponsor can be measured by calculating the proportion of its total support provided by this particular source.[4] In some large Japanese enterprises, managers were able to run down a list of their contractors and give the exact degree of dependency for each. This calculation was important because it reflected the extent of the firm's obligation to a particular contractor. In some cases managers could also provide the contractor's current grade with regard to quality of work—"A," "B," "C," etc.

☐ In sharp contrast, American society gives little official recognition to the existence of organizational dependency relationships. When attention is directed to them, it often reflects a suspicion of improper practices, for example, a

---

[3] Michael Aiken and Jerald Hage, "Organizational Interdependence and Intraorganizational Structure," *American Sociological Review, 35* (1970), 912–930.

[4] Of course, the extent of dependency is reflected in outputs as well as in inputs. The output of a highly dependent organization will represent largely the sponsor's work.

Congressional investigation of "overly close" relationships between a government agency and a large contractor. Organizations in the business world are supposed to be independent, "able to stand on their own two feet." This feeling is so prevalent that some managers quickly take offense at the use of the term dependency.

☐ While dependency is conceptually simple, its management can be fairly complex. In the United States, dependency relationships present problems and contradictions in part because they are not clearly *hierarchical,* relating superior to subordinate. Instead, such relationships involve individuals or groups who consider themselves to be the equal of those upon whom they depend. In a number of instances, the political or social value system affirms that they are, in fact, equals.

☐ Perhaps to some degree because of the value conflicts involved, American business has been almost totally disinterested in the administration of dependency relationships. In societies that stress hierarchical position, this type of relationship is taken for granted. Managers often become quite skillful in the administration and control of subordinate dependent entities, such as subcontractors.

☐ Research on advanced technologies has shown an interesting combination of dependency relationships and egalitarian sentiments regarding relative status, for scientific and professional values stress the inherent equality of those with comparable technical competence. In this context, social or economic power can become a matter of small importance.

☐ The extent to which technical skill determines status in a given relationship was revealed when a very small but top-quality optical-coating subcontractor returned the designs of its main customer, a large aerospace firm, and insisted on doing its own. If the mammoth concern would not agree to this arrangement, the tiny company confidently predicted a delay of months or even a year. This type of dependency relationship is quite different from those involving the small contractor who performs routine or standardized tasks. Clearly, the administrator, no matter what his system of values, cannot rely on traditional principles for control, that is, those flowing from the fact of hierarchical inequality.

The Affluent Dependent

☐ The sponsor of an advanced-technology program must adopt some strategy for the control of dependency, for he finds himself faced with a variety of these relationships, the most important of which involve fairly large and/or technically sophisticated organizations. Complex endeavors have brought into being a new breed of rather affluent, high-level dependents, working in modern buildings located on beautifully landscaped R & D campuses. All are heavily involved with the programs of their sponsor, and without these programs most would lose their current reason for existing. Moreover, most of these organizations recognize their dependent status, accepting it as an inevitable concomitant of their participation in a new and complex endeavor. The manager of an R & D establishment with 3000 employees remarked: "We don't run ourselves, even though we feel we must be hardnosed when there is disagreement on a technical question. We are an extension of the contracting agency, willing to be extra hands and minds."

☐ The organizations allied to a given sponsor have a variety of origins. Most closely connected to the sponsor are those specifically created to serve in the mission-oriented programs of government bodies, such as the Department of Defense, the National Aeronautics and Space Administration, and the Atomic Energy Commission. Examples are the Rand Corporation, the Aerospace Corporation (serving the Air Force), Bellcomm, Inc. (serving NASA), and the Sandia Corporation (serving the AEC). Another large group includes divisions of big corporations, units especially established to undertake contract work in advanced programs. Examples include the aerospace divisions of firms such as Hughes, TRW, Boeing, Douglas, North American Rockwell, Lockheed, and Bendix. Finally, there are the smaller "spin-off" companies brought into being to play the role of contractor in one or more major programs. Founders of such enterprises frequently are former employees either of a sponsoring agency or of an organization closely allied to a sponsor.

Dependency and Organizational Needs

☐ In the uncertain, changing world of development work, dependent organizations can give a sponsor the commitment, responsiveness, flexibility, and predictability needed to make the project a success. This kind of congruent behavior cannot be preprogrammed. In this context, responsiveness means more than just a willingness to be agreeable. It means the ability to be quick to criticize and challenge, to fight for what one believes to be technically right in terms of the program's goals—behavior that requires thorough immersion in the sponsor's work.

☐ From the standpoint of a sponsoring agency, a satellite with a fairly high degree of dependency (say, 70 percent or more of its total effort is devoted to the sponsor's work) is much more apt to structure its organization and procedures to meet the sponsor's specific requirements. When the sponsor walks into the dependent satellite's plant, he finds a shiny new project office set up especially for his work. A less dependent company might simply distribute the task among a number of its existing functional divisions. In the past, in visiting these establishments, some sponsors have reported disappointment at their inability to detect evidence of any project effort, despite the award of a sizable contract.

☐ Of course, organizations that spring up—or are brought into being—specifically to do a sponsor's work are bound to be the most adaptive. The sponsor feels entitled to approach them at almost any time with a request for changes, and he anticipates a ready response to his demands. Although dependency often is a hard pill to swallow in a society such as ours, such organizations will at least grudgingly accept some of these conditions.

☐ In addition to the increased responsiveness the sponsor hopes to obtain from a dependent organization, he also looks to it as a much-needed source of flexibility. Frequently, the sponsor is a large government agency with legislatively imposed limits on the size of its staff. Moreover, civil-service regulations introduce rigidities in the employment relationship that are inconsistent with the needs of development programs. The successive stages in a program require different skills and numbers of personnel. Thus, the sponsor seeks organizations that, in essence, will serve as extensions of in-house resources. (Critics sometimes derogatorily refer to these as "body shops.")

☐ On the other hand, the dependents enjoy a privileged status. They work primarily for a famous sponsor. The R & D work they are engaged in is part of a prestigious venture, and the sponsor may rely upon them for the performance of an extremely important function. For instance, their dependency status may have been dictated by the fact that they provide advice on crucial policy matters, and thus it would be inappropriate for them to appear to capitalize on this role in other relationships.[5] Such dependents may see their position as one of a protected monopolist. They belong someplace: they do not have to go the rounds, knocking on

[5] Other aspects of this particular type of relationship will be discussed later in the chapter.

doors, seeking new sponsors. Like the famous artists of bygone eras, they relish having a patron.

Economizing on Commitment: The Japanese Approach

☐ In our society there is a pronounced tendency to solve organizational problems, such as the inducement of responsiveness in collaborating organizations, by developing competitive alternate channels for a given function. Everything is expendable. There is greater emphasis on starting a new relationship and less stress on nurturing the old. This reaction, in part, is a function of the psychological framework of the American manager. He sees himself as operating in an unlimited environment. To fill needs, he relies on negotiations in the marketplace.

☐ By way of contrast, in countries such as Japan, managers see themselves as operating in a restricted economic environment, organized on an emergency basis. They emphasize ensured cooperation, firm organizational linkages, and precise systems of control. Within a hierarchical matrix, dependency relationships are developed to serve these basic needs. Thus, dependency is an important part of their organizational design and strategy.

☐ The Japanese manager economizes by placing his dependency relationships in a structured environment. He relies very little on improvement via chance factors or drastic shifts to new relationships. Instead, careful administrative procedures are a way of life. He *economizes on commitment.* Close ties with the firm's lifetime inside workers are buffered by a variety of other insiders of lesser status, temporary workers, and contractors' employees. In a similar manner, key related companies and dependent contractors are cushioned from economic shock by the firm's assignment of work to companies with whom they have only a temporary relationship that can be cut off in times of depression. The parent concern feels an obligation to provide members of the core group with work, and they in return feel obliged to accept orders on demand.

☐ Dependency relationships tend to be incompatible with certain competition-oriented business practices. As we have seen, a dependent will design his organization and procedures for the work of a particular sponsor. The dependent is thus hampered in competing for contracts from other sponsors. Moreover, the major sponsor may be loathe to share with others the knowledge and expertise his dependent has gained while working for him. In principle, he may advocate competition to assure the best work at the lowest price, but in practice he will place limits on his dependent's mobility to other relationships. Whereas the Japanese recognize that competitive procedures must be muted in the case of dependents, Americans seem to expect dependency and competitive behavior to somehow manage to coexist.[6]

DEPENDENCY AND PROGRAM DEVELOPMENT

☐ Like his Japanese counterpart, the manager in the United States also must cope with dependency relationships. However, the American is less apt to definitively structure these relationships and more apt to have them thrust upon him as a result of events connected with the historical development of a given field, a process which begins with the initiation of any new program.

Relationships in New Programs

☐ New programs often have mammoth dimensions and constitute a tremendous drain on resources. Sources of support are limited. Required skills are scarce. The parties involved are few in number, and the members of this small group find that they basically are engaged in a process of learning together. All are excited about the new field, but at the same time they are highly uncertain about its prospects. Heavy investments are being made, while the question of return is still problematical. Critics may be launching a vigorous attack. To further complicate the picture, the sponsor himself may be less than a pillar of strength, for he may be dependent for support on one or two users or political figures whose enthusiasm ebbs and flows.

☐ As members of the numerically small family of a new program, the sponsor's satellites feel quite dependent on one another. The options in the system are few. The subcontractor on today's project may be the prime on tomorrow's. Because status relationships are continually shifting, it is difficult and even dangerous for any one of the parties to take full advantage of the power he may have in a particular situation. One manager of a large aerospace corporation noted that, as a participant in this early phase, he was very cautious about his relationships with his fellows: "We never force anybody. If we have a contract, we never take a company to court. We never know when we might be their poten-

---

[6] See the case of Systems Engineering, Inc., later in this chapter.

tial subcontractor. We treat each other with great respect." In general, conflicts among the parties are muted because this is not the time to "test" relationships.

Dependency in Mature Programs

☐ On the whole, conditions in our economy tend to be unfavorable to the long-term continuance of a particular interorganizational dependency relationship. Long-time participants—in a mission-oriented program's truncated time dimension this might mean four or five years—repeatedly use derogatory phrases to refer to their dependency relationships. One frequently heard phrase is "locked in." Another is "captive," or "slave."

☐ These descriptive terms reflect the fact that dependency relationships tend to generate feelings of anxiety and hostility on the part of the dependent party; if this development is not controlled, the dependent can begin to feel a strong desire either to escape entirely or to withdraw by reducing the extent of his commitments.

☐ As a new technology develops, opportunities arise to "escape" to better worlds. The options in the system increase. The sponsor who has regarded himself as the captive of certain large contractors now can initiate relationships with others. A highly dependent contractor who felt locked into his relationship with a sponsor can use the experience he has gained to diversify into other, related fields.

☐ The manager of one such concern made the following remark just as his company was reaching a decision point regarding its relationship with its sole sponsor: "I don't think we should perpetuate the ten-year role of 'slave contractor.' It's not good for us or for Sponsor B. We need other challenges for the stimulation of our personnel."

☐ In the United States ambitious employees of technologically advanced firms often leave the parent concern in order to start their own enterprises. In the same manner, a company that has developed capability in systems engineering while working for one sponsor may decide to shift this talent to others in newer, more promising fields. For example, one contractor considered moving from the military space program to environmental research and development—air and water pollution control.

☐ Given the ambivalencies inherent in dependency, there is a basic instability in these relationships that seems to generate a steady procession of moves toward freedom. But this statement applies only to trends in existing relationships. The need for the tailor-made, responsive dependent persists, and thus, as old relationships go sour, sponsors proceed to adopt new dependents, and key satellite organizations attempt to capture new sponsors. The cycle repeats itself.

□ An administrator in a sponsoring agency expressed real concern about the problems involved in this process of acquiring, losing, and then replacing satellite organizations:

Those aerospace contractors who start out with the system adapt more readily because most of their work is for us. But then they diversify operations so they won't have to be so dependent. The trouble is, we also become their captive, and unfortunately, we can't replace them as you can a contractor that makes nuts and bolts.

How can we better manage these relationships over time? What can we do when things begin to go sour?

□ Paradoxically, in some cases the very success of a relationship dooms it. As a key dependent advisory group begins to receive public notice, it becomes so closely identified with its sponsor that it loses its value as a source of "independent" judgment.[7] In this, as in other instances, managers clearly see the need to somehow control this process through which modern technology induces constant change in the structuring of relationships between and among organizations.

THE MANAGEMENT OF DEPENDENCY

□ It seems apparent that high-dependency relationships have both positive and negative values in the organizational world. In any case, most sponsors can afford to maintain only a limited number of such connections, for if the dependent is to serve as a readily available source of support for the sponsor's activities, the sponsor must furnish the backing needed to keep the dependent continuously functioning, and this may involve financial aid as well as provision of a steady flow of assignments of a quality sufficient to permit the retention of high-level personnel. Moreover, the sponsor is obliged to continue to use dependent organizations even if they are no longer needed or are obviously not fulfilling

[7] Bruce Smith, *The Rand Corporation*, Cambridge, Mass., Harvard Univ. Press, 1966, p. 140.

their intended purpose. A sponsor is held responsible for the decision to "adopt" a particular dependent. If the dependent were suddenly dropped, it would be an admission that the sponsor's judgment was bad.

☐ Dependency relationships increase the sponsor's ability to respond quickly and to engage in a concentrated effort, but the investment and obligations involved in nurturing dependents also can lead a sponsor to literally become the captive of such a relationship. The wise sponsor learns to ration parsimoniously the number of times he initiates such relationships.

A Program for Administration

☐ Dependency, in reality, has two sides. If units of financial support (inputs) are translated into units of work (outputs), one side can be measured by the extent to which a sponsor monopolizes the work of another organization. In the same manner, the other side, the dependency of a sponsor on other organizations, can be measured by the extent to which these other organizations monopolize the performance of one of the sponsor's key functions. Decisions regarding the extent to which a sponsor "adopts" dependents to perform a function, relies on his in-house resources, or becomes a dependent himself are clearly related to the nature of the function in question.

☐ Five basic functions serve as the building blocks of advanced technological systems: (1) advisory functions, (2) scientific-research functions, (3) systems evaluation and integration functions, (4) design, development, and production functions, and (5) operations and support functions. (See Figure 1.) Each of these five basic functions has its own distinct requirements. A wide range of skills is involved. The advisory function demands high-level knowledge and experience that can serve as the basis for planning future technical and managerial goals and directions. On the other hand, some operations and support functions involve primarily routine maintenance and housekeeping activities. The qualities of a dependent organization may be useful for some of these functions, but not for others. It is essential to develop criteria upon which to base a strategic approach to the use of dependency relationships.

☐ As a first step, *the manager in the sponsoring organization must determine which relationships should be placed in a fairly dependent status and which should be assigned to freer agents.* The manager must (a) examine each major

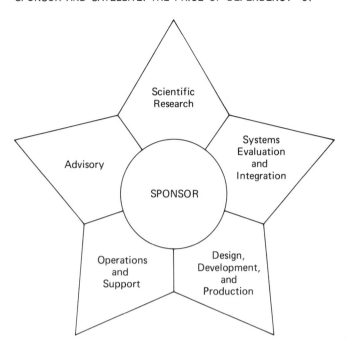

Figure 1. The five basic functions in advanced techno-logical systems.

function critically to determine whether a high- or a low-dependency relationship would lead to better organizational performance. Immediate needs and results must be balanced against long-run implications. And (b) he must judge the policy for each area in terms of its impact on the total system.

☐ In connection with point (a), it may at first appear most attractive to meet the needs of current programs by setting up a completely dependent nonprofit organization to perform *systems evaluation and integration functions.* (The Aerospace Corporation established by the Air Force is an example.) However, the manager in the sponsoring agency must consider the fact that, once established, such relationships are not easily severed. He then must ask himself whether technological developments within the next ten years, say, might render such an arrangement useless.

☐ If the answer to this question appears to be "yes," reliance on more tentative commitments might be preferable. (Reliance on more tentative commitments might also be preferable if the requirements of the technology appear to dictate an active role for the sponsor in this area.) Thus, the sponsor may ask a large contractor to set up a temporary "systems evaluation and integration program office" for the use of a given project. The task force would be staffed by men who would resume their employment with the contractor after the assignment was completed. One example of this approach was the use of Boeing to perform technical integration and evaluation for the Apollo Program.

☐ With regard to point (b), the impact on the total system of policy for a given function, the sponsor may decide that if he attempts a strong in-house effort in the *scientific-research* function, he may only scatter his resources and still not be able to duplicate the quality found on the outside. Thus, one sponsor elected to become highly dependent on universities for this function. As far as the top manager was concerned, this decision had no unfavorable aspects. He noted, "I don't worry about being 'locked into' relationships with universities. They have high quality, one-of-a-kind talents. We can't duplicate them, or perhaps we could, but the drain would be enormous."

☐ Complex endeavors are avid users of specialist knowledge and advice, and they are also quite willing to become dependent on these functionaries. However, there is a rather fine line between *dependency* on high-level groups and *control* by these same elements. Thus, in the case of NASA, scientists pushed for a Space Research Corporation that would have permitted such a group to take over many of the functions of the space agency. (Other examples of this conflict have been cited in the previous chapter.)

☐ For the scientific-research function, the manager quoted above chose to be dependent on highly independent outsiders, who could be maximally creative in this role. However, he felt that the total program would benefit if his organization were active in the *design and development functions.* Internal strength was needed to effectively coordinate and integrate contractor activities, especially in the early stages of research and development. He also saw no advantage to becoming a captive of a particular group for design and development work because, in contrast to fundamental research, these functions make use of talents that are available on a fairly widespread basis. He noted, "I believe in having several contractors working along on the same developmental problem. If one doesn't come through, there's always the chance that another will." In this case the sponsor also rejected the notion of having the development function performed by a few highly dependent organizations. For this work, a number of competing sources, including an in-house "yardstick," seemed to be the best strategy. Thus both sponsor and contractor dependency was maintained at a comparatively low level.

☐ In countries such as England and Canada it has long been a tradition for government laboratories, such as the Royal Aircraft Establishment, to undertake the major part of design and development work, leaving for industrial contractors largely the *production* phase of this basic function. However, in the United States sponsors have been more inclined to involve outsiders in the total effort of design, development, and production, so that the treatment of the production function is not radically different from that of design and development. However, as might be anticipated, very few sponsors are interested in engaging in actual production activity. In most technologically advanced countries, this work is done by contractors. Moreover, traditional restrictions on the functions performed by contractors are gradually giving way. For instance, government establishments in England and Canada have been loosening their hold on design and development work, in part to increase their international competitive power by broadening the range of skills available in industry.

☐ Of the five functions mentioned above, the *advisory function* is the only one that by its very nature must be turned over to outsiders. The main question concerns the type of dependency the sponsor will elect. Will he concentrate his dependency by using a single advisory group or disperse it among many? Will he create a satellite advisory body or employ the services of a number of independent outsiders?

☐ The *operations and support function* seems to be the kind of routine, though in some cases very highly skilled, activity that lends itself to contracting out. On the surface it also seems that dispersing the function by employing a number of contractors would be just as desirable as concentrating it in the hands of a few. However, in terms of impact on the total system, this may not be true. Sponsors such as NASA have encountered troublesome jurisdictional disputes among the various support contractors working on the launch pads. This development in turn has led to moves to reduce the number of contractors in order to cut down the number of friction-producing interfaces.

☐ A sponsor's activity in this area may be heightened by conditions unique to his organization. For instance, military sponsors have a built-in source of manpower that can be quite readily used for operations and support-type functions.

☐ The sponsoring agency organizing its work in relation to the five basic functions has a wide range of options. However, since sponsors serve more as initiators, coordinators, and integrators than as "doers," sponsor involvement in what might be described as the physical side of ongoing activities is bound to be limited. Of the five functions, design, development, and production lies at the heart of a mission-oriented sponsor's programs. If a sponsor does become more deeply involved in any area, this would seem to be the appropriate one.

☐ There is no question, however, that the use of outsiders is so pervasive that the extent of sponsor dependency and the extent of sponsor use of dependents are crucial issues. *These dependency relationships must be approached from a systems standpoint.* If a sponsor elects high-dependency relationships for a particular function, such relationships must be buffered with those involving fewer obligations. Few, if any, organizations can afford to have the majority of their relationships in the high-dependency category, especially in the sense of having others highly dependent on them.

☐ Even in large programs, the number of highly dependent satellite organizations usually is small, and this group of (hopefully) cooperative dependents generally is counterbalanced by a collection of freer agents. These freer agents may or may not be as responsive, but they can be "cut off" more easily, thus providing the sponsor with needed flexibility.

☐ Similarly, the sponsor who becomes overly dependent on outside organizations can progressively lose his ability to manage and may finally become little more than a figurehead. Sponsors must control their own dependency in order to preserve their status as free agents, capable of exercising independent judgment in matters concerning their programs.

☐ All sponsors eventually develop their own characteristic pattern of high dependency, moderate dependency, and low dependency in their relations with other organizations. The process is not random, but at the same time there are no set rules. The pattern that is developed—the extent to which the sponsor permits himself to become dependent and the extent to which he acquires dependents—will be a reflection primarily of two key factors: (a) the nature of the technology in question and (b) the stage of development of an endeavor. Dependency needs in the early stages of a complex endeavor may be (and often are) greater than in later periods.

Decision Criteria

□ The following six questions can be used as guidelines for decisions concerning dependency relations for a given function:

1. Is this function a core function (integral to the mission) in the eyes of the sponsor? If it is, the sponsor should consider assigning it to a dependent organization. (Using its in-house staff is an equivalent alternative.) If it·is not a core function, then the tables can be reversed and the sponsor can place himself in a position of dependency on others. The answer to each of the following questions can be patterned in the same way.

2. Is this a key function in the sense that it is time-critical? Can a halt in this function stop activities throughout the system?

3. Does this function involve work that must be integrated with the activities of others? (The converse of this is the completely separate function.)

4. Does this function require expertise that should be internal to one's own organization because of the confidential nature of certain aspects of it?

5. Are the tasks associated with this function primarily managerial?

6. Is this an essential program-oriented service function whose precise future dimensions are still in the process of definition?

□ Application of these criteria might lead a sponsor to conclude that it would be appropriate to assign the scientific-research function to independent organizations upon whom the sponsor, in turn, will be quite dependent. This work is not a core function for the sponsor, nor is it time-critical; it does not have to be integrated with the work of others. Finally, the function is not a managerial one, nor is it a program-oriented service function currently under development.

TECHNOLOGY AND THE STYLE OF THE DEPENDENCY RELATIONSHIP

□ The pattern of dependency relationships that emerges in a given complex endeavor clearly is related to technological factors, especially to the difference between *production-type* and *one-of-a-kind* systems. Production-type advanced technological systems are those engaged in large R & D programs, with substantial follow-on operations or production (e.g., missiles). One-of-a-kind advanced technological systems have relatively small R & D programs and very little follow-on production (scientific satellites).[8]

Table 1
Relationship Between Type of Technology and Extent and Type of Sponsor Dependency on Outside Organizations for the Five Basic Functions of Advanced Technology Systems

Function	Extent and Type of Dependency	
	Production-Type Technology	One-of-a-Kind Technology
Advisory	Dependent (100%) (concentrated)	Dependent (100%) (dispersed)
Scientific-Research	Dependent (dispersed)	Dependent (dispersed)
Systems Evaluation and Integration	Dependent (100%) (concentrated)	Dependent (dispersed)
Design, Development, and Production	Dependent (100%) (concentrated)	Independent (dispersed)
Operations and Support	Independent (dispersed)	Dependent (dispersed)

Note: The rating "dependent" is received if more than 90 percent of the effort is conducted by outside organizations.

□ Table 1 presents the relationship between the type of technology and the extent and type of sponsor dependency on outside organizations for the five basic functions of an advanced technology. A sponsor is rated as dependent if more than 90 percent of the total effort is contracted out. A mere 10-percent sponsor effort may seem to be a strange dividing line between dependency and independence, but in terms of the programs of advanced technologies this figure represents substantial sponsor involvement. If the sponsor has no real in-house effort, he is rated as 100-percent dependent.

[8] The term "small R & D" is used here in a relative sense. In 1967, NASA, a one-of-a-kind advanced technology agency, had a total R & D budget of $4866 million, while that of the Department of Defense, a production-type, was $8049 million.

□ The table also indicates the manner in which the sponsor's dependency is structured. The rating "dispersed" indicates that a number of outside organizations are used for the function in question. On the other hand, a rating of "concentrated" means that only a few outside organizations are involved. Especially in the case of the advisory and systems functions, the "concentrated" rating often reflects a situation in which the sponsor uses a single satellite organization brought into being to serve his needs exclusively.

□ Examination of the table reveals that while both production-type and one-of-a-kind advanced technologies are highly dependent on outside organizations, the production-type system has moved further in this direction and has favored the "concentrated" structure rather than the "dispersed" structure preferred by the one-of-a-kind type. To assure retention of control when the sponsor itself has no role in a given function, the production-type system relies to a much greater extent on the creation of 100-percent-dependent outsiders, on whom it in turn is 100-percent dependent.

□ These differences in the use of outsiders in part reflect the fact that the production-type system experiences less severe technical constraints. Operational failures are not as critical. A particular missile may be produced in the thousands. Testing and operations are overlapping procedures. An initially successful flight of a spacecraft is a much more critical matter, especially if it is manned.

□ Generally speaking, although one-of-a-kind technologies are obliged to use numerous outside organizations in all their functions, their managers are less keen on this system. These men tend to prefer an active role, especially in the design, development, and production function. Wishing to retain a fairly free hand for themselves, they also prefer to disperse rather than concentrate dependency relationships. They almost seem to fear overdependency on any one organization. In their relations with their satellites, they see themselves more as a competitor among equals.

□ This high involvement in technical matters is not necessarily a matter of preference for the one-of-a-kind sponsor. However, an agency intent on building an object such as a spacecraft, which must function continuously, error-free, and for long periods in a hostile environment, may well discover that existing standards of industrial workmanship are not adequate. To meet these stringent needs the sponsor is obliged to exercise constant surveillance and to engage in intense, protracted relationships with his contractors.

□ As a result of concerning himself so fully with technical matters, the one-of-a-kind sponsor may find that he is in dire need of assistance in the systems function. In contrast to the "concentrated" approach of his counterpart in the production-type technology, the one-of-a-kind man will probably prefer to bring in several rather independent outsiders. Moreover, he is apt to favor commitments that persist only for the duration of the task in question over long-term arrangements.

TYPES OF DEPENDENCY RELATIONSHIPS

□ Let us turn now to the satellite's dependency on the sponsor. Such relationships would seem to be least complicated—"cleanest"—in the case of the single company entirely dependent on a single sponsor. In this situation the dependent has a classically unambiguous status. However, such relationships are rather rare even in the world of space shots and atom smashers, and most of them have been deliberately brought into being.

Plural and Incompatible Dependencies

□ More typically, one finds *plural* dependencies in advanced technologies. Moreover, some of these dependencies, such as a contractor's simultaneous dependency on production and one-of-a-kind sponsors, may be incompatible with one another. This phenomenon is especially apt to occur when two or more sponsors are operating in a given field. The space activities of the Air Force and NASA are an example.
□ In other cases a particular dependency relationship can set the tone for all others in which a satellite company participates. Thus, if a contractor is 80-percent dependent on a production-type sponsor, the 20 percent of its efforts devoted to the interests of one-of-a-kind sponsors may be bogged down by a production-type orientation with regard to management systems and the like. Tailor-making procedures for the one-of-a-kind sponsors would escalate the costs to them. Thus, the work of these parties is inevitably affected by the sometimes incompatible values and attitudes imposed by the dominant relationship.
□ A large contractor, who was highly dependent on Sponsor A for 90 percent of his total workload, was always scornful of Sponsor B, who furnished the remaining 10 percent.

Quite naturally, the contractor used A's management system and was continually irritated by what its managers described as the "sloppy" and "undisciplined" approach of Sponsor B. One of this contractor's managers remarked: "B never seems to learn anything. It is an organization that seems to be incapable of learning. On the whole, their people are bad managers who don't care about systems and prefer instead to mess in the actual workings of a project. Their entire management function is in a state of disarray."

☐ In reality, Sponsor A was a production-type organization that relied mainly on a "management system" and as a result interfered very little with the everyday work of its contractors. B, on the other hand, was a one-of-a-kind sponsor with a much more active approach to management, including a good deal of participation in technical questions at all levels. B's involvement in design matters literally knew no bounds. Even small standardized parts such as toggle switches and transistors were discussed in detail with contractors. In making his unfavorable assessment, this contractor in all likelihood was reacting to the fact that the second sponsor, with its much smaller official commitment of time and energy, demanded so much more of both because of the day-to-day interaction it required.

The 100-Percent-Dependent Organization

☐ When one considers the problems involved in sharing a dependent, it is not surprising that sponsoring agencies continue to seek exclusive dependency relationships. Because such relationships are tailor-made to meet the sponsor's needs, he is almost always directly or indirectly involved in their creation.

☐ In part because of this initial close connection, the relationship between sponsoring government agencies and 100-percent-dependent high-level service units has been a frequent subject of heated Congressional debate. Their dependency often seems an incongruous state in light of the advisory and systems-management functions they serve, functions that are supposed to require the utmost in independent judgment. It is not surprising that these dependents themselves express ambivalence regarding the role they play.

☐ As far as origins are concerned, some 100-percent dependents have "ancestors"—an industrial parent company who provided the organization; others are "foundlings" brought into being by the sponsor. The foundlings generally are nonprofit organizations, while those with ancestors may have either a profit or a nonprofit status.

The Foundling

□ The totally dependent "foundling" organizations seem especially uneasy about some aspects of their status. A manager in one of these establishments professed great envy of those dependents who possessed "ancestors," for they had someplace to return to if work with the sponsor became unbearable. On the other hand, managers of competitors who had to make profits in the marketplace expressed great jealousy of this particular foundling. They regarded it as a "kept" organization, with free buildings and unlimited support. All were convinced that it was little more than an expensive toy, performing tasks at theoretically cheaper but actually much higher prices.

□ One might anticipate that their secure position would lead such dependents to become confident, almost arrogant, pets. But beneath the surface almost the reverse is true. While managers of foundlings do not deny the support they receive from their sponsor, they are apt to be disturbed at the manner in which their future is so tied to the other. Moreover, if the sponsor's interests shift, or if it fails to continue to obtain support for them, they could be left out in the cold. In a world that advocates healthy competition, such organizations may feel isolated, trapped in their own private economy of both plenty and scarcity. It is not surprising, then, that a 100-percent-dependent foundling organization may attempt to escape, at least in part, from what an outsider would consider a "soft" situation. A few have been successful in diversifying into other relationships, although at some cost to their rapport with the sponsoring agency. Others remain "locked in," patiently awaiting the day when their spectrum of relationships can be broadened.

The Dependent with "Ancestors"

□ The foundling relationship obviously cannot involve dual and potentially incompatible dependencies. On the other hand, the dual dependency structure may be an extremely important component in the life of the 100-percent dependent with "ancestors." Sponsors have many reasons for not wanting to be an organizational "parent without a partner." If a sponsoring agency joins with a large industrial concern in the creation of an affiliate designed to serve the sponsor's needs exclusively, this dual arrangement gives the sponsor the benefit of the strengths and resources of the other "parent." For instance, the industrially based parent concern can meet peak workloads by drawing men from his permanent facilities. Then too, when the sponsor wants to sever its connection with the affiliate, the latter can be simply reassimilated by its industrial parent.

□ However, there are indications that this arrangement has drawbacks as well as advantages. For instance, the affiliate is a dual dependent, and this circumstance gives it a built-in hedge. Early in the game its management can begin planning for the day when the sponsor may turn to another source or for some reason seek to alter the terms of the relationship. As the manager of one such affiliate put it, "It's good to feel that we have an anchor. We can't be set adrift."

□ It seems apparent that the initial structuring of these dependency relationships has a profound impact on their subsequent history. Was the dependent provided with industrial "ancestors" or was it simply dumped on an organizational doorstep as a foundling venture? The strategy chosen has a great effect on the dependent's view of the world—and on his reactions to organizational problems. There is no one best structural arrangement, but the sponsor must be certain that the structure chosen does not actually impede the purposes for which the relationship was initiated.

Managing the Sponsor, or "We Don't Pump Gas!"

□ Thus far our analysis has centered on the sponsor's problems in dealing with dependent satellite organizations. But there is another side to this coin—the countermoves on the part of the dependent to control the sponsor. Of course, all contractors, dependent and fairly independent, feel this urge to some extent; but a "locked-in" relationship of strong dependency serves to highlight the phenomenon. Countermoves of this type are probably healthy as far as development work in advanced technologies is concerned because the field demands contractors who can take an independent stand and who can, on occasion, forcefully tell the sponsor that he is dead wrong.

□ How are controls bargained over and devised in the day-to-day interaction between sponsor and contractor? It seems clear that the highly dependent satellite is particularly strongly motivated to establish ground rules that will permit him certain freedoms. One such dependent affiliate was created by a government agency and a large utility company. The agency was a one-of-a-kind sponsor with a preference for a more tentative type of relationship. It wanted a completely dependent organization to whom it would not be bound for life: In fact, the sponsor wanted to be able to *increase, decrease,* or *terminate* the relationship at will! Specification of these conditions involved an implicit trade-off between the sponsor's demands and some of the customary benefits of dependency, particularly the potential for "unlimited" flexibility and responsiveness. It is not surprising that the affiliate created under these conditions responded in kind. Systems Engineering, Inc., as we shall call it, steadfastly refused to increase the number in its employ beyond a figure small enough to permit easy return to the parent organization. The same line of reasoning led it to be cautious about the scope of the activities in which it engaged: These had to be either central to the purpose set forth in the original agreement with the sponsor or central to the parent utility's interests.

□ On the other hand, the affiliate was neither ambitious nor restless. Rather than seeking credit for its work, it had a strong desire for anonymity, conditioned in part by fear of Congressional investigators curious about its protected status. S.E., Inc., saw itself only as a high-level service group; and indeed, it performed very well in the limited role it had carved out for itself.

□ However, S.E., Inc.,'s self-imposed limitations on the scope and depth of its efforts in the advisory function caused considerable disappointment to some members of the sponsor's house. They attempted to prod the affiliate by having it bid against others for assignments, but S.E., Inc., resisted this effort, citing the inherent incompatibility between dependency and competitive procedures. It argued that it was precisely the special, skilled group that the sponsor had wanted. If the sponsor no longer needed it, or sought to introduce an intolerable condition (such as bidding), the affiliate would simply return to its other home.

□ Initially, these two dependencies seemed to be compatible. The potential for return to the utility parent made the tentative conditions set forth by the other parent acceptable. However, this basic situation really prevented the governmental sponsor from getting the services it wanted, and in time, severe incompatibility developed.

□ As the relationship with the sponsor dragged on, S.E., Inc., became restless. The programs on which it was working were being gradually phased out, and the sponsor gave no indication of what the future might hold. (In part, of course, the sponsor's silence reflected its own insecurity about its programs.) Although they were cautious and conservative in some ways, S.E., Inc.,'s managers deplored the sense of drift; they now regretted what at one time would have seemed a trivial omission—the failure to include a termination date in their agreement with the sponsor:

These things can go on forever. You can't specify an exact date, but we should have picked a definite point such as "after the first successful mission." You need a fixed limit that establishes a time for new discussions about your future.

You have to have a new mission, a new goal. If not, you tend to drift. Your work becomes "do what we tell you to do."

□ Moved from its essentially defensive position by the sponsor's inaction, S.E., Inc., spent a good deal of staff time deliberating over possible future roles for the organization. A wide and rather surprising range of options was considered:

1. Go out of business.

2. Continue in the relationship with the government sponsor.

3. Cease being a "contractor" and become a division of the sponsoring organization.

4. Become a division of the parent utility company.

5. Become a division of another corporation.

6. Work for another sponsor in another advanced technology field, such as environmental science.

7. Become an independent contractor and seek commercial systems-engineering business.

□ Considering S.E., Inc.,'s cautious approach to problems, rejection of alternatives 5, 6, and 7 was to be anticipated. In the end it settled on a strategy that did not unduly disturb its current situation. It planned to gradually reduce its 100-percent effort on the sponsor's behalf to something less than 50 percent and to devote the capacity that became available to work on special projects for the parent utility company. This ultimate choice clearly was in keeping with its customary protected life style.

□ In making this move, S.E., Inc., led from a position of considerable strength because its stand was always buttressed by the implications of its relationship to the parent utility. Whereas it managed its sponsor very adroitly, not all dependent contractors can afford to be equally firm. However, it would appear that they all aim to achieve similar kinds of controls. This finding is a reflection of the phenomenon referred to in the beginning of this chapter—dependency relationships that do not fit into a clearly sponsor-dominated hierarchical authority system. In these non-hierarchical sponsor-satellite relationships, the tendency toward equalization of status is often stimulated by an essential equality of technical competence.

☐ Dependent contractors center their efforts for control on three basic areas: administration, the program itself, and communications. To draw a parallel with the industrial-relations field, these are not traditional "bread and butter" issues. Rather, they concern basic managerial and technical matters.

Administration

☐ There are inevitable differences in the viewpoints of sponsor and satellite: The sponsor looks upon the dependent as a *resource* whose use he wants to broaden; the dependent, on the other hand, seeks identity and independence or limitation of commitment through pursuit of a specialist role.

☐ It is not surprising that administrative matters often serve as a testing ground for these differences. *Employment size,* for example, is a strongly contested issue. Limiting the number of one's employees may seem to be simply a conservative business procedure, but in reality dependents use it to control the nature of the functions they perform. They can then argue that they lack the manpower to conduct unwanted tasks. For instance, S.E., Inc., never acceded to persistent requests that it hire more than 500 employees.

☐ The question of the sponsor's voice in *personnel selection* raises similar issues. Some dependents consistently refuse sponsor requests to hire certain individuals, often persons currently in the sponsor's employ. In the case of hierarchical dependency relationships (e.g., in Japan), sponsors regularly send personnel to the dependent companies, who routinely, if sometimes unenthusiastically, accept them.

The Program

☐ Conflicts in this area seem to present the most serious problems. Decisions concerning the program structure the satellite's entire operation, for they specify its basic assignments. Dependents of one-of-a-kind sponsors are especially

apt to feel discriminated against in the matter of assignments. One of them, voicing a frequent complaint, noted,
"Sponsor B wants you to do the jobs his technical people
don't want to do." Another contractor remarked, "We tell
them, 'We don't pump gas!' " Even those who somewhat
grudgingly accede to most sponsor requests seem to share
this universal desire of the technically skilled to delimit their
functions to those included in their field of specialization.

□ Contractors most frequently justify exceptions to "the
principle of specialization" by arguing that their personnel
could learn, or benefit from, an offbeat assignment. One
contractor used this reasoning when it undertook a long-
term planning assignment that fell outside the scope of its
regular activities: "Choosing future missions is Sponsor B's
job, not ours, but we did it partly because we thought we
would learn something that would help us in our own decision processes. We debated whether to do this job or not for
a long time."

□ As one might have anticipated, S.E., Inc., took a firm
stand with regard to program decisions. Although it made a
few exceptions in emergency situations, it generally held to
the rule that it would perform only "upstream" tasks—tasks
that involve specification of a sponsor's future actions in a
given program—and that it would not undertake "downstream" tasks, such as analysis of the data gathered in a
program's previous missions. The byword was, "stick to
your mission" (as defined in the initial agreement between
S.E., Inc., and the sponsor). As one S.E., Inc., manager
noted, this particular affiliate had been progressively narrow-
ing, rather than broadening, the range of tasks it was willing
to perform, apparently as a defense against anticipated
future sponsor pressures for expansion. (Note the contrast
with what is assumed to be traditional business practice.)

Communications

□ Although this area might seem to be the least crucial of
the three, in reality it presents some of the knottiest problems. From whom in the sponsor's house will the contractor
take direction? What access should the sponsor have to the
contractor's internal management data or staff meetings?
Interestingly, contractors who felt almost honored at being
invited to important meetings in the sponsor's program
office were highly resistant to the idea that the sponsor
should be present at similar conferences in the contractor's
house. Contractor recognition of the latent authority structure expressed itself at this point.

☐ In the same vein, informal means for promoting sponsor-contractor interchange were also resisted: "We have no desk in the sponsor's shop and they have none in ours. They would like to have us there, but you lose your independence. Something like that quickly grows out of bounds."

☐ In the communications area, contractors frequently wrestle with problems concerning which types of information shall be given to the sponsor and which shall be withheld. In one case a sponsor asked that a contractor furnish the names of all persons receiving raises greater than 12 percent. However, the contractor felt that this request constituted an infringement on its freedom to manage its own personnel: "After debating for months, we finally gave the sponsor averages, and the number above and the number below. The sponsor said he had that data from other contractors, but we told him our agreement said nothing about this matter. That settled that. There were no more requests for this type of information."

☐ But the key issue concerned *the question of taking direction.* Especially in the case of the highly dependent contractor, the sponsor tends to feel that managers at all levels should be able to give technical direction. This sentiment is consistent with the policy of treating the satellite as a resource whose use one is attempting to maximize. As one contractor noted, "The lower people in Sponsor B's house want to tell you what to do. They want to use you for their purposes. 'Here is a resource we can command.' They try to twist our arm. They say Contractor X will do it or Contractor Y did thus and so for us."

☐ However, few contractors want to be exposed to multiple direction from a large number of individuals at various levels in the sponsor's shop. Most prefer to have one established point of contact with the sponsor. Again, S.E., Inc., was obstinate on this point. There was nothing in the original agreement about sponsor direction, but when the issue arose, the affiliate first wanted to accept direction only from the major program head. It finally agreed to accept one other man, who it agreed was also technically qualified, but this arrangement was to continue only so long as this particular person held that assignment. Thus, S.E., Inc., was able to limit the number of points of contact by accepting direction only from those whom it deemed "technically competent."

☐ Again, it should be noted that not all dependent contractors are or could be as forthright as S.E., Inc., but almost all of them are concerned about these same issues and even the very timid have made surprisingly strong stands on some points.

GIVE-AND-TAKE: KEEPING THE
RELATIONSHIP "ON COURSE"

☐ Certainly, the data presented above indicate that those managers in the sponsor's house who deal with contractors cannot content themselves with the role of mere order-giver. The drive for autonomy found among even very dependent contractors (and perhaps especially among such contractors) almost forces these managers to concern themselves with determining the manner in which they can best guide the relationship to keep it on course and to prevent the emergence of "withdrawal" or "escape" syndromes.

☐ If not properly managed, long-term, dependent-based service relationships—those that demand the highest professional qualifications as well as those involving only menial housekeeping functions—quickly become occupied with "power struggle" issues similar to those found in labor relations. As a matter of fact, some of the primary characteristics of the typical union-management relationship are just as apt to be found in one-of-a-kind advanced technologies, where the sponsor's managers tend to become heavily involved in the day-to-day activities of the contractor. These managers often create a basis for coercive comparisons by conducting competitive in-house efforts. Or, they may stir up defensive reactions, as S.E., Inc.'s sponsor did, by treating 100-percent dependency as a tentative arrangement. Thus, there is fertile soil for disputes over questions of the scope of an assignment, jurisdiction, rights, and authority. This is strikingly similar to relationships in traditional craft technologies, in which there are almost continuous arguments over boundary lines (e.g., debates over who shall hang a steel door). On the other hand, in a production-oriented technology, the contractor has a considerably smaller "working interface" with the sponsor, and thus there is less occasion for issues of this type to arise.

☐ Sponsors initiate relationships with 100-percent-dependent satellites in order to have a responsive, reliable organization to perform key functions. In essence, they want a group on whom they can depend, and they must concentrate on developing an effective relationship to that end. Because the dependent has only one source for its workload, it may come to feel somewhat like a wastebasket, an object basically designed to receive a miscellany of scraps (task assignments). Its attitude then tends to become one of a disgruntled subordinate, rebelling against an arbitrary supervisor.

☐ An organization that is constantly supported cannot count on a steady flow of only the highest level work (a type of work that is characteristic primarily of the early stages of research and development). However, it must be placed in an environment that encourages it to be flexible. An occasional downstream job, which may actually provide some valuable experience, need not constitute a threat if the dependent is certain that the original purpose of the relationship remains the same. The satellite-contractor should be invited to participate fully in the planning of assignments—much more so than a contractor serving a number of sponsors, for participation in multiple relationships provides the latter with a built-in source of freedom and discretion.

CONCLUSION

☐ In this chapter we have discussed the chief characteristics of the interorganizational dependency relationship common in new and advanced technological systems. But in this universe, as in all others, dependency relations are in a constant state of flux. Sponsors engage in a continual process of bargaining both to obtain dependents and to free themselves from unwanted degrees of dependency. Conditions in our particular economy tend to militate against long-term interorganizational dependency relationships. But the need is there, and thus the process of adopting dependent contractors (and of capturing or monopolizing sponsors) goes on.

☐ Unfortunately, there is a weakness in the management of interorganizational dependency relationships in our society. We tend to solve problems by developing new sources, alternate channels for a given function. Too often we look to new relationships for answers, instead of attempting to cope with the old. The former is often more costly and adds new complexities. To remedy this situation, the manager of a sponsoring organization must, as a first step, determine which functions need a strong dependency relationship. Each of the five basic functions of an advanced technology imposes its own requirements. Dependency requirements are also related to the nature of the technology involved. There are significant differences between the production-type and one-of-a-kind advanced technologies. The manager then must proceed to employ skills that will enable him to economize on and to manage interorganizational commitment. Because of the demands high-dependency relationships place on the organization supporting them, the number of such connections must be strictly limited, and they must be buffered with "freer," more expendable relationships.

□ Organizational dependency relationships are rarely simple. Advanced technological systems exist in a world in which plural, incompatible dependencies are the rule rather than the exception, yet little consideration is given to these structural problems.

□ We have examined in some detail the sponsor's interest in seeking relationships with 100-percent-dependent contractors. Obviously, the initial structuring of these arrangements is extremely important in determining their future course. Skillful management during the later stages of the relationship is equally important to prevent the emergence of either the withdrawal or the escape syndrome and the reverse side of this coin, to control the dependent's moves to manage the sponsor.

□ Satellite organizations clearly feel dependent on their sponsors. However, we also have cited various examples of contractor countermoves aimed at controlling and managing the relationship with the sponsor. Although on the surface these two postures may seem to be contradictory, they are actually consistent. In the final analysis he who controls the resources calls the tune. Hence the sponsor is generally dominant. On the other hand, we must recognize that there is a process of day-to-day adaptation within this framework. The contractor's maneuvering for greater independence within the boundaries imposed by the long-term realities of the relationship is frequently very effective.

INDUCING EXCELLENCE: THE SELF-FORCING, SELF-ENFORCING SYSTEM

FIVE

Crises related to engineering development problems seem to be almost a way of life in advanced technologies. The manner in which human ingenuity meets these emergencies by compensating, sometimes brilliantly, for such gross organizational defects as poor systems management both excites our admiration and reaffirms what we all desperately want to believe, that human judgment cannot be dispensed with. In one case a satellite that encountered difficulties in flight lasted ten times longer than it might have simply because a project manager remembered and put into the system an error command that had been used to right the paddles on an earlier version of the spacecraft.

☐ In the world of technologically advanced complex endeavors, it is the dream of nearly every top manager to "routinize" this ingenuity, to develop a system for achieving excellence—one that learns, corrects most of its own errors, including the human ones, and has its own internal means for keeping on course and preventing major distortions. The manager who wishes to achieve this goal becomes involved in the creation of the multifaceted pressure system that will be the major topic of this chapter. Devising a pressure system that will effectively control these endeavors is extremely difficult because of their multiorganizational structure, the necessity for continuous coordination, the mixture of key functions proceeding at differing paces, and the instability introduced by an incessant flow of changes, large and small. Traditional day-to-day supervisory techniques that may work well in a smaller, less technical endeavor become costly, irritating, ineffective, and, in a word, almost impossible as projects grow in size and complexity.

☐ In this chapter we will examine some designs for inducing excellence that specifically take into account the federal nature of mission-oriented advanced technologies and their consequent ability to defeat or subvert externally imposed controls. In essence, our point of view will be that of the top manager in search of ways of planning, coordinating, and controlling his organization. Chapter 6, "Achieving Excellence in the International Project," will pursue the question of attaining excellence in international efforts, in which problems of coordination and integration become even more severe. The material in Chapter 6 also underlines the fact that more than one type of excellence is relevant for the functioning of the mission-oriented endeavor.

□ Our prime concern, of course, is with the achievement of excellence in a technological sense. But any mission-oriented project has a further objective—ensuring the utilization of what it has developed; and in this sense it must achieve another type of excellence, *organizational excellence* in the building of future links to sellers and users of the items being developed. There are actually two tasks in which the mission-oriented endeavor must excel: (1) technical achievement and (2) exploitation and dissemination of this achievement.[1] The second task is especially difficult because it requires the extension and testing of relationships in areas and activities that lie beyond the life of the project itself and the scope of its immediate purpose.

□ Clearly, controlling the program to induce excellence is an ever-present need for the mission-oriented advanced technology. A tremendous investment in human life and effort turns on the success or failure of one space shot. Tightly interlocked systems are extremely vulnerable; even a single source of difficulty may ruin a program. The Apollo fire of 1967 and the aborted Apollo 13 provide dramatic evidence of this fact. Unbelievably small matters can defeat the mighty. The British pioneered the development of nuclear reactors, and yet in 1969 they found to their dismay that corrosion of some hardly considered steel bolts was reducing the output of their Magnox Reactors after almost a decade of successful operation.[2] Similarly a toggle switch worth a few pennies came close to ruining a major NASA project, while Canada's deuterium (heavy-water) plant has been plagued with so many start-up problems that the 100-million-dollar facility has never produced a gram of product.[3]

□ All these appear to be cases in which mechanical and physical design trailed an advanced technology. How can advanced technologies move on to the point where managers will literally be able to achieve excellence in every respect—to anticipate every vital problem? Is this an impossible goal?

[1] Problems related to the second task are discussed in Chapters 6 and 7.

[2] *Financial Times,* September 24, 1969.

[3] *New York Times,* April 26, 1970.

CONTROL SYSTEMS AND PERFORMANCE

☐ Control systems designed to encourage excellence of performance are a key managerial tool. Traditionally, those creating such systems have been most concerned about standards to assess the quality and quantity of output. For the manager these standards are a major means of coercing those under him. He becomes dependent on their use, and if one group of these surrogate indicators does not produce the desired results, he seeks others, often hoping to find a solution in greater refinement and greater complexity of the measures.

☐ However, none of the various surrogate performance stimuli and indicators typically utilized give more than a slight clue as to what is actually happening in the shop or laboratory. The standards reassure the manager that he is being diligent in his pursuit of quality, but they do not provide him with a measure of the actual situation at a given time, an element which is of crucial importance in managing advanced technology. The huge investment involved and the importance of a successful mission demand that the actual situation be known and that it alone serve as the basis for action.

☐ In fact, these standards may not only be irrelevant for the problem at hand; they may serve to distort behavior and thus impede the pursuit of excellence, in a number of ways:

1. Standards predetermine decisions. In effect, the sponsor's incentive systems serve to make decisions for his contractors before the actual situation is known. The sponsor thus forces action based on information which is less than that possessed by the man "on the firing line."

2. Inevitably, more than one set of standards and controls apply to a given situation, and more likely than not, these will conflict with one another. For instance, multiple-incentive systems are designed to give the contractor freedom in making trade-offs that will permit him to earn the highest possible incentive award. Thus, he may decide to lose something on meeting the prescribed schedule in order to produce a higher-quality product. However, other controls may deny him this choice. For instance, the sponsor may have imposed a requirement that the contractor take technical direction from members of the sponsor's program group or from a designated outside organization, and these individuals may insist that the schedule be observed. It is obvious that this latter source of control can vitiate the contractor's ability to make effective use of the trade-offs available under the multiple-incentive system.

3. Externally imposed controls often induce optimization of the subunits that compose the total system. However, the potential for integration of these units may be sacrificed as subsystem objectives come to dominate those of the whole. For instance, the "cost-effectiveness" controls of the Air Force resulted in each unit of the F-111 being optimized, but when the individual units were brought together the total system failed to function properly.[4]

4. Generally speaking, externally imposed controls tend to focus attention on means rather than ends, on "how to get there" in a way that will look good in terms of the standard. In the process, the mission for which a project was organized may lose its "visibility."

☐ In a small-scale R & D undertaking, the sponsor's manager can reinforce standards-based judgments with first-hand observation of the actual situation, although even with a small group the independent spirit of the professional may lead to resistance to this effort. But the manager of a multi-organization large-scale system is faced with a truly difficult problem. Its federal structure means that the manager is faced with the problem of controlling to induce excellence in units not under his direct authority. Determining the actual situation is difficult, if not impossible. Attempts to intervene directly to gather this information may only lead to rebuffs.

☐ What kind of excellence-inducing control system does the multiorganization endeavor want to develop? What should be the major sources of the control a sponsor exerts over organizations participating in its programs? Is there a substitute for formal standards and regulations and contrived tests such as cost-effectiveness? One thing is certain. The managerial solution cannot be a simple one. Nor is a combination of simple solutions the answer. Strategies such as replacing an incentive system that rewards one type of behavior with a system that rewards several will not be effective.

THE SELF-FORCING, SELF-ENFORCING SYSTEM

☐ The top manager of a large-scale system is continually seeking a means of identifying problems when they first arise. As a first step, a major design change would seem to

[4] *New York Times,* August 17, 1969; December 20, 1969.

be required. He must create a system that will make both the organizations it embraces and the people in them want to do what is needed in a system that is *self-forcing* (for excellence) and *self-enforcing* (for control), a system that over time could literally learn to run itself.

□ To achieve this goal, a pressure system must be devised that will function to correct significant errors and prevent major distortions from arising. Relying heavily on indirect means, management provides pressure in the right direction so that most of the time the system will be brought back to its original course. Management of large-scale endeavors essentially involves the skillful creation of such a pressure system.

□ In this chapter we explore the use of indirect pressures. However, large-scale systems inevitably will oscillate between emphasis on these and emphasis on more direct pressures as the sponsoring agency responds to the need of a project contractor to elicit information indirectly from an unwilling associate contractor or to the demands of a Congressman for more rigid accounting controls. A single predictable strategy for devising a pressure system will not work for a large-scale system. Instead, the manager must operate in a multidimensional political, economic, and social arena. Inevitably, he comes to employ a battery of polar or even contradictory strategies that may cause oscillations in the system. Thus, at the same time he is moving to a self-forcing, self-enforcing system he may also be pushing quite different programs that deal with problems directly—for example, the increasing use of centralized external controls which require that virtually everything be "signed off" by a head manager. The mushrooming of externally imposed controls is reflected in the growing body of rules and regulations surrounding such matters as contractor compensation and engineering design changes.

□ The administrator of the large-scale system works to control it to the point where he can concentrate on forward direction of its missions. He recognizes that he always will be working with a relatively unstable system, and he seeks controls that will override the potentially detrimental effects of this built-in instability. The error-correcting pressure system must function well enough to enable the top administrator to proceed with another important part of his basic task (ensuring excellence): taking the lead and showing those involved in a mission how it can be successfully accomplished. (See Figure 1.)

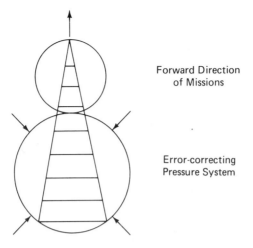

Forward Direction
of Missions

Error-correcting
Pressure System

Figure 1. Key components in managing
for excellence.

DESIGN STRATEGIES

☐ The large-scale endeavor's need for a self-correcting
error system is clear, but what are the key design principles
for such a system? How can one introduce indirect and
unobvious, but nevertheless compelling, constraints which
will somehow constitute an underlying authority pattern
(similar to the long beat in a musical score) that sets the
shape of relationships and encourages excellence?

☐ In designing the indirect components of the pressure system, the manager must determine the kinds of constraints he
wishes to employ. These will be a function of the kinds of
relationships the sponsor wants to cultivate in his milieu,
which in turn will be a function of the technology in question. The nature and extent of the sponsor's involvement in
the effort are major factors. If the sponsor wants to contribute actively to the endeavor, to be the dominant decision-
maker, and to engage in independent development work, he
may want to retain a relatively free hand for himself. In this
case he may favor *competition-inducing* constraints to set
the shape of relationships and develop excellence in the
system.

☐ On the other hand, if the sponsor is willing to dispense
rather completely with traditional lines of authority and responsibility and to accept a fairly high degree of involvement with his satellites and associates on their level, he may
select a *cooperative strategy.* Cooperative strategies force

sponsors to surrender some of their freedom as independent decision-makers as they move into much greater interaction with the total system and participate in reciprocal systems of interorganizational control. In other words, collaborating organizations may turn the tables and seek to induce excellence in the sponsor's activities!

□ The new and therefore somewhat insecure sponsor is likely to favor at least some constraints aimed at nurturing competition. Full use of cooperative strategies may have to await the testing and maturation of relationships in a given advanced technology.

□ The top manager who wishes to develop a self-forcing, self-enforcing pressure system naturally wants to employ the most effective strategy. In almost all cases, however, he will be unable to scrap previous organizational systems; he will have to work with them, restructuring patterns of relationship among existing in-house and external organizations and personnel.

□ In some cases, in devising his plan for an indirect pressure system, the top manager will have to concentrate the resources expended. In others he will have to increase or reduce them. Generally speaking, bringing the more traditional aspects of relationships in the system into the new plan will usually involve either concentrating or increasing the resources expended in order to alter or redirect relationships. In line with the general philosophy of this indirect approach to the problem of control, those strategies serving to reduce the resources directly expended by the sponsor are the most innovative and crucial because they tend to confirm the fact that the parts of the system are learning to respond to internally generated controls.

□ Obviously, the specific strategies employed will vary, depending on the technology in question and the stage of development or maturation achieved by the sponsoring agency. Table 1 illustrates a program for creating a self-forcing, self-enforcing system and lists specific strategies for resource allocation. This list is by no means exhaustive, but we present it to illustrate the fact that development of such a system is a complex undertaking and that a simple one-shot, one-strategy approach will not work.

Concentrating Resources:
Promoting Organizational Interdependency.

□ The first of these excellence-inducing strategies involves concentrating on qualities to be found in some existing relationships. Promoting interdependency can also serve to

Table 1

Strategies for Creating a Self-Forcing, Self-Enforcing System

Concentrate	Increase	Reduce
on qualities in existing relationships	the number and variety of relationships	the number and variety of relationships
1. Promote interdependency to induce cooperation	1. Promote parallel efforts to induce competition	1. Substitute group pressures for formal standards in the control function
	2. Promote alternate sources to provide continuous support for collaborators	a. Induce collaborators to join the sponsor's programs via heavy penalties for staying outside
		b. Create a self-operating "visibility" system of control

promote excellence. Organizations can be said to be interdependent when there is interaction between their inputs and/or their outputs.[5] The less interdependence there is, the greater the degree of self-containment; the completely self-contained organization is independent of everything. However, a mission-oriented large-scale system cannot tolerate in collaborating organizations much of the behavior that the self-contained independent state produces. In fact, constraints promoting cooperative behavior are essential to overcome the effects of the ever-present "sovereignty factor."

☐ Contractually imposed requirements are of little use in building such pressures, for there is no way of defining in advance the amount and quality of interchange needed between two organizations that must cooperate to assure the successful completion of a given project. For instance, when condensation appeared on the camera lens of one orbiting spacecraft, the immediate and close collaboration of two major contractors, one responsible for the spacecraft, the other for the camera, was needed. There was no time for either one to "wait out" the other in the hope that subsequent events would prove that the other was at fault. Ways to motivate such cooperation must be found, since it cannot be defined in advance. Of course, the sponsor can intervene to

[5] See Chapter 4, p. 72.

force various groups to work together, but this type of action should be necessary only on rare occasions. If such intervention were to become routine, contractor initiative would be destroyed.

☐ To some extent, the sponsor can achieve his goal of building-in cooperative tendencies by capitalizing on natural interdependencies. Thus, in looking for a working partner for Organization A, the sponsor may prefer Organization B to Organization C, although on the surface both appear to be excellent candidates. However, B's activities may complement those of A, so that the two can anticipate a continuing relationship apart from their temporary connection in this particular endeavor. On the other hand, A and C may be competitors engaged in the same kind of work. If the project appears attractive, A and C might be willing to accept the sponsor's proposition; but he can anticipate that each will be loathe to enter into anything more than an arm's-length relationship with the other. (In one case "Organization A," an aerospace engine manufacturer, was slated to be subjected to some fairly thorough systems engineering monitoring of its work. "Organization B," a large airframe manufacturer, was selected because the sponsor knew that A later would be looking to B for major subcontracts. Although technically equal to B and somewhat more experienced, another engine manufacturer, "Organization C," was rejected for this role because it was a direct competitor of A. The fact that A and B had a continuing need for one another served to at least partially soften A's resistance to what might be perceived as the "policing" aspects of the relationship with B.)

☐ In the absence of such interdependence, cooperation inevitably seems to be something less than wholehearted. In one case a large contractor received a crucial reliability-and-quality-assurance (R & Q) assignment from a sponsoring agency. To carry out this function, the contractor approached another giant firm, asking to be permitted to enter the plant. The latter immediately reacted to the fact that the R & Q contractor was a competitor in the aerospace industry, and entry was vehemently refused. Upon learning of this incident, the sponsor swiftly intervened. But even then the "receiving" plant's managers maintained a cautious attitude: "After all, they were our competitors. We weren't going to let them snoop around. We finally had to let them in, but even so, we were very careful about the assignments we gave them."

☐ Another pair of problem collaborators, far from being

competitors, operated in separate worlds. Company A was an aerospace manufacturer, and Company B specialized in cameras and optical instruments. But lack of long-term interdependence produced much the same effect. When A's work on the project was held up by B's failure to supply a key instrument on schedule, B refused to be hurried, saying, "We work 40 hours a week and that is it." Again the sponsor had to step in.

☐ In the selection of individual employees, natural interdependencies sometimes are regarded as cause for rejection of a candidate. Thus one finds rules prohibiting nepotism. However, inducing cooperation across organizational boundaries is a procedure akin to the nurturing of a delicate plant. A favorable soil is the first requirement, and to achieve it one may be forced to ignore the time-honored demand that parties to such arrangements be totally free and independent agents. In advanced endeavors that depend greatly on effective interorganizational collaboration, the risk of outright collusion may be deemed a lesser potential evil than the risk that two parties will be unable to cooperate.[6]

☐ The manager of a technologically advanced endeavor inevitably gathers into his enterprise many diverse, "sovereign" organizations. He is compelled to find some means of ensuring that those who must cooperate with one another will be sufficiently able to abandon their sense of sovereignty to collaborate effectively. As we have seen, one basic governing principle relates to the degree of interdependence among the units in the system. The greater the interdependence of the units, the greater is the probability that cooperative work relationships will develop and a self-forcing, self-enforcing system will emerge. Conversely, the more independent the units are, the harder it is to weld them into a single system designed to achieve the sponsor's objectives. The manager of the endeavor is thus apt to consider interorganizational nepotism an issue of only secondary concern. Instead, he capitalizes on natural interdependencies, nurturing them whenever he feels it will further the effectiveness of a particular relationship.

Increasing Resources: Developing Alternate Sources

☐ As we noted above, the potential for development of cooperative-type strategies is a function of the technology involved and the degree of maturity of relationships in the

[6] See Chapter 4, "Sponsor and Satellite: The Price of Dependency."

sponsor's satellite group. Indirect pressure systems aimed at generating a self-forcing competitive process represent an alternative strategy that is especially apt to be found in new large-scale systems and in one-of-a-kind technologies. The competitive approach to developing a self-forcing, self-enforcing system often involves the creation of a kind of organizational redundancy—building in alternate sources for the accomplishment of a particular objective.

☐ Of course, the sponsor incurs expenses when he acts to generate his own competitive process. This strategy may involve investing in the capabilities of other organizations in order to create a group of competitors in a given field. Or the sponsor may develop a competitive in-house effort in certain areas. Strategies of this type are hardly new, but their use by managers of advanced technological endeavors reflects the particular problems of these programs. For instance, a sponsor's manager may learn that a major project will be delayed two years if a sticky technical problem is not solved within a period of six months. If a single contractor tackles the assignment and fails, the two-year delay may be unavoidable. On the other hand, if several organizations simultaneously take different approaches to this problem, the probability of an on-schedule solution is increased greatly.

☐ Maintaining parallel efforts to induce excellence may seem a very simple strategy, but both cultural and economic factors have acted as barriers to its implementation in these endeavors. A manager in a country with a small but very good advanced program noted:

We do everything in series, not in parallel. We are used to planning only a little way ahead and then we count on working hard to make up for our lack of foresight. We have to learn to do things in parallel. But one problem is lack of money. Doing things in parallel may be cheaper in the long run, but the taxpayer often thinks we are managing our money better if we finish one thing, start another, and so on.

☐ But even the better-endowed programs have trouble supporting parallel efforts. In addition to the cost factor, there is a danger of introducing through competition one of the very elements the system is attempting to overcome, the sovereignty factor.

☐ However, forcing excellence via the development of alternate, competitive sources has a "soft" as well as a "tough" side. On the "soft" side, the sponsor's actions are directed at maintaining the momentum necessary for the success of his programs. Advanced technological systems require huge expenditures and are a heavy drain on resources. They also operate in a rapidly changing external environment which generates demands that may drastically affect a sponsor's sources of support. This is especially true when pressure-prone public funds are involved. Still, key contractors and scientists whose contribution represents a large investment in talent and resources cannot be allowed to drop by the wayside. If this happens, the system can lose its ability to perform excellently, and such a loss may take years to recoup. To maintain at least a competent core group, the manager of the endeavor must be able to develop alternate sources for meeting a satellite's needs. If one program is cut back, he must be ingenious in finding alternative means to achieve essentially the same objectives. Because techno-logically advanced endeavors often function in terms of projects and programs with set time limits and uncertain budgets, the manager has to counteract the tendency of satellites to treat the sponsor's work as a temporary assign-ment and encourage them to think of their involvement in the field as a long-term commitment.

□ The sponsor can achieve this goal by ingenuity in marshalling a battery of alternate activities. The temporary nature of specific contractual commitments is then over-shadowed by the industrial or scientific satellite's sense of sharing in some way the sponsor's permanent involvement in the field.

□ The need to provide alternative activities leads to actions that seem to go completely against the time-honored notion of pure and independent competition. In one case Con-tractor X (the generally able systems division of a large electronics manufacturer), which had been assigned a key systems evaluation and integration function at Site A, was doing an unsatisfactory job. X was replaced at this site by another contractor, Y, but was not thrown out in the cold. The sponsor maintained X's capacity by giving it a different, but also major, assignment at Site B.

□ Of course, the system has to tolerate some losses of participating organizations. Organizations who are on the periphery of a new technology's key interdependent sponsor-satellite group sometimes attempt to gain entry to the field by investing their own funds to develop various aspects of proposed programs. If the program does not materialize or if they are not selected as participants, these "independents" may simply lose out—or they may be urged to enter the program at a secondary level, as subcontractors. This pattern for maintenance of the excellence and capacity of key participants and encouragement on a more tentative basis of those on the periphery is reminiscent of the Japanese approach to the management of commitment discussed in Chapter 4.

☐ Thus far, we have outlined two elements in a design for a self-forcing, self-enforcing pressure system. In one case the technologically advanced endeavor attempts to ensure a sufficient degree of interorganizational cooperation by selecting for and nurturing interdependence. In the other it stimulates participants to excel by developing alternate sources to challenge and support their efforts. In both cases, results are achieved by strategies that serve either to concentrate or to increase the resources expended.

Reducing Resources:
The Indirect Approach to the Authority Relationship

☐ This final group of strategies is aimed at eventually decreasing the resources expended in the direct exercise of authority as less direct "self-generating" pressures are instituted. Faced with the sovereignty problem, the sponsor of the multiorganization large-scale endeavor tends to feel that the subtle approach will be most effective. Thus, he seeks to design situations which by their very nature will have a compelling effect on the organizations concerned. The initial investment in some of these controls is not insubstantial, especially if computer hardware is involved; but if they are successful, the substitution of group pressures for administrative effort could result in a tremendous saving. Two strategies of this type are (1) the creation of heavy penalties for staying outside the system and (2) the "visibility" system of control.

Heavy Penalties for Staying Outside the System

☐ In the first place, how does the sponsor attract the kind of top-quality collaborators he wants and needs? Money is a very effective persuader, but it alone may not serve to convince a group of noted scientists that they should devote their time and energy to a sponsor's program. The independent nature of such men is well known. Therefore, a simple positive approach may be less effective than one with a negative slant. In essence, the situation must be so structured that there are heavy penalties for staying out. While the recalcitrant is not subjected to direct coercion, he suddenly finds himself, on the outside, unable to engage in significant activities. He discovers to his dismay that he has no real access to a new and vital field.

☐ The members of a certain scientific body are a good case in point. Initially, some noted astronomers refused to participate in a proposed venture unless the sponsor acceded to their demands regarding the conduct of the program. Nevertheless, the sponsor went ahead with his plans. After a while, as the astronomers realized that the program provided all sorts of professional opportunities and gave them access to scientific data that they could gain in no other way, they quietly rejoined the project. In another instance, one of four top officers at a sponsor's major operational center refused to cooperate with a new management system for data collection and processing. The officer in question was independent. Since he had his own budget and his own contractors, he saw no need to "waste" his time supplying data to other parts of the system. But he soon found himself out in the cold. He was forced to yield because, as others adopted the new procedures for reporting and analyzing problems, he became unable to communicate in his old manner with men in his own organization or with managers in cooperating contractor organizations. In both cases, instead of expending effort to negotiate the matter, the sponsor let the situation "speak for itself" as it began to generate its own pressures.

The "Visibility" System of Control

☐ How does the manager of the complex endeavor get problems that only he can deal with effectively out in the open quickly enough to take timely action and ensure that all those actually and potentially affected will have the information they require? It is difficult to achieve excellence when information crucial to a problem is locked behind someone's door. Intense monitoring and surveillance by the sponsor's personnel is one answer, but in addition to being time consuming and expensive, these procedures are still liable to error. Other sources of pressure are needed.

☐ Complex endeavors cannot seem to escape the problems created by organizational boundaries. Thus it is little wonder that managers in this business have searched diligently for some *impersonal* means of achieving *visibility* for troubled areas. If a problem becomes so apparent that everyone concerned can react to it almost simultaneously, its very visibility creates pressures for its solution. Such impersonal pressures can serve as an ideal means for achieving a self-forcing, self-enforcing system. The difficulties that occur when one major organization attempts to give orders to, or report on, another are avoided.

☐ In this vein, some major projects employ rather simple procedures to give visibility to men who would prefer to exercise their opposition covertly. For instance, procedures may be enforced by a requirement that changes cannot be made until they have been "signed off" by the key functional managers. However, under this system a man can take a negative stand without revealing his hand. He merely exercises a pocket veto by not sending in the papers in question. NASA's project heads defeated this strategy by assembling all the functional managers in a common meeting room and requiring anyone who disagreed with a proposed change to justify his stand in front of the others. This is a very unsophisticated example of the visibility system of control. In an ideal system information would be transmitted via means far less personal than face-to-face meetings.

☐ According to the visibility system of control, a party with a problem is pressured to take care of it because the matter is known throughout the entire system. If a problem cannot be hidden—if it is something routinely entered in a data bank—then it must be handled. Under the visibility system the manager does not have to issue orders to the offending organization. As one manager put it: "Organization A knows it, Organization B knows it, Organization C knows it, I know it, and the offender knows that we all know it. He feels compelled to take action."

Making the System Operational

☐ However, visibility continues to be a difficult concept to make operational. The data most amenable to collection and processing are not necessarily those most vitally needed. The facts surrounding a troublesome matter are seldom clear-cut; just when one desperately wants an answer, one encounters ambiguity.

☐ Then, too, the automatic aspects of the information-processing system stop short right at the doorstep of the ultimate sources of data. Is there some self-forcing means for getting the various organizations involved to generate and then provide information that should be highly visible? It is quite normal for organizations to attempt to withhold information from others, even from those who are members of the same system. There seems to be an almost universal tendency to resist sharing information. Computers and data banks appear to be impartial and ultimately fair sources of coercion, but project personnel may see feeding information to these electronic monsters as the first step toward potential trouble. They may cynically regard visibility as a process that does no more than disguise the real authority it represents. Those who are asked to cooperate remember unfortunate past experiences. As one top manager noted:

We realize people have been hurt in the past. Someone from headquarters goes to a site, and the next thing you know a man at the site is getting a call from the Program Manager at headquarters asking, "Why are you doing thus and so?" They develop a strong resistance to giving information and they rationalize it by saying, "They don't need it."

☐ The familiar sovereignty factor may force the manager of the large endeavor to use some of the strategies discussed earlier to gain cooperation for the visibility program. He must show key satellites that participating in this system will be useful to them—that the information made available will help them solve their own problems—and that they will suffer if they stay out.

☐ Despite some less-than-perfect starts, electronic devices may eventually provide the basis for potent "indirect" control systems for advanced technological endeavors. Certainly there are top managers who are eagerly awaiting this day. One man at least in the space program was convinced that a powerful management-information system was the only answer if he was to do his job effectively. Like many others in his position, he constantly had the feeling that everyone in the organization knew what was going on better than he. What was needed, he reasoned, was a system in which all management information—especially data concerning problems he alone could handle—would flow to the top. He turned to a large communications firm for help, only to be told that realization of such a plan would have to await future developments in the software field. One of the top men in the company remarked: "Actually, we couldn't do this job for our own organization. We had the equipment but not the skills to design what was wanted."

☐ Managers in other countries have shown a similarly high degree of interest in the use of visibility-type pressures to pry out vital information. These become especially appealing to adopt in any society in which the normal desire to conceal failure is reinforced by heavy cultural stress on the importance of maintaining one's honor at all costs. One foreign manager expressed the hope that a data bank would eliminate some of these problems:

Right now I am working on a data bank, partly to get around the NIH factor. There will be no hidden information. Everybody can know everything. But it's a big problem finding out what information people need, and how can we get them to report failures? We need to introduce a new system. The man with the most failures gets the most honor. He failed the most. He is the most honored! This is the information we need, but now it is very hard to draw it out.

Visibility and the Key Manager

□ The day when top managers can enjoy electronic omniscience is still some distance away. In the meantime, the self-forcing, self-enforcing system needs some short-cut procedures for gaining visibility for ideas and problems. Imaginative use of key personnel is one means of accomplishing this. Despite efforts to treat information impersonally by using data banks and the like, communication is still basically a personal matter and very much a function of the relationship between those who have information and those who need it.

□ The important ideas in most programs are generated and propagated by men, not organizations—by individuals who become advocates of a particular concept or of the use of special measures to cope with a problem. Too often, especially in large programs, these men are confined to their own cubbyholes when they could be used to give a significant idea, concept, or problem systemwide visibility. Thus, a complex endeavor might place key men at several focal points in the system where they can serve to tie problems together, see relationships, and make comparisons.[7] Or a single man can play multiple roles in a given program. (In one case a manager was moved for this purpose into four different organizational components of the same program.) The Japanese, who excel in the field of organizational innovation, employ this device, sometimes shifting a man's organizational level so that he plays both superior and subordinate roles in a given project. For instance, one man was superordinate as head of the electronics division handling a radar project, but in another role he was subordinate to the project manager. The insights he obtained in this lesser capacity improved his handling of general administrative functions. Experience in several roles increases the manager's sensitivity to the many sides of the problems with which he is concerned.

[7] In NASA the executive secretariat was created to serve this general function.

CONCLUSION

☐ The manager of the large-scale, multiorganization endeavor has a real need for a pressure system that will induce excellence of performance in his far-flung empire by correcting errors as they occur and preventing major distortions. The top manager is understandably intrigued by the idea of a self-controlling, foolproof system because standards and other externally imposed controls commonly employed do not provide him with a measure of the actual situation. This is a serious failing in view of the huge investment involved and the critical need for mission success. The actual situation at a given time must be known and must constitute the basis for action. Instead of relying solely on intense surveillance and monitoring by members of his staff, the manager tries to create a system that will make the organizations involved and the people in them want to do their utmost to cooperate to achieve the sponsor's objectives.

☐ The top manager intent on developing a self-forcing, self-enforcing system naturally wants to employ the most effective strategies. Working with the resources at hand, he will concentrate and increase some of them and reduce others. Those strategies serving to reduce the resources directly expended by the sponsor are the most innovative and crucial because they tend to confirm the fact that the system is learning to respond to internally generated controls and that reliance on externally imposed controls is being lessened.

☐ Will the top manager finally obtain a true measure of the situation? Even with the achievement of the perfect self-forcing, self-enforcing system, the top manager in the sponsor's house may not be able to determine what actually is happening in all parts of the system all the time. However, those problems that merit attention will surface in time for the appropriate parts of the system to correct them.

☐ The strategies presented here are by no means the only ones possible, nor are they necessarily the best possible strategies, but they are typical of the managerial approaches and programs used to attain this objective.

☐ It is not surprising that, as yet, no one has succeeded in creating the perfect self-forcing, self-enforcing system. One can find the beginnings of this type of system in various technologically advanced programs, and, in fact, such endeavors seem almost to require a system of authority tailor-made to their own specific needs. Nevertheless, as we have seen, top administrators and those below them continue to rely heavily on procedures adapted from more traditional management systems. Obviously, "direct" controls have not been abandoned in the anticipation that self-management under an "indirect" system is near at hand.

☐ However, the management of multiorganization advanced technological systems has continued to move toward the development of a self-controlling, or as we have styled it, a self-forcing, self-enforcing system. Both cooperative and competitive approaches have been used. The choice of strategy appears to be a function of the technology involved, the role played by the sponsor in the enterprise, and time, with the newer programs leaning toward a competition-inducing plan. In developing such indirect pressure systems, the management of advanced technological endeavors has begun to depart significantly from the old and familiar patterns of supervision and control.

ACHIEVING EXCELLENCE
IN THE INTERNATIONAL
PROJECT

SIX

☐ A deeper understanding of the management of complex endeavors can be derived from exploring the problem of achieving excellence in the international project. In many ways these efforts constitute a supreme test of managerial skill, for bridging international boundaries compounds the customary difficulties of coordination and integration. At the same time, the multinational structure has the advantage of making explicit much that is implicit, or taken for granted, in projects conducted at the national level, just as union-management negotiations make explicit much that is hidden in the ordinary employer-employee relationship. In addition, the very important but often obscured view of project management as a political decision-making process comes to the forefront.

☐ The material presented here is based on studies of several international atomic energy and space projects, including one which achieved a high degree of excellence. (We have given this latter effort a pseudonym, the Satan Project.) There are certain factors that appear to be associated with the achievement of excellence. At this stage we offer no proofs, only evidence that those projects which achieved excellence had the characteristics in question, while those that failed in this regard did not. Our analysis will begin with a discussion of some of the major characteristics of the international technical project and the environment in which it operates.

INTERNATIONAL TECHNICAL PROJECTS:
WORKING UNDER FIRE

☐ A headline in *The Economist* wearily took note of a well-known international project with the following headline: "Concorde: It's Been a Ten Year Slog."[1] Not unexpectedly, the article decried the long period of time taken by the project, the escalating costs, and the uncertainty of the market for the supersonic plane when it finally became

---

[1] *The Economist,* April 12, 1969, p. 67.

available. Of course, these problems are not unique to international advanced-technology projects. They are characteristic, as well, of development programs conducted within a single country. All have long lead times; all tend to cost more than originally estimated; and, as the technology they employ is based on rapidly advancing fields, all face the danger that new developments will make the end-product obsolete and pre-empt prospective markets.

□ But despite similarities to national efforts, the international project is an especially inviting object of attack. The very name calls forth visions of ministers conniving for political advantage and of foreign industrialists scurrying home to exploit illicitly acquired information. It is not difficult to dismiss these projects as little more than political adventures. One cannot deny their problems; but the simplistic description of them as "all politics" does not do them justice. In fact, it has become increasingly apparent that the effort needed to make them work may be definitely worthwhile.

□ International technical projects date back to the early nineteenth century, but not surprisingly, the major thrust of the effort has taken place since the mid-1950s, a period of amazing growth for large-scale endeavors in fields such as space and nuclear technology. As far as international efforts are concerned, the most popular game is named "technological independence." Smaller countries play by banding together to share the risks and expenses of developing nuclear power reactors that will free them from the continuing dependency involved in purchasing equipment from the United States, with its associated commitment to buy U.S.-produced enriched uranium.

□ Another game involves the creation of new markets. A country such as Britain may lead in developing technology yet not have enough domestic customers to support a growing nuclear-reactor industry. However, in seeking business abroad, she is likely to find other countries inclined to shun dependency on a relatively unknown "foreign" technology. On the other hand, if the technology is shared through a joint developmental project, the "lead" country can build relationships with its various governmental and industrial partners that produce both potential customers and contractors.

□ Clearly, participation in these projects has advantages. At the same time, they can create unparalleled management problems. The perennial problem of inducing excellence of performance that will justify the effort expended becomes particularly complicated.

Does the International Basis Make a Difference?

☐ Managerially speaking, one might be tempted to maintain that an international project involving several European countries is not much different from an effort like the U.S. space program, which requires the close collaboration of program centers and contractor companies thousands of miles apart. Indeed, some cross-national projects may seem infinitely simpler. Moreover, individual companies engaged in national projects are notoriously quick to defend their sovereignty and guard their secrets.

☐ On the other hand, when different countries are involved, the sovereignty factor has much more force and the parties feel they can defend it with honor. Moreover, intergovernmental relations, in which the sovereignty issue dominates, tend to take precedence over all others. International efforts are constantly plagued by the question, "Who will make the ultimate technical and economic decisions?" to resolve this issue, the parties must sometimes threaten either to reduce their participation or to pull out entirely. Unsatisfactory "standoff" decisions are often the only alternative.

☐ In view of these attitudes, it may be surprising to learn that the international project has survival value and can even be a stabilizing force. For countries other than the major powers, the involvement of more than one government and more than one large manufacturer adds considerably to the overall stability of a program.

☐ A European industrial manager noted that he had discovered one central virtue in international projects: When his government was on an economy drive it was more apt to cancel internal programs and less apt to touch international commitments because of potential repercussions in other aspects of relations with the countries involved! The international endeavor may not be another world, organizationally speaking, but its political-technical milieu does introduce new constraints, new requirements, and most surprising of all, new freedoms.

The Question of Excellence: Pursuit of a Chimera?

☐ Many of these points relate to the ability of an international project to endure rather than to excel. To confound the question of excellence, some experts see this quality as lying largely in the hands of the gods. Sir William Penney, in his role as Chairman of the British Atomic Energy Authority, remarked in a Parliamentary hearing: "The success as a project and as a wonderful effort of international collaboration seems to be almost random; some go beautifully, some do not."[2]

☐ A hypothesis favoring randomness places all projects on an equal basis as far as potential for achievement is concerned. However, there is evidence that the formulation of objectives and the design for structuring relationships and systems of control can definitely add to, or subtract from, the probability of outstanding achievement.

☐ One can challenge the statements of those who categorically deny that excellence is possible when collaboration among governments is involved. There are definite indications that the international project can produce a high degree of excellence. Projects fail to achieve a level of excellence not because they are international, but because they neglect certain basic conditions. Two factors seem especially important: (1) a sense of purpose and (2) a good structural design.

HOLDING THE PROJECT TOGETHER

Developing Motivation Through the Formulation of Objectives

☐ Like many collaborative efforts involving various groups, cross-national projects tend to lack flexibility. They cannot easily redirect their activities, for changes can compromise a vast network of commitments. In fact, cross-national efforts are especially vulnerable on this point. If they are to rise above the level of mediocrity, they require from the very beginning a sense of having a significant objective or target, as we noted in Chapter 2.

☐ Projects that do not possess a sense of significant purpose tend to level off at what might be called the *multinational* stage, in which national identities and interests dominate most other considerations. If there is only agreement to develop jointly a fighter plane, a European launcher, or a low-cost power reactor, with no challenging concept to explore, then vested interests can readily grab hold.[3]

☐ When a group of nations are presented with an objective that is too general to give much guidance on means, the

---

[2] *United Kingdom Nuclear Reactor Programme, Report from the Select Committee on Science and Technology, Session, 1966–67,* London, Her Majesty's Stationery Office, 1967, p. 25.

[3] One example of a concept that provided challenge is the European Nuclear Energy Agency's Dragon Project. The multination project was organized to explore the feasibility of a high-temperature gas-cooled

range of solutions appears to be proportionately large. Thus, there is great temptation for men from each country to say, "We have an investment in Internal Technology X. Let's get the international project to use that." Each party holds to his own design until the last minute, hoping that the others will become insecure and, fearing his pullout, give in. Of course, a highly general objective often is no accident, for it can increase the chances of getting an initial agreement among the various parties. A highly specific objective also can lead to a leveling off at the multinational stage. The narrowness severely constrains the range of means, and in essence, this may simply be a way of specifying the use of existing capabilities in the countries involved.

□ It is not surprising, then, to find that whether the objective is highly general or highly specific, subsequent technical decisions become intertwined with politics. Ministerial conferences are organized to determine the program, and the remaining possibility of developing a ground-breaking effort disappears as battles are waged over where funds should be committed. National considerations breed competitiveness, which, when unregulated by constraints resulting from properly set objectives, may readily degenerate into acrimonious dispute. "Fair shares" for the participants, not excellence, becomes the basic organizational principle. Most commonly, task areas are carved out and distributed among countries in accordance with their economic contribution as well as their existing technical capabilities and investments.

□ Politicians are not eminently qualified to plan advanced-technology projects, and there is no reason to believe that they relish doing so. But in the case of the ill-defined project, they are almost forced to take over the planning. Quite naturally, they look at the problem from the standpoint of intergovernmental relations. Each government views its industrial firms almost solely as agents for carrying out its part of the bargain. Cooperative work relations within the multinational group of industrial firms are neglected, and this neglect undoubtedly is one reason why project groups tend to break up when the point of commercial exploitation is reached. No basis for later joint production and marketing is established. The ultimate, user-oriented goals of the

---

reactor that would employ graphite instead of metallic canning and structure within the core and would use the inert gas helium as a coolant. Scientists and engineers saw that if a reactor based on these design principles were successfully brought into operation, a high thermal-power density could be achieved. This in turn would permit a compact, low-capital cost structure as well as low fuel-cycle costs.

project are readily set aside. Thus it is easy to drift into a situation in which the technical design evolved by the international group is never exploited commercially because it appears to threaten existing technology in the various countries.

□ However, it is possible to escape this seemingly inevitable fate. If a project starts out with a technically interesting concept that has been developed sufficiently so that it can be grasped by others and they can see its value, then the probability of fixation at the multinational stage is greatly lessened. Such a concept creates expectations about the future and about the kinds of commitments needed. Objectives, then, are more apt to be set that are neither too general (thus inviting political interference) nor too detailed (overly constraining the choice of means). The project can move on to what might be described as a true *international* stage, in which project objectives control the actions of the parties involved. Figure 1 illustrates the consequences for

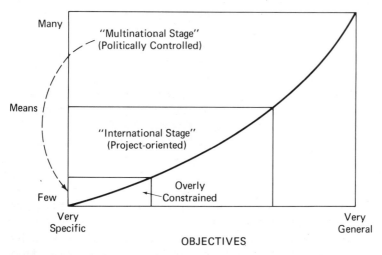

Figure 1. Consequences for project functioning of the relationship between objectives and means.

the functioning of the project of the relationship between objectives and means.

The Satan Project

□ The Satan Project, mentioned earlier, is a case in point. Satan had propitious beginnings. Because its objectives were based on a significant concept, they were set in the proper range, and planning could be conducted from the standpoint of the project rather than special-interest groups. In the mid-1950s a group of scientists and engineers in Country A's research laboratory evolved an idea for a uniquely designed nuclear power reactor. The concept involved many unusual features that needed to be worked out experimentally, but Country A had committed her resources to the development of other types of reactors. Internal facilities and staff appeared to be in short supply.

☐ At the same time an international developmental organization was searching for a reactor project to sponsor. This organization had considered another design but had rejected it (fortunately, for it turned out to have little merit). When representatives of Country A offered their unique concept, it was accepted, and the Satan Project was off to a good start, with two years' background work under its belt. In all, a dozen countries were involved in the project, whose mission was to prove that a reactor based on the new concept was commercially viable.

☐ Another factor contributing to the success of the Satan Project was the decision, at an early stage, to pursue a systems approach to the structuring of relationships, thus avoiding the prevalent practice of focusing the lion's share of attention on agreements among governments and leaving almost entirely to chance industrial cooperation in the post-developmental stages. The project's management encouraged both formal and informal interchange among industrial collaborators. Relationships among the major contractors' operating personnel were developed by having the men travel together to visit work sites in the various countries. Moreover, a group of private companies from five of the countries formed an association to develop and market Satan-type reactors on a worldwide basis.

Project Organization: Creating the Right Environment

☐ Certainly nothing can substitute for a good technical concept—and nothing can compensate for its lack. A significant group objective propels a project above the divisive influences of the sovereignty factor. But in addition to the essential requirement of a good technical concept, the members of an international project group also need an environment that will enable them to work together effectively. The experience of a number of projects indicates that disruptive pressures, political and otherwise, which stop the work flow must be minimized so that the group can devote its energies to achieving its mission. To be most effective the project must develop an internal, self-enforcing regulatory system. Overdependence on external controls can lead to endless delays and frustrations. In one project, most staff members and contractors either languished in uncertainty or acted on the basis of educated guesses because official decisions from a high-level ministerial council could involve delays of up to six months. As the manager noted, "We have people all over, working on what they guess the plan to be."

☐ To avoid this type of problem, a kind of "sovereignty," not for the individual components, but for the project as a whole is needed. Autonomy appears to be a significant requirement for the international project intent on excellence. And financial autonomy is perhaps most important of all. Satan had a five-year budget with provision for three-year extensions. During these rather substantial periods of time, the group had a fixed sum of money to work with as it pleased. This was one of the project's strong points—and perhaps one of the reasons it was able to accomplish the rare feat of staying within its budget. It did not have to go back to the signatories every year, in the fashion of Euratom, to engage in an annual battle for funds. Satan's management did get some feeling for the extent to which such negotiations can create uncertainty and disrupt the flow of work when the first renewal was under consideration. Not knowing what would be in store for them, some members of the staff actually returned to their former positions in their home countries.

☐ Satan also had other advantages. The project was completely independent of any individual signatory in the planning and execution of its program. It was responsible not to the individual governments, but only to its own Board of Management, composed of representatives from the various countries. Thus the project managers were able to operate with considerable freedom. In fact, one manager remarked that the situation was almost idyllic. He felt that there were few places where he could function with such a free hand. Like most staff members, he had been temporarily transferred from a post in his own country and on returning there would be faced once again with more involved procedures, such as the necessity of checking every proposed expenditure with the finance ministry.

☐ The Satan Project was essentially self-contained, despite the almost 3000 research and plant contracts awarded to firms and organizations in the twelve countries. Of course, many of the contractors and contracts were very small. In all, there were about 150 major contracts and 15 major contractors. By U.S. standards the ten-year project budget was very modest, roughly $75 million.

□ The relatively small size of the project undoubtedly contributed to its ability to achieve a high degree of integration. Satan was not burdened with the communications difficulties and the lack of visibility in regard to technical problems that commonly plague larger efforts. The Satan Project site in Country A served as a focal point for the geographically widespread group. At this site, where the Satan Reactor was constructed and placed in operation, a closely knit group of 100 or so scientists, engineers, and technicians from the various countries worked together to learn and develop a new technology. There was extensive participation within this group, for a great deal of responsibility was delegated to small project teams at the site, and their progress was reported to a large number of committees.

□ We observed the same closely knit, collaborative work group in those successful national projects which had multiagency sponsorship. Normally such diffusion of responsibility among agencies and such complex lines of authority guaranteed failure, but when the operating people could separate themselves from the several headquarters' groups, they evolved precisely this type of organization.

□ Structurally speaking, Satan represents a highly integrated form of international project. It contrasts strikingly with those at the other end of the "integration scale." For instance, Concorde has dual British and French management, production, and sales structures. The Technical Coordination Group is the nearest thing to a joint body in the supersonic transport project.

Concentrating Administrative Responsibility

□ It was sometimes jokingly said in reference to Satan that the best international projects are really national! Actually, Country A supplied roughly half the funds, and the other countries matched this amount. This 50–50 formula seemed to prevail generally. About half the technical and scientific staff at the reactor site were from Country A, and half were from other countries. However, in order to avoid creating a new international legal entity, the Satan Agreement provided that all legal acts were to be performed by Country A's atomic energy organization, on behalf of the signatories. This provision did not encompass the employment relationship, and thus members of the project staff continued to be paid by their original employers. In this way assurance also was provided that the benefits of the project would be infused into industrial and governmental organizations in all the signatory countries.

□ Contractually speaking, Satan was a success. The project stayed within its budget and finished its task on schedule. In essence, Country A's atomic energy organization acted as a contractor performing general administrative and auxiliary and support functions. Its engineering division handled all the design engineering and construction, and its contracts division, the contract letting and administration.

□ If, as it would seem, it is easier to obtain international agreement on technological than on administrative matters, then "farming out" contract administration to one country may have been an ideal solution. Procedures were introduced, implemented, and monitored by the same party. In an international project in which administrative activities were conducted separately by the various member countries, a top manager who attempted to introduce common procedures brought about near-chaos. The govenments concerned were not about to change their administrative systems to accommodate the needs of this one project.

□ In its contracting, the Satan Project departed from the usual procedure of making awards on the basis of a country's economic contribution. Instead, a system of international competitive bidding was employed whenever feasible. Each country prepared a list of potential bidders. From the proposals submitted by them, the project awarded a contract to the lowest offer that was technically acceptable. Interestingly, and in part because the factors that determined the extent of a country's involvement in Satan were also reflected in the number of qualified contractors available, the awards matched rather closely the proportional shares contributed.

□ During a visit to the Satan Reactor, the cross-national nature of the entire enterprise is evident. One sees a valve pipe flange from one country fitted on a pump made in another, and a number of control panels lined up, each one made in a different country, reflecting the design tastes of that nation.

Establishing Control Procedures

□ The Satan Project employed a battery of meticulous controls to ensure that procedures were being followed and that work was being done properly. Four sets of monitors were used: engineering, contracts, inspection and procedures, and safety.

□ One manager remarked that if the controllers and controllees had stayed behind their desks, writing letters to one another, things would have started off on the wrong foot. Instead, the entire enterprise was characterized by large numbers of personal visits that included even the smallest contractors. The personal relations established by these visits helped to check problems as they arose and made it much easier to uncover difficulties before they became serious. One might also imagine that, in view of language and geographic barriers, a company could easily exaggerate its expenses; but again the detailed data assembled through Satan's face-to-face monitoring system prevented this from becoming a problem. Satan, then, did not involve the separation at the working level that the term international project suggests.

□ Controls in an international project would be most effective, of course, if they were part of the basic structural design, rather than being externally imposed on members of such a diverse group. Yet in this case certain common procedures were accepted with relatively little difficulty because Satan was administered in a way that was internally consistent and at the same time seemingly tailored to the project's needs. The zeal for conducting business on a face-to-face basis contributed to this acceptance.

□ Quite surprisingly, the sovereignty factor, which is often blamed for the troubles of the international project, also can be turned into a source of self-generated control. National pride serves to induce good performance. One project manager noted that the desire to make a good showing led the countries to send their best people. Moreover, failure to produce a satisfactory component had an added note of disgrace attached to it because the poor performance was visible internationally.[4]

□ The extent to which national pride can serve as a spur to correct poor performance was particularly noticeable in another project. A large firm's contract personnel had fought hard to obtain an important contract, but the general managers seemed to have no enthusiasm for the assignment. However, when these men were informed that they were doing badly, they were dismayed by the prospect of "losing face." They then turned about and even erected a new facility, in part for the project's work. Every component

[4] See Chapter 5.

received a painstaking "gold plating." Spurred on by national pride, the former slackers turned in an excellent job.

☐ Heightened visibility in the international project also promotes an extra sensitivity in the matter of fair treatment. The project management often is extremely eager to have a favorable reputation in this regard. The hard and fast "sticking to the rules" that might be demanded of a local contractor generally is avoided. If a firm asks for more money because design changes have upped its costs, it is apt to receive at least a token payment. At the same time, the firm attempting to realize a large claim because of cost overruns will be examined very closely. If such a claim is granted, others will demand similar treatment, almost as a matter of national honor.[5]

☐ If national visibility were a sufficient element of control, then all international projects would function beautifully. Clearly, this is not the case. The sense of national pride involved in this control factor can lie dormant unless it is stimulated, Satan-style, by a fairly substantial number of personal contacts among the participants.

FROM DEVELOPMENT TO OPERATIONS: THE CRUNCH APPEARS

☐ As projects move from the development stage to the "user" stage, the self-interest aspects of the sovereignty factor become increasingly evident. The sense of sharing engendered by the development stage is replaced by an increasing competitiveness as the time for commercial exploitation of the item draws near. The attitudes of the signatory countries toward one another and toward the project begin to change as they make plans for taking the fruits of the joint effort back home.

☐ As one international project approached the user stage, the attitudes of participating countries appeared to harden a bit. They became reluctant to share information. And as commercial prospects moved to the center of the stage, the project managers found they were losing control over decisions to the individual countries, who now demanded a bigger voice in determining the future of the project.

☐ Member countries are forced, at this stage, to begin to take into consideration the "realities" of the outside world.

[5] The current Lockheed/Rolls-Royce dispute over the RB-211 jet engine for the Tri-Star airbus is another case in point involving national honor.

Some have to face up to the existence of competing interests on the home front. A unit serving a similar purpose may be under development there. Countries with this type of problem may attempt to delay the operations stage of the joint enterprise by insisting on the need for more testing and checking.

□ It has been noted somewhat cynically that international projects which look interesting from a scientific or technical, but not commercial, viewpoint are apt to be the most successful when it comes to achieving excellence and advancing "the state of the art." The rules of procedure are quite different when commercial considerations are absent. For instance, in "far out" experimental programs such as Satan, the parties are more willing to permit free interchange of information because they do not see how the data can have any practical value.

□ It is discouraging to think that groups can only work together harmoniously when the product of their work is not commercially useful, although this may be a form of compensation for the lack of monetary gain. As the Satan Project moved along, it too became of interest commercially. When the project group concluded that its unique reactor design was commercially viable, it became increasingly subject to some of the pressures it had managed to avoid in the days when it was regarded as "far out" and "experimental." On the positive side, however, there were still the close bonds forged between the countries and companies cooperating in the developmental phase and the possibility that some of these partners would undertake seriously their planned collaboration on the industrial aspects of Satan.

CONCLUSIONS ON THE ACHIEVEMENT OF EXCELLENCE

□ Technical projects sponsored by several nations operate in a political-technical milieu that introduces new constraints, new requirements, and new freedoms. They create special problems, but they also have built-in advantages. A properly designed international project can provide a favorable environment for the R & D effort, for it provides opportunities to:

1. set up a new work environment without the procedural red tape found at the national level;

2. capitalize on self-forcing control factors such as international visibility; and

3. achieve greater stability and continuity of effort, especially among smaller countries, since a number of governments and large companies are involved.

Essentials for Success

☐ As the Satan Project and others have indicated, excellence can be achieved in international projects. They are not by any means doomed to mediocrity. Furthermore, there most certainly is more than one approach to the achievement of excellence. However, a study of the history of various projects suggests that certain conditions must be met. Two factors seem especially important: (1) care in the formulation of objectives and (2) a proper structural design.

Objectives

☐ With regard to the first point, there seems to be no substitute for a good technical concept, one that immediately gives rise to certain expectations about the future and about the kinds of commitments needed. Objectives, then, are more apt to be set that are neither too general nor too detailed. A highly general objective, because it gives too little guidance on means, fails to constrain competition arising from national considerations. On the other hand, too-detailed an objective unnecessarily limits the range of means. In either case, the project is apt to level off at the *multinational stage,* in which national interests dominate most other considerations.

☐ The Satan Project began with a challenging concept, and this in turn permitted the specification of objectives in the proper range. The project was thus able to establish itself at what we have described as the *international stage,* in which project objectives control the actions of the participants. The parties can begin to work on a truly joint effort instead of merely dividing up the work pie and then proceeding with individual efforts as usual.

Structure

☐ Control of structural factors is important in developing an "international" project. An obvious structural factor, *modest size,* undoubtedly contributes to the potential for building effective relationships among the working partners, especially when international boundaries must be bridged. A common work site serves the same function.

☐ However, *autonomy,* particularly freedom from continual dependency on political decisions, seems to be even more important, especially where finances are concerned. Without this freedom, projects tend to lack the sense of being an integral unit. While participants in the Satan Project, like all those involved in joint ventures, were obliged to surrender some of their autonomy to gain access to needed resources, the project group was able to govern itself sufficiently to prevent its becoming mired in dependency relationships.

☐ Structurally speaking, it also appears advisable for the parties to concentrate their joint efforts on achieving the major objective and to "contract out"—perhaps to a single outside organization—specialized functions such as contract administration. In this way the pulling and hauling that inevitably accompanies the process of working out mutually agreeable means and methods is avoided.

Controls

☐ The multinational structure often is cited as a reason for the difficulties of the international project. But this situation can be turned to advantage. The manager can design controls that will both capitalize on the structural strengths of these projects and compensate for their structural weaknesses. For instance, the fact that one's accomplishments are visible internationally can be a powerful spur to good performance. However, care must be taken to bring this control factor to the fore. It can lie dormant unless it is stimulated by a fairly large number of personal contacts among the participants.

☐ Liberal use of personal contacts can compensate for structurally created problems in the area of technical and contractual controls. Meticulous controls are needed in advanced-technology projects, and yet crossing national boundaries raises questions about the value of some of the more traditional and legalistic approaches. In the Satan Project a face-to-face monitoring system was extremely effective in uncovering and solving problems at an early stage, while at the same time providing the informality that permits the saving of national "face."

☐ Structural design thus can serve to promote the project orientation of the international stage and decrease the nationalistic tendencies found in the multinational stage.

The Two Dimensions of Excellence

☐ In the world of the international project there are two key measures of performance: (1) technical excellence and (2) excellence in promoting utilization of the technology under development. Technical achievement is a prime concern because failure in this regard precludes the realization of other goals. But any mission-oriented effort has a further objective—ensuring the utilization of what it has developed. Thus there is another, distinct type of excellence that must be achieved—organizational excellence in the building of links for the future to potential sellers and users of the items being developed.

☐ Entering the utilization phase is thought to be a perilous step. Some who make formal agreements to undertake such a step never follow through (as in the case of Euratom). The harmonious and productive relationships developed during the development phase of the Satan Project were credited to the fact that nothing commercially useful was being produced at the time. We have described the transition from development to operations as "the crunch," a period in which the sense of sharing that characterized the development phase is replaced by the competitiveness inherent in commercial exploitation. Is there a way out of this dilemma? Can an international project group cohere to move on to joint participation in the user stage?

☐ The experience of the Satan Project suggests that the achievement of technical excellence may increase the potential for achieving excellence in the user stage. The kinds of working relationships that produce technical excellence in an "international" project automatically increase the chances of effective transition to the next step: dissemination and use of the project results. (A more complete discussion of the problems inherent in the transition to the user stage is presented in the next chapter.)

Political Decision-makers and Political Decision-making

☐ If in this chapter we have seemed to be critical of all things political, it should be remembered that we have aimed our fire at *decision-making by politicians,* which for the international project may mean an overemphasis on governmental objectives at the expense of others. (The Satan Project was fortunate in having this activity kept at a low level.) On the other hand, *political decision-making* in the sense of gaining agreement about means and objectives among all the parties is of key importance for the international project.

☐ Those planning and conducting these projects are apt to bog down on procedural and technical questions, while leaving political matters unresolved. The stage is preempted by discussions of technical issues ("Is the reactor reliable?" "Will it produce the results required?") or procedural matters ("How can we put this to use in our country?"). Unfortunately, political questions, differences in goals and interests, that are left unresolved during the development phase are apt to rise up at the user stage to prevent a project from achieving the hoped-for results.

☐ Machinery for getting agreement among countries to use the item being developed and among industrial partners in the various countries to coordinate marketing and production is of the essence if a project is to become more than an exercise in—or an attempt at—cooperative behavior. The strongest foundation for this machinery is the close working relations developed at an earlier stage of the project.

FROM DEVELOPMENT TO OPERATIONS: RELATIONSHIPS WITH USER ORGANIZATIONS

SEVEN

Although our analysis concentrates on interorganizational relationships, we have given only limited attention to the actual implementation of new technologies. In large, one-of-a-kind development efforts, such as the U.S. manned space program, the sponsoring organization tends to be self-contained. It is both developer and user, and for this reason, it faces little of the challenge that confronts programs with the strong production or operational orientation one finds in military R & D and in some British and Japanese advanced-technology programs. Smaller programs, operating on tight budgets, obviously cannot be self-contained. It is not surprising that they are highly user- or customer-oriented.

☐ However, even an organization, like NASA, that is committed almost solely to the development phase must give some attention to actual or potential users. In fact, there is increasing emphasis in the space program on applications: for example, using earth-oriented satellites for communication and navigation, for geodesy or metereology. But these applications also involve other government agencies and private organizations whose current jurisdiction includes radio and telephonic communications and weather prediction, for example.

☐ Examining sponsor-user relations also provides another opportunity to explore the basic problems of program management: bridging organizational interfaces and maintaining some common responsiveness among diverse elements with unique and sometimes incompatible interests and traditions.

DEVELOPER-USER CONFLICTS

☐ The shift from development to operations poses many problems. There is a good deal of evidence that even on the technical level the transition is not an easy one. There are always a whole new array of difficulties in translating successful innovations and prototypes to operational models.[1] The need for continuity, for operation by less skilled or committed technicians; the impact of hostile environmental factors; cost and maintenance problems—these and a host of other factors that are not present in the carefully insulated world of R & D can convert a successful experiment into a production disaster. Often a decade or more passes before a "proven" new technology is implemented successfully.[2]

□ The development organization has good reason to want to be protected from the nervous demands of the user. Development-oriented professionals may want to experiment with a wide range of possibilities, including highly sophisticated experiments that may have no immediate application. They are likely to seek broad solutions to problems that will reveal diverse uses. A particular user, on the other hand, wants a very specific application with limits placed on sophistication to ensure meeting production schedules and cost targets.

□ Taking into account these differences in perspective, there is a reasonable likelihood that professionals of good will on both sides will differ substantially in what they consider functional solutions to a continuing stream of threatening technical hangups.

Arguments for Separation and Coupling

□ Development personnel can cite many cases in which nervous or skeptical users attempted to dissuade them from trying out ideas that became the basis for highly successful new products.[3] The development process, they claim, will always contain disappointments, and users are likely to be the first to lose faith and demand compromises that may degrade the experiment. Further, it is difficult to predict the eventual uses to which really new technology will be put until the development process is quite far along. Most forecasting turns out to be erroneous.[4]

[1] See Donald Schon, *Technology and Change,* New York, Delacorte Press, 1967.

[2] This was about the time required to implement operational weather-observation satellites, for example.

[3] Within NASA, earth-orbiting, synchronous satellites (which appear to hover over a fixed location) are one such example. Potential users argued that this was not a feasible technique for communications.

[4] See Schon, *op. cit.*

□ Thus they argue that close coupling of development and user organizations inhibits more than it encourages real achievement. True breakthroughs require freedom from interference; users persistently understate the risk and the effort needed to prove out a new technology.[5]

□ But there are good arguments for more coupled operations as well. These come into play particularly when users are expected to finance or to help finance development programs. In such cases the user's doubts and questions must be satisfied; he must be reassured that the development organization is both responsive to, and realistic about, user needs. Even so, there will still be strong perceptual biases on each side. Thus it is easy to predict a continuing stream of misunderstandings: "We were sure that the new antenna wasn't really needed; it just gave the engineers a chance to do something they had always wanted to do and cost a lot of bucks."

THE NETWORK OF DEVELOPMENT AND USER ORGANIZATIONS

□ Of course, it is a vast oversimplification to talk in terms of just two organizations: the development organization and the user organization. In large endeavors, particularly those involving advanced technologies, there may be layers of contractors and sponsors. In addition there are often regulatory agencies like the Atomic Energy Commission, the Federal Aviation Agency, and the Federal Communications Commission who must either approve or license the new technology.

□ There may also be several competing users and development organizations. NASA's early work with the Weather Bureau (ESSA) was affected by the fact that the Defense Department was an alternative and sometimes competitive development organization as well as a potential user. Defense has its own R & D competence and also obviously requires accurate weather forecasting.

□ The situation can get still more complicated. For example, improvements in air-traffic control depend not only upon the R & D competence and jurisdiction of several

[5] Of course this is also one of the reasons some companies, and even some countries, have found patent licensing so attractive a policy: One need pay for the license only after the developer has proven the commercial feasibility of the item; one does not pay anything for all the failures.

government agencies but on the work of private aerospace-equipment firms. These firms are also potential consumers for the innovations developed in governmental laboratories. In addition the commercial airlines who will have to use and/or purchase complementary avionics, the airframe and jet-engine industries, and their related suppliers all have legitimate vested interests in affecting the flow of new ideas through the implementation stage.

□ The significance of these complicated interrelationships may be appreciated by examining somewhat superficially the lagging development of new short take-off and landing airplanes designed to reduce congestion at major airports and provide swifter short-distance transport.

A Case Example: V/STOL

□ Recent Congressional investigation of why the apparently highly promising V/STOL (Vertical and short take-off and landing) technology has not been implemented discloses that the number of organizations and the number of unresolved parameters of a potential civilian system has created a stalemate:

Existing manufacturers and development organizations have produced a number of competing designs for both the engine and the aircraft (e.g., propeller-driven and jet planes).

Some reasonable standardization is required to create a large enough market to justify private investments in manufacturing capacity.

Such standardization depends upon the airlines' decision as to what criteria they will use in evaluating competing designs.

In turn such criteria depend upon CAB and FAA certification and operating requirements, which must be determined in advance so that airlines and manufacturers can receive adequate assurances that their work will not be wasted.

The choice of an approach also depends upon the types of air-traffic controls and on-board avionics that will be required and can be provided, as well as the kinds of airports and supporting facilities that will be available. (Some advocate central-city and some suburban airports, but this decision is also a function of the costs and operating characteristics of future aircraft.)

□ All these factors are, in turn, also dependent upon the type of governmental R & D support, facilities support, and the degree to which this new network will be coordinated with actual or contemplated ground transportation.[6]

□ So among the more visible organizational participants are these:

. . . government agencies—NASA, the FAA, the CAB, the Bureau of the Budget;

. . . other government units—airport authorities, the FCC, planning and zoning boards;

. . . private manufacturers of airframes and avionics;

. . . private manufacturers of jet and propeller engines; and

. . . commercial airlines.

□ Thus one's opinion concerning engineering studies and the relative cost-efficiencies of various designs depends upon what one assumes with regard to passenger preferences; airport location and design; certification limitations; and consumer, manufacturer, and airline propensities. It is difficult to specify the appropriate sequence of decisions, and Congress is frustrated over "the industry's" inability to resolve the stalemate.

□ Where the national interest is clearly involved, Congress or the Executive Branch may take it upon itself to resolve the deadlock. Generally, a "blue-ribbon" study group is appointed to investigate ways of reducing the circularity and interdependencies. The committee's report is based on certain assumptions and accepts or rejects the evidence submitted by the interested parties. Because such arbitration procedures are costly and time consuming, an *organizational system* by which new ideas are evaluated and accepted or rejected in a regular, predictable fashion is desirable. Such a system would tie the various contributors into a predictable implementation process.

ALTERNATIVE PATTERNS OF RELATIONSHIP BETWEEN DEVELOPERS AND USERS

□ We have tried to suggest some of the more obvious problems in moving from development to implementation where several organizations are involved. Now let us look at

[6] These and other problems are discussed in *Issues and Directions for Aeronautical Research and Development,* Report of the Sub-Committee on Advanced Research and Technology of the Committee on Science and Astronautics, U.S. House of Representatives, 91st Cong. 2nd sess. Washington, D.C., Government Printing Office, 1970, pp. 74–82.

some of the structural solutions—variations in the structural relationship among the participants in the process—in systems terms. For the sake of simplification (a necessity for all models) and for the reader's (and the authors') sanity, all the intermediate organizations, such as regulatory commissions and component manufacturers, are omitted. Accepting this major analytical convenience we can categorize the relationships involved as follows:

I. Clear Separation of Development Organizations and Users
   A. User organizations utilize a "pool" of knowledge and expertise provided by R & D groups.
   B. Development organizations communicate their findings through mass-dissemination techniques.

II. Sequential Relationships
   C. Marketing relationships: Development organizations actively seek "consumers" for their products and expect to work closely with them.
   D. Agent relationships: Users prescribe what they want done and monitor the results.

III. Integrated Relationships
   E. Full partnerships: New concepts are developed and implemented through shared projects and programs.
   F. Junior partnerships: One organization, usually the development organization, is dominant.

Each of these relationships will be explored at some length in the remainder of the chapter.

Clear Separation of Development Organizations and Users

Development-Technology "Pools"

□ One frequently observes company R & D laboratories that are not closely allied with production, manufacturing, or even marketing divisions. In fact, one of the hallmarks of progressive, research-oriented companies like AT&T, Eastman Kodak, and General Electric has been their operation of university-like laboratories that pursue a somewhat independent course. Their function is to explore a number of natural phenomena, in part related to the company's interests, very broadly conceived, and in part related to the unique research interests of the staff. Their development work comes close to what is usually termed basic research: fundamental studies with no immediate commercial payoff anticipated.

□ In turn the more "commercial" departments of the corporation can draw on the laboratories' basic research to help them cope with unanticipated technical problems, for suggestions for new, product-oriented development projects. They can also use the highly expert laboratory staff as a consulting service. Such an arm's-length relationship, in which the "user" can dip into the "pool" of knowledge or data base filled by the laboratory, approximates the role of NASA's predecessor, the National Advisory Committee for Aeronautics (NACA). NACA's essentially service relationship with airframe and engine manufacturers reflected the easy, comfortable style of this structural arrangement.

☐ No close coordination is required, and the initiative for full-scale development typically comes from the "user," who finds it highly desirable to have this pool of expert knowledge available. Ideally the research-oriented development organization, being somewhat removed from the immediate pressures of the marketplace and the constraints of the balance sheet, can devote its time to anticipating future commercial needs. For example, NACA's wind tunnels pioneered certain aeronautical-design developments, and NASA has sought to carry forward this approach in its work on noise suppression and wing design.

☐ Under this structural arrangement, the user typically keeps the major implementation effort under its own jurisdiction. The R & D organization only comes into the picture when new or untried problems or requirements need evaluation. Obviously under these circumstances the R & D organization tends to undertake more modest projects, is less pilot-plant- or prototype-oriented, and is perceived as a major source of strength by the outside users. Relationships are easy and supportive (for example, users may aid their research arm by favoring large budgets), and the situation is reasonably stable.

☐ Of course, few organizational relationships are stable in perpetuity; restlessness is part of the human condition. Here the stimulus for change usually comes from the R & D side. One hears comments about how "we are nothing but a job shop," which, when translated, means that the users, for the most part, determine what major new work is to be done, and large, self-supporting continuing developmental programs are a rarity.

☐ One of the major differences between NASA and its predecessor organization, NACA, is the shift away from this service-and-support role. Some might even argue that the shift has been too complete and it is now difficult to get backing within the agency for projects that will *not* result in major pieces of flight hardware. NASA has become a mission-oriented agency, and its own momentum can make deferential, support activity unpopular.

☐ It is not difficult to understand how a talented, technically oriented organization subtly begins to shift the emphasis from support and service activities to those where it is more independent. Here is a relevant example cited by a high-level technical manager:

In the old days we were the ones they would ask about feasibility. In fact the government agency responsible for approving all new technology in this field would send us the proposals they received for our technical assessment. Frankly we don't think this is our greatest contribution. What we should be doing is not telling them whether this or that proposal is workable but rather what is the *best* plan that can be evolved.

☐ Translated from the altruistic to the organizational, this means a shift from responding to outsiders to taking the initiative. To decide what is "best" means not waiting for other technical organizations to do the preliminary work (which the service-oriented researchers then evaluate), but rather doing it themselves. In our terminology this is a shift from a "service-and-support" activity to a "marketing" posture. The R & D organization seeks to do the fundamental early conceptual work, which is then "sold" or conveyed to others who will hopefully provide both the approval and support needed to translate the original conceptions into a useful, operational technology.

Mass Dissemination

☐ Another arm's-length relationship is one we have termed *mass dissemination,* in which there is little effort to adjust to individual user needs. Rather the emphasis is on broad distribution of the new technology created by the development organization.

☐ Some of this dissemination is highly indirect, almost a byproduct of the developmental process itself. For example, contractors associated with the space program have learned new techniques for ensuring reliability in the manufacturing process (e.g., "burned-in" components) and have been stimulated to use computers in novel and sophisticated ways, all growing out of their experience with NASA's demanding manufacturing and check-out requirements: "Virtually every on-line, direct-access commercial computer system in the world today is American, and reflects the space guidance and check-out requirements of some years ago."[7] This *diffusion* process occurs because once a technique or an approach is mastered in one context, it is likely to be repeated in other contexts.

☐ Even more mass-communications-oriented are efforts to make computer data banks and research funds directly serve the user community. Thus NASA initiated a grants program for universities and a public-affairs program that, in part, serves secondary and elementary schools. These efforts are designed to persuade students and faculty to take a greater interest in space science and engineering. The eventual result could be better-trained employees and better-informed and more sophisticated citizens. NASA also encourages other countries to expand their R & D efforts in the space field.

☐ In a similar vein, NASA has a Technology Utilization Program that seeks to broadcast new engineering accomplishments that could have implications for fields other than aerospace (e.g., new heat-resistant paints and heart pacers).

☐ In all these programs only a minimum of effort is devoted to catering to the user organization, and there is little in the way of on-going relationships. As a result at least some portion of these efforts is wasted. As some critics would put it, "They send out thousands of solutions looking for problems." Some university grants are not used for the purposes for which they were designed; many of the computer print-outs of new technology are not followed up. In response NASA has tried to reduce the impersonality of its "missionary" tactics by developing retrieval programs for the technology-utilization activity tailored to the needs of individual firms. Similarly a great deal of effort goes into negotiating university grants that are consistent with the character of a given university. Nevertheless, some question remains as to whether such efforts have anything but a modest impact.

☐ Also, as in our relationships with underdeveloped countries, there is always the lingering suspicion that it is somehow degrading to be dependent upon the largesse of a much stronger or wealthier donor. This in turn induces a fear of manipulation, of being used to strengthen political support for the not-so-altruistic sponsor.

[7] Thomas Paine, NASA Administrator, in a statement to the Committee on Aeronautical and Space Sciences of the U.S. Senate, April 6, 1970 (mimeo).

Sequential Relationships

Marketing Relationships

☐ The unsatisfactoriness of mass-dissemination techniques can result in a move toward more closely linked structural forms, but forms that still leave the initiative with the development organization. Again using NASA as our example, there has been recent experimentation with what they call *Technology Application Teams.* These teams endeavor to adjust existing or on-the-threshold NASA technology to the problems of user organizations. The users have been such diverse "customers" as hospital groups, law-enforcement officials, and fire-fighters. An organizational process something like this emerges:

1. The development organization builds contacts with high-level managers in the user organization, who can pinpoint responsive and informed insiders with whom they can work and legitimize the development organization.
2. Joint user-development professional teams explore existing user problems for which there might be an answer in the development organization's technology.
3. Proposals are implemented. This may require, among other things:
(a) additional development work,
(b) seeking out and persuading fabricators,
(c) extending the market to other customers to permit economical production, and
(d) the funding of users by development organization to encourage them to solve problems associated with implementing the new technology.

☐ Clearly, this puts the development organization squarely into the marketing function. Here marketing is largely selling, and the basic development function of the initiating organization is little affected. The transfer of technology takes place after development, not during or before.
☐ If the user is itself a major organization comparable in size and power to the development organization, buyer resistance can be rather substantial. Assuming that the new technology will have a major impact on the user, its cost effectiveness must be carefully calculated:

When NASA was endeavoring to convince the Weather Bureau to "buy" a particular new development satellite (Nimbus), the Bureau questioned whether its additional cost was worth the additional benefits it would provide over the existing satellite system (Tiros). If they waited a while longer they might be able to acquire a much more sophisticated apparatus than Nimbus, and it was also tempting to stay with what they had, Tiros. Further there was always the chance that another development organization (the Defense Department, which was itself a user) might come up with a still better system, but it was not clear whether both "users" had compatible needs.[8]

☐ The user must always make many more adjustments than the developer originally believes or promises. Implementation requires a major effort over a prolonged period even after the technology is perfected, and it often conflicts with established routines and professional skills in the user organization. Also the users often prefer to do their own innovating if they have professional competency and resent either the dependency or the inferiority implied by taking on an outsider's innovation. (For example, COMSAT is no longer dependent on NASA spacecraft development although it must still use NASA launching technology.)

☐ Thus gaining acceptance of a new development is not simply a matter of demonstrating that a concept will work. It requires some exploration of the other organization's needs and methods, the building of relationships with key people, and a willingness to live with reciprocal, as distinct from very one-sided, relationships. The development organization's managers have to accept ideas, proposals, and criticisms from the user side and cannot take the position that they are colonials granting technical superiority to the natives.

☐ In part, this is a communications problem. Even within technologically oriented organizations, many facets of the work will not be explicitly specified. Routines, requirements, and technology may reside partially in the minds and work habits of the members of the organization. Further, group attitudes tend to become more rigid in the face of efforts on the part of other organizations to impose a new technology upon them, for the personnel of the user organization are sensitive to the impact of this new technology on their work routines and careers. Here are some typical problems the space agency experienced in these relationships:

[8] For this and other data concerning the NASA-ESSA relationship during the 1960s, we are indebted to Richard L. Chapman's superb Ph.D. dissertation, *A Case Study of the U.S. Weather Satellite Program: The Interaction of Science and Politics,* Maxwell Graduate School of Citizenship and Public Affairs, Syracuse Univ., 1967.

NASA's research on all-weather landing techniques involving on-board computers prompted complaints from users that the effort was poorly coupled to real-world needs. For example, it was claimed that it was unrealistic to expect general-aviation aircraft to carry such elaborate equipment when much less costly electronics would do a somewhat similar job.[9]

NASA's research on synchronous satellites brought comments from users (primarily military during the early development phase) that it was unworkable and unrealistic, that it had been tried and wouldn't work, and that it was a waste of money.

NASA's research on geodetic spacecraft was criticized by users (the Departments of Agriculture and the Interior) as going too slowly; the space agency was attacked for "researching it [the spacecraft] to death when we could use it now." NASA replied that it wanted to perfect the system before freezing the design and pointed out that there was some question as to whether the departments in question had tooled up to use the kind of information that might be collected.[10]

NASA's research on meteorological spacecraft met the following response from users (ESSA): "NASA doesn't seem interested in an operational satellite. We need a lengthy series of pictures; we tend not to get them because NASA prefers to do its own experiments instead. They tend to go it alone; development work is preprogrammed, so it is hard to get our special needs attended to." NASA replied that it was difficult to obtain the very detailed requirements it needed from users—for example, it asked for things like resolution power required and received conflicting data. NASA was also somewhat suspicious of the other agencies because it had discovered that satellite photographs did not fit into their preexisting work procedures.

☐ With so many internal components to adjust to and be responsive to in implementing a major development program, it is hardly surprising that energies can flag and appropriate organizational techniques are limited when it comes to this final work-flow stage. Technologically, as many—if not more—mutual readjustments, negotiations, and trade-offs may be required than at the earlier stages of the development cycle. There is a big gap between proving a concept and developing a successful, economic application that will be self-sustaining within existing, ongoing organizations. But it is still tempting to say, "The tough work has been done, developing this new technology; now it's up to

[9] See *Aviation Week and Space Technology,* October 21, 1968, p. 84.

[10] See *Business Week,* July 13, 1968.

them to make use of it. After all, it's a marvelous new tool, far better than anything they now have."

☐ As a development organization grows more accustomed to the marketing role, it is likely to reduce the effort devoted to being a catalyst in favor of systematically exploring user needs.[11] The user organization, to explain its operations and requirements, may also establish advisory boards and panels or committees who can speak for "the user community." Such groups are usually relatively passive sounding-boards and information sources, although at times they can make demands upon the development organization. However, because the boards often represent a variety of users with differing needs, they find it difficult to speak with a forceful voice.

☐ On the other side, an astute "marketer" encourages the consumer to begin exploring for himself his own future requirements and the problems of implementation. Thus NASA financed efforts by Weather Bureau personnel to begin developing procedures for the operational use of satellite cloud-cover photographs. (The assumption—which proved correct—was that ESSA, once involved, would take over this financing.)

☐ The development organization can grow impatient with the lack of sophistication of the user's technical staff. Effective marketing, it is argued, requires an in-house competency even to converse with users. From there it is only a short step to conceiving of exceeding the user's own level of competence. As one development manager told us about his "user" experience:

Frankly, we relied much too heavily on their knowing their own needs. They had never even thought through the implications of a total system and we now have the technical competence in-house to do things they could never do.

☐ Obviously marketing philosophies will differ, and it is easy to get too far ahead of user technical abilities. It may be better simply to encourage the user, perhaps by funding his efforts, to develop internal technical strengths. Excessive dependency on the user's part, as in the area of international economic development, breeds hostility and distrust. But it is easy to understand how in any professional field, enthusiasm encourages a group to take on functions that had

[11] This begins to approximate the "partnership" structure we shall describe on pp. 151–155.

been performed by outsiders but which are part of what the insider perceives as his legitimate jurisdiction. This is part of the long-run counterpoint observable in so many areas of organizational behavior:

Specialization → gradually broadened jurisdiction → complete autonomy → increasing specialization and willingness to use outsiders → increasing distrust of outsiders → gradually broadening jurisdiction again.

□ In the marketing role some broadening of function is undoubtedly useful; too much puts the outsider-user on his guard. There is a vast difference between learning the user's business and telling him what it should be!

□ One additional word about the user's viewpoint is necessary here. They, as we have noted, always face a dilemma. In highly technological fields, progress, at least at the conceptual level, can be quite rapid. Any commitment a user makes to purchase or acquire or adapt to some new equipment forecloses, for some period of time, the opportunity to take advantage of further breakthroughs. It is difficult to decide how long to postpone commitment while waiting for the next generation of technology. Also, the user's ability to get their preferred system depends upon relative dependencies. Where there is a monopsonistic structure (only one user), the chances are improved substantially. But satellite communication systems, for example, have several users— the television and telephone industries, for example, as well as the military—and each may have to modify its optimal requirements wherever there is a shared development program.

Agent Relationships—You Need a Customer in the Loop

□ The agent is almost the direct opposite of the large, relatively self-contained development organization that relies on marketing or mass dissemination of its ideas. The latter is occupied with serving its own internally generated market. Nominally, the agent has charge of a developmental enterprise, but in practice he is dependent on the initiative of others. (As a result his size is modest, too; his staff usually numbers in the hundreds rather than the thousands or tens of thousands.)

□ The potential user is a key participant in the development process. He provides funds and furnishes designs and key personnel. The agent provides the facilities and the expertise needed to direct the work. A potential user may be a

department of agriculture wanting a satellite for crop surveillance, a weather bureau seeking a meteorological-satellite
system or a postal and communications agency interested in
a communications satellite.

☐ The job of the "agent" is usually very delimited. For example, in the aerospace field, it may be the furnishing of a
slightly modified production item like a booster. The cus-
tomer-user (say Comsat) then provides the payload-
spacecraft. Of course, there are still some modest interface
problems, but all the initiative is on the side of the user. The
agent system is typical of small programs with limited
budgets. This procedure has strong supporters overseas
who feel that this is the only way to conduct an effective
development effort, in terms of meeting the practical needs
of a society.

☐ The agent system also serves to bridge immediately the
gap between sponsor and user. It does not guarantee an
amicable relationship, but it sets the stage for an active joint
venture. An agent-type sponsor's program manager who felt
that a definitely superior product resulted from such collaboration said, "You absolutely need a customer in the
loop. A closed loop is no good. When the [sponsor] is de-
signer and customer, there's no check." He spoke with great
enthusiasm about a coming project involving collaboration
with the postal service. The postal service planned to supply
half the funds, and of course, this aspect of the joint enterprise was most welcome.

☐ However, the life of the agent-type sponsor is not entirely
a bed of roses. Managers complain that potential users
within their own country are far from loyal. Users are seeking the best bargain, and if they find a cheaper price abroad,
they are apt to place an order with a foreign competitor.
Such competitors frequently are found in countries that have
developed a given technology far beyond the point achieved
locally. One manager of an agent-type operation remarked
mournfully that the education ministry was his only sure
source of support. Other ministries displayed only a limited
loyalty to the local effort.

☐ As a result, most agents tend not to remain pure agents.
They are pushed into developing an in-house program to
compensate for the vagaries of user support. Therefore, it is
not surprising to find that in the United States the relatively
self-contained NASA was preceded by an organization that
had some of the flavor of the "agent."[12] This predecessor,

---

[12] Arthur L. Levine, *United States Aeronautical Research Policy 1915–
1958, A Study of the Major Policy Decisions of the National Advisory*

NACA (National Advisory Committee for Aeronautics), which was founded in 1915, attempted to reserve at least a small portion of its total effort for in-house research, but it shared another common complaint of agents, that the need to be responsive to the immediate needs of users left little room for innovative work. As a result, the aeronautics field developed rather slowly. In part to meet this criticism, NASA was designed as a mission- rather than a user-oriented agency.

Integrated Relationships

Partnership Relationships

☐ The most integrated type of development-organization–user relationships involves a partnership in which initiative is shared relatively equally. Neither organization dominates the other; operational and R & D needs are given rather equal weight, and the relationship presumably extends over the entire life cycle of the program, from conception to operations. In many ways this might be construed as almost an *ideal* or even an *idealistic* relationship, with two or more organizations with quite different conceptions of priorities and their objectives able to work closely during an extended, often grueling, developmental and implementation effort.

☐ It may be instructive to look more closely at one such effort: NASA's relationship with ESSA during the development of the Nimbus satellite.[13] (We have referred to this relationship elsewhere because at various times it has assumed almost all the structural forms we have been describing.) This case illustrates many of the problems of partnership relationship.

☐ At the first stage of the cycle, requirements for the project have to be established—in this case, what the satellite would have to do. One might assume that this would simply be a matter for the user to determine, but this was not how things turned out. Particularly in technologically advanced programs, there are uncertainties both as to what can be accomplished (what is feasible) and what would be desirable. NASA and ESSA disagreed over the number of satellites that would be required to provide adequate global coverage, the

---

Committee for Aeronautics, Ph.D. thesis, Faculty of Political Science, New York, Columbia Univ., 1963.

[13] Chapman, *op. cit.* The paragraphs that follow on Nimbus are derived from Chapman's work.

appropriate orbits (which also affects coverage), the frequency with which information should be collected from the
satellite, and the best of time of day for this and other operations.

Figure 1. The project work flow in a partnership relationship.

□ Design is generally the province of the developmental
organization, because of its greater technical engineering
strength. But here ESSA, the user, had inputs it wanted to
make, particularly because of its concern about both developmental and operating costs. Higher orbits (than NASA
proposed) would mean less costly ground stations. NASA's
optimistic assumptions about the impact of radiation belts
were disputed. Nuclear power, ESSA reasoned, might give
the satellite a much longer life, as would passive stabiliza-
tion (in contrast to gas-powered jets). NASA, for its own
technical reasons, objected to most of these ideas, in some
cases because they were beyond the state of the art, in
others because they thought ESSA's calculations were
wrong.
□ Following requirement specification and design comes
the actual engineering development itself, carried out, of
course, by the development organization. Again, one might
assume that this would be an easier stage of the cycle for
collaboration since the roles of each party appear relatively
well defined. And again one would be wrong. Assuming, as
in the case of Nimbus, that the user also has its own budget
and operational needs to consider (it has to have completed
equipment ready to go on-line in a reasonable time), it will
require timely and detailed reports and feedback from the
development agency.
□ In this case NASA apparently was reluctant to provide as
full a reporting or as full access to the ongoing project as
ESSA would have liked. Like any nervous sponsor, ESSA
interpreted this sparse feedback as meaning that the project

was in trouble; it redoubled its efforts to monitor the work and also began to consider alternative hardware.[14] On its side NASA found the implied distrust disconcerting and indicative of a lack of sophistication in regard to the natural ups and downs of the developmental process. Also, with plenty of technical problems to solve, any development group is resistant to suggestions from the outside.

□ There were also disagreements over how much ESSA should participate in the establishment and modification of schedules. NASA preferred sending ESSA reports and comments; ESSA wanted to observe firsthand and participate fully. There were arguments over who was competent to interpret what, and what the relevant legal responsibilities were. Again, the relative sparsity of such partnership relationships and the complexity of the work-flow process makes any paper explication of roles and lines of demarcation relatively useless.

□ Of course this pulling and hauling also reflected uncertainties concerning the partnership relationship. NASA, as the major engineering organization with substantial space success to its credit, sought to play the more dominant role; ESSA, in part at least, probably saw NASA as its agent and resented its own junior status. (Both had also carried the struggle to Congress, where there had been long discussions of who should do what.)

□ Again one might assume that collaboration would be easier during the operations phase. But complex technologies usually contain another booby trap for the old-fashioned organizational-procedures expert: The interfaces blur. In the case of a weather-satellite system, for example, at what point do routine operations begin? Operations include the satellite's collection and periodic transmission of data, ground-station reception, usually some preliminary aggregation of the data (although this can sometimes be done in the satellite before "dumping" of the data), and transmission to the user's premises for further analysis and interpretation. Who gets what? When does the user come into the picture?

□ To simplify the Nimbus dispute, NASA wanted to control the satellite throughout its useful life, as well as during launch and orbit placement and correction; ESSA wanted to

[14] In the Nimbus case alternatives included a modification of the existing Tiros satellite, which had already proven successful. The proposed new Tiros, called Tiros "Wheel" because of some of its engineering features, was a more conservative approach, based as it was on a previous success, than was Nimbus.

take over the satellite after it had been successfully placed in orbit and data transmission was assured. NASA also felt it should have the ground stations because of the intimate linkage between them and the spacecraft; this, of course, was strongly resisted by ESSA.

□ An interesting summary of the last stage of the NASA-ESSA Nimbus partnership, which extended over several years in the early 1960s, is provided by Dr. Richard L. Chapman. Chapman is describing the period *after* a variety of Nimbus technological and organizational problems had caused ESSA to propose the Tiros "wheel" as an alternative to Nimbus:

The complex, subtle blending of scientific and political forces is evident in NASA's rejection of the TIROS "Wheel" proposal advanced by the Weather Bureau in the summer of 1963. First, the proposal originated from the political and scientific needs of the Weather Bureau. There was increasing user (primarily Defense) pressure for weather satellite data of the kind that the TIROS Wheel could provide. Weather Bureau inability to fulfill its role in meeting user needs could encourage DOD unilaterally to enter the weather satellite picture with its own program, thus diminishing the Weather Bureau's own role. Then, there was the scientific need (in order to study and experiment with data utilization) for weather satellite data on a more regular rather than the sporadic basis that could be expected if sole reliance were placed upon the NIMBUS R & D launches.

Second, from the NASA viewpoint, the initiation of a TIROS Wheel program posed a probable drain on Goddard resources which would have to come from the NIMBUS program. A diversion of NIMBUS resources to the proposed TIROS Wheel posed a threat to NIMBUS. It would delay the NIMBUS program, stimulating pressure to meet planned launch dates, and possibly forcing less desirable technical choices to gain time. If a successful TIROS Wheel were launched before NIMBUS the new data (not available from the standard TIROS) might further reduce program support for an untested NIMBUS in favor of the TIROS Wheel as the program of prime interest. If both a diversion to TIROS and operational pressures could be held at bay, the whole problem might be resolved by a successful NIMBUS first launch.[15]

□ As we saw in Chapter 6, such interorganizational suspicions, jurisdictional concerns, and struggles for preeminence can be accented in large international programs where national prestige and sovereignty are complicating

[15] Chapman, *op. cit.*, pp. 295–296.

factors. Most of the recent history of COMSAT and Intelstat is a reflection of these endemic "partnership" problems.

□ On the other hand, successful partnerships can occur where the project has very low visibility and is outside the mainstream; where there are few, if any, institutional jurisdictional concerns; and where *personal relations* predominate. The head of one such project describes the organization:

In the ——— project everything was done with handshakes. There weren't even any formal interagency agreements. Everyone was an equal partner, and we really got to know each other and respect each other's competence. Key managerial assignments were intermixed and we solved most of our problems at weekly meetings. There were no formal reviews; equipment was scrounged, and most of top management in the agencies weren't involved and probably didn't even know much of what was going on. The whole project was finished in 18 months, but upper management wasn't too happy with the extent of the informality.

□ There have been many recorded instances of such slovenly informality besting formal structures, both during and since World War II, but it is worth repeating that this can happen only when the project is small. Informality will not solve the problems of the large project.

□ One characteristic of a partnership relationship is the use of project managers from *both* the development and the user organization who report to a common manager. This can be the outward form of an integrated program as distinct from a coordinated program. There are many examples of coordinated programs in which liaison activities tie together two halves or other fractions. Where the interfaces are truly blurred and a great deal of interchange is needed to make the parts "fit together," integration is required.[16]

Junior-Partner Relationships

□ In theory, a partnership relationship implies equality between the two sides, but in practice it is difficult to maintain these equalities. Thus in the space program, the best example of what we have called a partnership relationship involves the collaboration of university and other outside

[16] Observers of the consistent technical failures of boosters under development by the European Launch Development Organization (ELDO) have noted ELDO's lack of strong and internal *integration* organization. It has endeavored instead to *coordinate* the various parts of a program being handled by one or another country's teams.

scientists, largely with NASA.[17] They are the *users* of the flight hardware, whose major purpose may be to fulfill the requirements of a number of scientific experiments. But in time even these tend to become "junior" partnerships, or at least so the scientists assert. A great deal of effort on the part of intermediaries, such as project scientists, is necessary to prevent a complete rupture. Scientists feel their experiments are degraded in the interest of engineering expediency, and their project-manager counterparts assert that scientists make unreasonable demands, ignore cost, time, and other interface requirements, and expect to be treated like prima donnas.

□ Fortunately, the key aspect of the partner relationship is the need that both sides have for one another during the developmental process, and therefore they often come to recognize the importance of continuing the relationship. The principal investigator or the guest investigator has to learn about the special requirements and rigors of space experimentation, and the engineer must learn about the nature of science and the academic tradition. In addition to direct contact and constant meetings to iron out inevitable conflicts, other events may serve to strengthen the partnership. Both sides may begin to deal with those who stand "behind" their counterparts. Scientists may meet with headquarters personnel who can facilitate their special claims for attention, and project heads may have to work with university officials and the heads of the laboratories with which the scientists are affiliated.

ALTERNATIVE IMPLEMENTATION STRATEGIES:
CONCLUSIONS

□ Previous industrial research suggests that companies differ (on the basis of technology) in the manner in which they handle the marketing function.[18] So-called *unit-production organizations* (which make items one at a time, and to order) handle their marketing function first, before development and manufacture. *Process-production firms* (where production is continuous and automated and there are no discrete manufacturing stages) handle their marketing last.

□ On the surface it would certainly appear as though most

[17] Only brief reference to this important relationship will be made here, since it is covered extensively in other chapters.

[18] The following is based on Joan Woodward's *Industrial Organization,* New York, Oxford University Press, 1965.

of NASA's work is closer to unit production, and therefore one might anticipate more efforts to work with potential users *prior to* the development process. Of course, this is done in the case of principal investigators (experimenters on unmanned satellites), who are one kind of "user"; but the same organizational approach could be extended, for example, to communications, meteorological, and geodetic satellites.

☐ One must maintain a balanced view of these administrative problems. On its side NASA has many organizational problems that may not be comprehended by the actual or potential user. These are not only the typical budgetary and programmatic restraints, but also the distinctive implications of earth-oriented space hardware. There are a number of defense, foreign-policy, and economic implications associated with almost any communications or sensing satellite. Eager implementers may be too willing to ignore these important peripheral considerations and relationships. However, it would be most unfortunate if difficulties in this regard so handicapped a sponsor that it would appear to the public at large as being indifferent to applications.

☐ Successful fulfillment of the "marketing" function, however, *also* requires the developmental organization to be able to shift drastically between two extremes. As we have already noted, the organization must be willing to develop a sufficiently intimate and continuing relationship with the user so that it will be able to tailor some of the specifics of the development process to the user's future needs. This means learning a good deal about the user's operations, its hardware, procedures, and problems, and perhps even modifying experiments and prototypes to make them more suitable for the future user.

☐ At the same time, particularly in high-risk ventures going beyond the "state of the art," the developmental organization must take care not to become the captive of the user. The very experience and exposure of the users also can make them shortsighted and parochial; real innovations may be discouraged or even ridiculed.

☐ It is hardly comforting to the developmental administrator to conclude that he must be able to alternate between encouraging interorganizational "closeness" and "distance" in effecting the translation of innovations into useful applications.

☐ In any case "marketing" relationships require much more contact than is now programmed by large, self-contained agencies such as NASA. Particularly during the "induction period," when a new technology is being introduced into an older organization, there are enormous numbers of problems, some stemming from irrational fears and jealousies, but many from real technical barriers to effective implementation. Those most familiar with the new equipment, its idiosyncracies and potential, that which is modifiable and that which is not, ought to be involved in working with the "customers." The latter know their own needs and capabilities and resent one-sided relationships which imply that the more highly sophisticated developer knows what is best for the more backward user.

☐ There still will be the specter of competition. New technologies inevitably upset the equilibrium of existing organizational relationships. Some institutions stand to gain ground; others, to have their status and influence reduced. However, the existence of this power struggle is no excuse for neglecting the administrative chores of accommodating potential and actual users.

☐ As contrasted to mass-dissemination, marketing relationships must be tailor-made and conducted on an individual basis. Unlike "partner" relationships, they can never be intimate; and the timing must be more carefully contrived since there is an inherent intermittency about the flow.

☐ Even in the "hard" fields of science and engineering men and women of comparable training and good will can differ widely on key technical parameters. What are safe (for humans) dosages of radiation, the ecological implications of heat pollution, the probable orbit life of a satellite, are just a few of the many issues on which "experts" may differ. To the outsider it always comes as a shock that internecine quarrels among professionals, who presumably share common values and knowledge, are more intense than disputes between those in different fields. It is no wonder that there are strong impulses to keep the "outsider" out, particularly, as we have said, when he represents a concerned user worrying that his budget, schedule, and other commitments may go down the drain if those crazy development people fail to "shape up."

☐ Technical progress is uneven, is probably not even linear. What may appear to be insurmountable problems can be solved, but outside pressure to keep down costs and meet schedules may not contribute to, and may handicap, solutions. Therefore a nervous partner or one who is like a severe sponsor, not sharing problems but only seeking results, is not usually welcome.

☐ We all know many of the complications involved in moving from development to successful application, no matter how well-worked-out a concept has been. In the computer field, a specific industrial application of a well-proven technology may take years (although the experts promised months). New agricultural seeds or animal breeds may require years of additional experimentation before they are adaptable to the unique weather, soil, and farming techniques of a given area.

☐ Large, one-of-a-kind development organizations can be less than enthusiastic about the additional challenge of working closely with users. It is very tempting to shift most of their user relationships into the mass-communication or junior-partner category. After all, with so many organizational interfaces to monitor in advanced technologies, something has to give. Nevertheless, for both political and economic reasons, there should be an administrative mechanism for working out and monitoring "marketing"-style relationships in which there is mutual give-and-take and in which actual and potential users are directly assisted in adopting, and adapting to, new technologies, even though the development organization foreswears operations for its own account.

☐ Of course, the development organization must concern itself also with backward integration on the part of the user. COMSAT, for example, has sought to make itself independent of NASA's spacecraft-development competency, just as industrial firms generally attempt to decrease their dependence on outsiders by vertical integration.

☐ Conceptually it is rather easy to describe the movement from new ideas to actual operations and the satisfaction of human needs. As we noted in Chapter 2, the theory is a simple one. New ideas and concepts lead to experimentation, then, at least for major hardware systems, to proof of the concept or pilot-plant operations, then to qualification and final designs and specifications, and, at last, to operations. But this intellectual flow, or system, need bear *no* resemblance to the actual organizational system.[19]

☐ For example, as we have described, the last stage (operations) can be the initial, or first, step in the system. The users go to the research and development people and get them to respond to their (the users') needs, specifications, and requirements. On the other hand, a good deal of basic

[19] Unfortunately, as we have noted frequently, there is a naive tendency to extrapolate organizational systems from engineering-like flows describing communications systems or the development process. There need not be, in fact, there usually is, no correspondence between the two.

research and development is undertaken without these user initiatives, and then the development organizations must seek out potential users to either take the newly minted "technology" as is or join forces with them to make it operational. And, of course, there will be many in-between cases involving joint efforts of users and development organizations.

☐ The table below summarizes the sequence of initiatives (who gets involved when) in the three distinctive implementations patterns we observed.

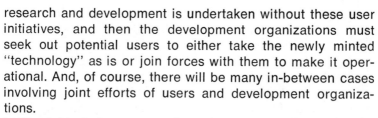

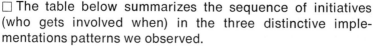

Agent	User Organization → Development Organization → R & D Project
Marketing	Development Organization → R & D Project → User Organization
Partner	{ Development Organization / User Organization } → R & D Project → User Organization

☐ The first two approaches may appear easier to the actual participants. The development organization, having perfected some new technology or technique, looks for a "customer" who can use it. Alternatively, a potential user organization with an unfulfilled need (or unsolved problem) looks for an agent who can provide an answer. However, neither of these relationships is likely to be as effective as a partnership-type relationship.

DESIGNING
THE INTERNAL STRUCTURE OF
THE SPONSOR ORGANIZATION

EIGHT

By this time the reader should be impressed with the significance of one of the most obvious characteristics of advanced technologies: They require the collaboration of many
independent organizations. Management of the interfaces,
the boundaries that both separate and connect diverse professionals and technical personnel, is a continuing challenge.

THE SPONSOR'S NEED FOR INSIDERS

□ But in most of these complex endeavors there is also a
significant central organization, controlled by the sponsor,
which not only assumes a major role in the management of
the widely dispersed program but also carries out a number
of operational activities itself. Thus, in the case of NASA, our
prime example in this book, thousands of engineers, scientists, technicians, and administrative personnel are employed in laboratory and field-development work, in basic
research, in launching and tracking spacecraft, and in a
whole host of support activities. While outsiders employed
by contractors may comprise 90 percent of the work force, a
critical amount of designing, testing, planning, and "operating" is conducted "in-house" by NASA personnel. Further,
NASA believes, with substantial justification, that outsiders
cannot be successfully stimulated, managed, or coordinated
without a technologically sophisticated internal organization. Technologically sophisticated organizations appear to
refute the old saw that "a manager is a manager is a manager. . . ."
□ To communicate with, and influence, the thinking and
actions of a highly trained professional, the manager must
have somewhat comparable training and experience. Elements of mutual respect, professional camaraderie, and
simple comprehension all seem to be involved. To put it
most directly, "They don't tell you very much unless they
think you can really understand; and even if they do, unless
you know a lot that they aren't telling you, you'll end up
being fooled or mistaken." Thus a certain amount of redundancy in both personnel and activities is necessary if a

central client organization is going to manage dispersed contractors and support groups. A lot more has to be done, as we shall see, than simply assigning tasks, agreeing on who gets paid what, and waiting for the item to be delivered. The insider must be a catalyst, a conscience, and a confidant.

☐ Unfortunately the "shelf life" of technical expertise is very short in dynamic fields like science and engineering. It cannot be stored (obsolescence is too rapid), and therefore talented experts cannot be hired by the sponsor solely to monitor and guide the activities of the contractors and the other outsiders who will be doing the lion's share of the work. Unless the insider has substantial challenging work to perform, his own skills will deteriorate, and he is likely to leave for a more active post.

☐ In fact, as we shall see, it is difficult to draw hard-and-fast lines between insider's and outsider's jurisdictions. For example, it is simple to propose a division of labor in which the sponsor does the key planning and the contractor does the implementing. But, if the contractor has highly motivated technical personnel, they will not be content merely to follow someone else's plans. On the other side, in the course of the program, problems will occur that will call for the expertise of the insider.

☐ In planning and design and development, the insiders play critical roles. While the outsider may predominate in the production stage, there will still be a variety of testing and support activities provided by the sponsor for itself, and of course, in the case of NASA, the operational stage (launching, tracking, controlling) is entirely under Its Jurisdiction.

☐ In actual practice, particularly in larger programs, internal NASA personnel (often with informal advice from outsiders) will review a number of alternative means and technologies for accomplishing an objective, say an unmanned landing on the planet Mars. Several of what appear to be promising alternatives are then explored by competing contractors, who seek to develop preliminary designs for implementing these concepts. Thus the planning is an intricate process of give-and-take involving NASA technical personnel and those employed by outside contractors. In addition "expert" committees composed of distinguished outside scientists, the National Academy of Sciences, or the President's Scientific Advisory Committee may get involved.

☐ The same blurring of boundaries takes place at other stages of the work flow. However, as we concluded in

Chapter 4, one can make certain reasonable predictions about which functions are more likely to be performed by sponsor insiders and which are likely to be contracted out.

□ Of course the rationale for a highly competent, strong central organization is strengthened in public programs because of the enormous fiscal responsibilities. A government agency cannot shift to outsiders, particularly private institutions, the responsibility for the efficient and effective use of public monies.

□ Thus a significant central organization is required for a number of reasons:

Monitoring and control requires technical expertise, and this expertise can only be maintained in "working condition" if the possessor has his own research and development work to perform *in addition to* his control activities.

The inherent uncertainties and the complex technical problems associated with these programs necessitates a sharing of the technical burden, some of which must be shouldered by insiders who can supplement the skills and resources of the outsiders. In particular, in NASA, there is a need for specialized and very expensive test facilities.

Some stages of the work flow are probably best handled by insiders. Again, for example, in NASA, launch and mission control require a distinctive competency as well as unusual equipment, the cost of which is enormous. Neither is readily available in the private sector.

By their very nature, government programs have certain responsibilities (to Congress, taxpayers, and the Executive Branch of government) that cannot be delegated to private organizations.

□ Table 1 suggests some of the major structural decisions a focal organization like NASA must make in order to facilitate collaboration and coordination among the parts and to ensure manageable executive jobs.

Table 1
Basic Structural Decisions

---

1. What will be the organizational "backbones," the major vertical subdivisions of the total organization?

2. How will the operating work be institutionalized?
   a. In more permanent "homes" where technicians, scientists, and administrators will perform experiments and tests, do designs, monitor development work, etc.?

  b. In temporary project groups that will cut across other organizational subdivisions in order to bring together the resources needed to accomplish a specific mission?

3. What will be the division of labor between upper management and the lower levels of administration?

ALTERNATIVE ORGANIZATIONAL DESIGNS

☐ Although the technology of systems stresses interrelationships and interdependence, it is impossible to organize human resources without introducing compartments and separate jurisdictions. However, the various parts of the human organization cannot be truly autonomous; they depend upon one another and draw upon one another's skills and resources. Thus it is a challenging administrative problem to determine where the lines of demarcation shall be drawn, what the "natural" divisions are within what is essentially an interdependent whole.

☐ It should be remembered that the major function being served by these structural decisions is the shaping of goals and relationships. Personality and administrative effort can accomplish some things, despite the contrary inducements provided by structural arrangements. However, the best predictor of future events, of which goals will be emphasized, of who will collaborate and who will compete, of who will have prestige and who will be defensive, is the organizational structure.

☐ The central organization has a variety of structural decisions to make. Some of them we shall examine in depth, but others will simply be catalogued, to await more perspicacious observers.

☐ The most obvious, traditional, and primary structural choice concerns the major vertical subdivisions of the organization. In business organizations these "backbones" typically reflect the major products, processes, or geographic divisions of the firm. (Of course all three can be used simultaneously.) In NASA's case, however, the choices appear to be those in Table 2.

Structure Based on Work Flow

☐ The organization could reflect the major *work-flow* stages or processes that are characteristic of any development or R & D-oriented institution: Basic research leads to applied research and design activities, which are followed by hardware development, which is followed by operations (launch-

Table 2
Alternative Criteria for Structural Decisions

---

1. *Structure based on work-flow stage:*
   Basic research
   Applied research
   Hardware development
   Operations (launching, tracking, data processing, and mission control)
   Users

2. *Structure based on type of technology:*
   Aeronautics technology
   Launch-vehicle technology
   Spacecraft technology
   Supporting technology (e.g., electronics and avionics, data processing, on-board power sources, life sciences)

3. *Structure based on use or objectives:*
   Manned-space-flight programs
   Science-oriented programs
   Applications-oriented programs (e.g., meteorology, communications)

4. *Structure based on institutional affiliation:*
   Center A
   Center B
   Etc.

---

ing, tracking, and controlling) and/or transfer of control to a user organization.

☐ NASA's organization, for the most part, has not involved this type of vertical structuring. There has been a major organizational component called the Office of Advanced Research and Technology (OART), part of which has taken responsibility for basic research in electronics, lifting bodies, on-board power sources, and nuclear power. However, this has also been the division responsible for aeronautics development work at all stages, including the operational stage. (See Table 3.)

☐ There has been some debate over whether operations should be handled by a separate division, on the grounds that these very costly, continuing, and somewhat more routine (although certainly not simpler) activities deserve a separate organizational component. (For example, the handling of the tracking function represents the incorporation of a work-flow stage into a single organizational component.)

Table 3

National Aeronautics and Space Administration: Simplified Organization Chart

Office of the Administrator			
Program Offices			
Manned Space Flight	Space Sciences and Applications	Advanced Research and Technology	Tracking and Data Acquisition
Field Centers			
Marshall Space Flight Center	Goddard Space Flight Center	Ames Research Center	
Manned Space-craft Center	Jet Propulsion Laboratory	Langley Research Center	
Kennedy Space Center	Wallops Station	Lewis Research Center	
		Flight Research Center	

Structure Based on Type of Technology

☐ A second alternative is vertical division based on type of technology. A great deal of NASA's work is based on three major types of technology: launch vehicles (rockets and boosters), spacecraft (which carry the payloads of experiments, measurement devices, and men themselves), and airplanes (the experimental aircraft, including very high-speed and slow-landing craft). In addition there are certain across-the-board types of support technology such as electronic control and guidance equipment, data-processing equipment, sensing and recording devices, life-support systems, and on-board power sources. Sometimes these are common to both spacecraft and aeronautics, which complicates the organizational decision-making.

☐ At present NASA is partially organized on this basis. As we have already noted, there is a major grouping (OART) devoted to support technology, although it also controls all aeronautics research. But there has been little effort to develop common support technology such as sensors and tape recorders, although there is certainly a need for equipment to withstand the rigors of launch and space flight. (The NASA-wide need for unusually reliable electronic components did, however, spawn the ill-fated Electronics Research Laboratory.[1])

☐ Spacecraft are designed in many different organizational units within the agency, and work on launch vehicles is performed at several centers reporting up different organizational lines. However, within the largest subdivision of NASA, the manned program, there is a semblance of organization based on technology. The Marshall Space Flight Center (Huntsville, Alabama) was largely devoted to launch-vehicle design (the Saturn 1B and Saturn 5 rockets), and the Manned Spacecraft Center (Houston, Texas) had as one of its major missions the evolution of the Apollo spacecraft and lunar excursion module (the LEM).

Structure Based on Objectives

☐ At first blush NASA appears to have a very clear singleness of purpose. And, of course, the manned lunar landing by Apollo astronauts provided an unusually clear focus for the agency. But even during the period of Apollo's greatest build-up, there were competing objectives.

☐ Few organizations, beyond those that are very small or highly specialized, have single objectives. Most are multipurpose, and NASA is no exception. It is concerned with evolving the technology of space flight for both manned and unmanned missions, but it also has responsibility for aeronautics technology. In addition, some persons (within and without the agency) have proposed that it be given even broader interests in transportation.

☐ Technologies are themselves both ends and means. They are ends because we have come to view new technologies as essential to a strong, dynamic economy and connected to our status as a world power. But they are also means of accomplishing tasks that have (or should have) immediate human benefits: improvements in communication techniques, in weather prediction, in navigation. And there are those who would argue that NASA has evolved a managerial technology which is useful in dealing with an even wider range of scientific, social, and economic problems. The other "ends" of aeronautics and space technology are scientific, having to do with astrophysics and astronomy and exobiology, among others.

☐ NASA has established two major subdivisions reflecting these several objectives. The largest and most critical, of

[1] Late in 1969 agency budget tightening caused this Cambridge, Mass. Center to be abolished.

course, is the manned program (the Office of Manned Space Flight). The other "objective"-oriented division is the Office of Space Sciences and Applications.

□ There is some concern that the latter is too heterogeneous. Earth-oriented applications (navigation aids, natural-resource-identification techniques, communications satellites) may not mix well with basic science, although the two "unmanned" segments, when put together, are better able to balance the huge (in both numbers and funding) manned program.

Dispersion and Integration:
Cutting Through the Interfaces

□ While it may appear obvious that a profoundly difficult objective can be accomplished by creating a single organization devoted to this end, in our complex world there are too many private and public objectives for each to be institutionalized. Conglomerates are not new to government or business. Individual companies and government agencies have multiple objectives. Contrariwise, single objectives are dispersed among many institutions.

□ In 1957 when the Russians launched their *Sputnik,* the Army, Air Force, and Navy had rocket programs. In addition, the National Advisory Committee for Aeronautics (NACA) had an illustrious history of research and testing in related fields. It was not obviously necessary that a new agency (NASA) be created to give the United States an astronautical capability. Existing governmental units and their industrial support contractors already had both competence and established jurisdictional "rights."[2] In 1970 somewhat analogous concerns with ecology and oceanography have not produced new organizations.

□ Of course, the concept of using objectives as a criterion for designing organization has misleading simplicity. In the government a number of distinct organizations, including a variety of technical, military, diplomatic, and intelligence groups, have responsibilities for national defense. In recent years a supercoordinating committee has been formed, the

[2] For a meticulous history of the formation of NASA and its predecessors in rocketry see Lloyd Swenson, Jr., James Grimwood, and Charles Alexander, *This New Ocean: A History of Project Mercury,* Washington, D.C., NASA, 1966. NASA's ability to quickly assimilate a number of organizational units transferred from the Navy, Air Force, and Army, as well as the total NACA organization, was remarkable. This process is described in Robert Rosholt, *An Administrative History of NASA, 1958– 1963,* Washington, D.C., NASA, 1966.

National Security Council, but this integration has been matched by a growing differentiation in the number of federal agencies that have "defense" inputs, including, of course, NASA itself. There is also President Nixon's proposed Domestic Council, which would coordinate the Departments of the Treasury, Interior, Agriculture, Commerce, Labor, HEW, HUD, Transportation, and the Attorney General's office.

☐ In many ways, as we indicated earlier, this is the history of modern civilization: growing interdependence among institutions, with efforts at coordination balanced off by growing differentiation. As we shall see, the same process occurs *within* an institution like NASA. Neat lines of demarcation and specialization gradually blur as human ingenuity combines with the natural tendency of technical developments to exceed predetermined boundaries. Thus constant decision-making is required to determine the relative degrees of integration and differentiation which are desirable. Even though NASA was the nation's "aeronautics and space agency," the Air Force continued to have military programs and the Department of Transportation to have many legitimate concerns with commercial aviation. And as more of NASA's centers developed the capability to manage large-scale spacecraft-development programs, there were concurrent efforts to centralize and rationalize these capabilities.

Developing Institutional Homes

☐ The strategy that is chosen for creating and building institutional homes for the individuals in a program is highly critical to their functioning. In a reasonably large agency such as NASA most workers are employed outside the central headquarters. The latter is largely made up of top managers and staff support groups, while the real ·work is performed in a variety of field locations where appropriate facilities can be made available. These field locations then become the basic building blocks of the organization.

☐ Engineers find colleagues at, evolve social groupings in, discuss their work and receive admiration and criticism at, get office and lab space in, build their careers at, are evaluated and paid by, and develop their strongest loyalties to some specific "home." This can be a laboratory or center or field office, but it is a physical manifestation and an institutional reality that can be distinguished from the more amorphous and psychologically distant entity, the agency itself. The home base has a major influence on attitudes and motivation, and it is the place where most of the technical work gets done, at least the work that is done by insiders.

□ While it may appear obvious how to incorporate these "homes" into the organization, it is by no means so. For example, NASA is still debating whether all their field locations ought to report to a reasonably high-level official with agency-wide responsibilities or, as at present, to one of four program offices.

□ The argument for agencywide reporting is that the institutional needs of these critical centers are more likely to be attended to under this arrangement than when they are managed by executives busy with very explicit mission goals. The short-run time, cost, and performance pressures generated "in the heat of battle" are likely to outweigh longer-run concerns as to the growth and viability of any given center. Theoretically the principle that all centers are the property of NASA as a whole allows an easier and more flexible sharing of existing resources, particularly as program needs change. In actuality, however, when it comes to sharing facilities between one's own program office and any other program office, it is not difficult to predict who will get priority. For example, one executive at Program Office A reported: "We asked Center B for some additional support with our . . . problem, but they said they had absolutely no free resources although we knew they were stockpiling personnel."

□ Also, having centers report directly to top management would theoretically create a truer *matrix organization* in which mission-oriented projects and programs would have almost no "captive" resources. Of course, in practice the matrix model has its problems too. Difficult programs like Apollo may need to have substantial "captive" resources. Further, when everything is up for grabs, there can be excessive competition for institutional loyalties. NASA has already experienced some modest destructive competition between program offices having somewhat similar jurisdictions. Each has tried to get a specific center to commit itself more fully in one area of advanced research and development.

□ Whether centers report to program offices also relates to larger issues of organizational strategy. The emphasis given a function, a technology, or an objective will be in large measure determined by the amount of working-level support assigned to it. Thus it has been argued that NASA's unmanned space program suffered because it did not have sole jurisdiction over a group of centers, as did the manned program. What kind of balance maintains an appropriate dispersion of power but does not emasculate programmatic objectives is always difficult to decide.

☐ For the most part NASA treads a middle ground. Center budgets are partially programmatic (relating to specific projects which have been funded and are directed by project managers who may or may not be a part of that center) and partially general funds assigned by top agency management to each center to carry on a wide variety of research and development activities apart from projects.

☐ In private industry one finds strong pressures to assign clear, unambiguous missions to plants, laboratories, and other organizational units, thus making the evaluation of managerial performance easier. It is obviously more difficult to evaluate institutional managers' "effectiveness" when their activities contribute to a variety of products, programs, and projects, each of which may fall under the jurisdiction of a different headquarters division. Further, left to its own devices and without a clearly defined mission, each unit would seek to develop as broad a competence as the total organization.

☐ On the other hand, clarity of function is usually associated with greater specialization. In practice this means that expertise in a given field will be concentrated in a single organizational unit. This makes critical assessment of their plans and recommendations by upper management very difficult, since there are no comparably expert units to give testimony.

☐ Since the lunar landing, the position of the "narrower" centers has been in jeopardy. Up to that time Huntsville had concentrated an enormous proportion of its efforts on Saturn rockets, while Houston had been concerned chiefly with pulling the Apollo spacecraft, the LEM, and the astronauts through the difficult development and testing and practice stages. Both are now seeking new missions and would like to broaden their capability (particularly their scientific competency) in order to be able to take on a wider variety of projects and responsibilities. The older NACA-established centers like Langley and Lewis have a very broad range of aeronautics, spacecraft, space-power, and other activities. But it is unlikely that a program as complex as Apollo could have been completed if there were not a reasonably large aggregation of people in a single location supporting the project. This is part of the old struggle between short-run needs (and accomplishments are made in the short run) and long-run survival.

☐ Institutional structure thus appears as problematic as the more technological aspects of large-scale development programs. Within NASA one finds a number of unanswered structural questions concerning the centers themselves. Here are just several examples:

Is it desirable to combine in a single institution (i.e., a center) responsibilities for activities that represent vastly different workflow stages?

Are basic research and applied research mutually compatible in the same laboratory or center, or does one tend to drive out the other?

Can one have operational projects (in NASA's case this means flight projects) existing comfortably side by side with effective research groups, or is the result second-class research or poor flight projects?

Can centers with established jurisdictions and functions do the kind of advance planning that involves significant departures from established means and ends? How proprietary will centers become, and will those with the most unambiguous focus or jurisdiction become the most inflexible?

MANAGERIAL CROSSCUTS

☐ Cutting across these structural components are a series of staff functions. Some, like contract negotiations and public affairs, represent an operational work-flow element which has been centralized and which other components must make use of to the extent that they lack comparable "internal" facilities. Others, like budgeting, are more traditional control functions. Still others represent sensitive external relationships which must be maintained by the agency and which impinge on development activities: relationships with universities, other governmental agencies, and Congress, particularly.

☐ Like any large organization, the focal institution for a major development program must evolve a division of labor for its top managers. NASA has had to face questions like these:

What decisions should be made by the heads of the key programs, and what decisions should be made by the nonprogrammatic top management?

What controls should be placed inside the key program offices (and therefore under the direction of the head of the program), and which should be handled on an agencywide basis?

How much technical expertise is necessary at top levels to evaluate and reassess technical decisions and accomplishments and requests at lower levels?

☐ In practice top management has served largely a control function: the measurement, primarily after the fact, of the extent to which funds are being spent wisely; schedules are likely to be met; and whether all federal personnel, contracting, and other policies are being adhered to by both program offices and centers. A good deal of the time of the key top managers was devoted to external relations with various units of the Executive Branch, with Congress, and with key public groups representing private business, universities, the scientific community, and various international interests. The presumption that a continued broad base of support would be necessary to maintain reasonable budget levels and a viable jurisdiction was validated in 1969 when the successful moon landing appeared to exhaust public backing of the space agency's mandate.

☐ It is probably unrealistic to conceive of any fixed and clear separation of technical and administrative decision-making, separating the *what* from the *how.* A good illustration of the dynamic melding of the two is provided by an analysis of NASA's largest procurement decisions. Here we can see how informed technical judgment is intermixed with administrative factors.

☐ This decision-making process also contradicts the frequently heard observation that technically oriented, professionally staffed organizations are "upside-down" hierarchies because key decisions must be made at the bottom.[3] (After all, these "technocrats" argue, the technicians have first-hand and profound knowledge of the underlying data and theory, and their distant superiors, far removed from the "bench," have the choice of either rubber-stamping their recommendations or duplicating the costly and time-consuming analyses with a counterpart high-level staff of equal capability.[4])

[3] The most cogent statement concerning the inability of top management to exercise realistic control over lower-level technical personnel is provided by John Galbraith in *The New Industrial State,* Boston, Houghton Mifflin, 1967.

[4] It is true, however, that top-notch engineers are moved to headquarters to enable top management to "match" the sophistication of the centers.

A Case Example: Selecting Major Contractors

□ The large, multimillion-dollar procurement decisions at
NASA are made by an organizational mechanism that brings
lower-level technical personnel together with top agency
officials.[5] An ad hoc "Source Evaluation Board" comprising
a small team of informed center-level technical people is
formed to review the potential competency and efficiency of
the industrial firms competing for a given contract. After extensive assessment procedures, including discussions with
the potential contractors, the board presents its findings to a
panel consisting of the top three executives of the agency.
Using these assessments as its base, top management adds
its own knowledge of broader agency needs and political
factors and personal judgment to make a final choice:

The SEB process capitalizes upon an interesting division of labor
between the top three administrators and the Board members.
The Board members, having spent several months on the topic,
are intimately knowledgeable about the specific procurement
and understand in detail its cost, technical, and management aspects. Top management people, on the other hand, have a broader
view of the entire Agency, of the strengths and weaknesses of
corporate management, and of the political-economic climate. For
example, a company may be undergoing a reorganization. . . .[6]

There have also been instances where it seemed prudent to
base a decision on the need to have more competitors in a
given technical field.
□ At times the final decision will require NASA top management to undertake direct negotiations with the top management of one or more contending contractors if no proposal
is adequate. At other times there will be the need to respond
to contractors who feel they have been discriminated
against or who seek to know why they were not successful.
□ Thus this is a decision *process* involving not one but
many managers and technical people, not one step but several over an extended period, multiple organizations, and a
number of objective and highly subjective criteria. And while
it is clear who has the authority to make, and who an-

[5] Our analysis has benefited from the research of Willard Zangwill, sum-
marized in his article, "Top Management and the Selection of Major
Contractors at NASA," *California Management Review, XII,* no. 1 (Fall,
1969), 43–52. We were also fortunate in being able to observe several
such meetings during our own field work.

[6] Zangwill, *op. cit.,* p. 47.

nounces, the final decision (the top administrator of NASA), it is much more difficult to say who, in fact, *makes* the decision. It is the product of a complex process of interaction and confrontation in which technical, administrative, and broader political criteria are applied and in which both technical and managerial personnel participate.

□ The participants must persuade one another and move toward some consensus. The board members know that they cannot simply state that Firm A is better technically than Firm B; they must seek to provide evidence. Further, their ability to ferret out relevant data and to present it effectively in an intimidating confrontation with the highest-status members of their own organization will influence both the choice of contractor *and* the assessments that will be made of their own personal competence.

□ But top management also knows that it is highly visible in this process too and "that NASA personnel will analyze and debate its performance."[7] It cannot afford to make a choice that does not reflect the groundwork of the board without clear justification in the form of broader criteria and data that can be communicated and supported. Also, the meetings are used as training sessions for those in the lower levels of technical and administrative management. Seeing which issues, questions, and areas the discussion concentrates on during the board's presentation alerts and sensitizes them to the areas of major concern to top management. Thus communication, appraisal, and training are all combined with a broadly based decision-making process that integrates technical and administrative criteria. All parties involved are evaluated not only on the basis of the results they achieved (the data they collected and the opinions they expressed) but on the methods they employed and the way they went about doing their respective jobs.

□ Looked at in terms of pure interaction, the process represents the same balanced organizational network that Whyte identified over two decades ago as the basis for viable relationships both within and between hierarchies.[8] The concern as to "who" makes the decision in technically oriented organizations is thus seen as naive on the part of observers who fail to see the total decision process. The actual process involves visibility, confrontation, feedback loops, extended sequences of action and interaction, and

[7] *Ibid.,* p. 48.

[8] William F. Whyte, *Pattern for Industrial Peace,* New York, Harper & Row, 1951.

overlapping responsibility—nearly all the elements we have seen or will see in other aspects of the management of complex endeavors. Below we have endeavored to summarize this complex organizational process.

STAGES OF THE DECISION PROCESS

1. SEB undertakes field investigations that explore in depth proposals of various contractors and responds to presentations of contractor personnel.

2. Contractors assign top-management monitors to keep them informed of the progress of these SEB investigations.

3. SEB makes a formal presentation to the top three executives of the agency and responds to a variety of questions and probes. The board also receives insight into top management's concerns and criteria for this type of decision.

4. NASA top management undertakes final negotiation with one or more of leading contenders and/or responds to requests for justification of the award by unsuccessful bidders.

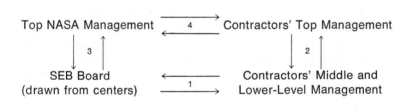

□ The extent to which "down-the-line" and "up-the-line" interactions balance and NASA and its contractors are bound together by lateral contacts is clearly indicated here. This process illustrates the naïveté of endeavoring to dichotomize organizations on the basis of whether decisions are made at the bottom (presumably in highly technical-professional environments) or at the top (traditional hierarchically functioning organizations). Decision-making is a process in which various organizational levels and interest groups compete for position in a sequence and to make their voice the strongest.[9]

[9] For a further discussion of this view of decision-making see Leonard Sayles, "The Manager and the Decision Process," *Managerial Behavior,* New York, McGraw-Hill, 1964, Chap. 12.

FUTURE STRUCTURES AND AGENCY UNITY

☐ Ideally there ought to be greater fluidity among the various legitimate bases for organizational structure. After all, one hallmark of complex technology is overlapping relationships: the absence of a clear compartmentalization of function and multiple affiliations. An engineer can be at one and the same time part of a scientific discipline or functional group (e.g., a thermal specialist), a contributor to one or more projects, a monitor of or an advisor to a contractor with technical troubles, a member of an intercenter panel, and identified with a given institutional base, usually in this case a NASA center. Over time some of these identifications become more salient than others as the frequency and meaningfulness of contacts increase. However, excessively strong commitments or long, unchanged relationships tend to impede adaptation to new problems and new organizational relationships.

☐ This does not mean that at any one time there should not be an identifiable structure. But these "backbones" should not be viewed as quite so permanent, and greater efforts should be made to emphasize the crosscuts. There is some evidence that structure tends to become more complex as technology becomes more complex. For example, the Mercury Program was under the control of a single field center, Langley, which made requests of other centers and coordinated their activities. Headquarters restricted itself to external relations. (There are some who assert that this delegation of responsibility to a "lead" center increases the technical excellence of decisions reached in the coordination process, since the best technical talent is in the field. When Washington has to undertake the coordination function [really program management], they say, the work suffers.) On the other hand, in Apollo a number of co-equal centers were responsible for various segments of the program. Only headquarters had the overview and took upon itself the responsibility for coordination.

☐ More recently, the early work on post-Apollo programs has shown another shift upward in complexity. It appears as though the effort to develop a reusable "shuttle" will involve a still greater blurring of interfaces. Whereas in Apollo a fairly clean line could be drawn between the procurement of propulsion units (managed by Huntsville Saturn-rocket experts) and that for the spacecraft (managed by Houston), the proposed shuttle involves a greater melding of rocket and spacecraft. The problems of interaction are enormous, since the boosters may not just "fall away" in space and there must be a reasonably common guidance system.

☐ Based on rather modest evidence, it would appear that the greater the inability to define interfaces, the more the agency must rely on relatively decentralized coordination. Headquarters cannot know enough about the technical aspects of the situation to make judgments. Thus the locus of control has shifted from the field level to the headquarters level and back again as technology has become more complex.

☐ As we noted at the outset, all structural lines of demarcation are artificial; particularly in advanced-technology organizations, all the parts are highly interdependent, not autonomous. Yet over time jurisdictional lines tend to harden, distinctive points of view become ingrained, and separate interests come to the fore. How can such trends be muted without destroying the required amount of identification with and interaction within smaller groups?

☐ A partial answer involves the planning process previously discussed. Structurally, NASA is now experimenting with new groupings of high-level officials that cross existing jurisdictional lines and unite, at least at the top, the key "line" officials. This is probably more efficacious than previous efforts to use high-level staff groups to monitor the amount of cooperation and coordination and to ferret out instances of needless duplication.

Is Decentralization Feasible?

☐ In recent years, the emphasis in American management has been on decentralization. It is assumed that the managerial task is simplified, individual managers can be held more tightly accountable, and the significant decisions can be made closer to the level of operating work if relatively independent clusters of activity are created by structural means. Thus in private companies a manager responsible for the sale of a given product may have the manufacturing, designing, testing, and advertising facilities for that product reporting directly to him. University departments are notorious for seeking autonomy. Each teaching department tries to control all the courses, labs, and training facilities its students will require even though comparable courses may already be given, say, by external statistics or math or language departments.

☐ As we move in the direction of more sophisticated technologies and larger, more complex endeavors it would appear as though just the opposite strategy has to be followed. It is very difficult to segregate activities and create semi-autonomous islands of activity. Everything appears to depend upon everything else. For example, the fields of space science and aeronautics are not neatly divisible; advanced electronics for the Saturn 5 rocket and for the C-5A airplane have a good deal in common.

□ As we have indicated, any organizational separations inevitably are artificial and begin to break down in technologically advanced systems. NASA, for example, has been moving in the direction of merging parts of its manned and its scientific programs. In the early 1970s a series of solar telescopes will be launched that will be pointed and serviced by astronauts in an earth-orbiting spacecraft (the Apollo Telescope Mount). The trade-offs between designs that favor astronaut training and convenience and those that favor scientific values cut across the major organizational backbones of the agency. Various institutional groupings (NASA field centers) are constantly having to make difficult choices between devoting resources to one major program or to another. At the extremes, the obvious dividing line between aeronautics and spaceships becomes artificial.

ROUTINE VS. MISSION ORGANIZATIONS: CONCLUSIONS

□ Organizations facing repetitive problems seek to regularize their activities through a variety of structural and control mechanisms. For example, knowing that separated groups tend to evolve highly differentiated norms and entrenched procedures that may be mutually incompatible, the executive seeks to extend his immediate jurisdiction as much as possible. This fact is reflected in the well-known trends toward vertical and horizontal integration. Such integrated structures are seeking to damp out the unpredictable perturbations that result from groups responding to different stimuli and evolving different norms. A monolithic structure is supposed to create mutually congruent responses from its members by building stable, informal groups whose norms reinforce organizational needs.

□ When successful (and that is an important qualification), a mission organization can depend upon more externalized direction. This direction comes from a common loyalty to the objectives of the mission and the willingness to watch for signs of difficulty and to do what is necessary to move the mission toward completion. All groups, regardless of their institutional affiliation, then, have a common external source of motivation: the relative progress of the mission. As we saw in Chapter 6, such identifications can overcome even national as well as agency and corporate boundaries. Out of self pride, the desire not to be considered as incompetent or as an impediment, individuals and groups put forth enormous efforts to help meet mission goals.

☐ Thus structural arrangements associated with building institutional homes for a mission-oriented agency like NASA ought not to work against this ideal. There obviously has to be some stability in structure, some base of operations, or *home,* for each participant; but these ought not to evolve into the rather rigid structures associated with routine organizations facing repetitive problems. In those, structure impedes change; stability works against adaptation.

☐ The routine structure is designed to operate after the major problems are solved, the instabilities eliminated by sound organization decisions and work procedures. The mission organization is designed to cope with an endless series of unpredictable problems. Given what James Webb has termed a "turbulent environment," it is possible to justify the search for structural arrangements that preclude the development of equilibrium. The argument can be made that the "digging in" by which a group surrounds itself with constricting norms, status systems, and proprietary self-perceptions militates against reasonable adaptability and responsiveness. "Stay loose" may be a better recommendation than seeking some semipermanent ideal form and procedures.

☐ Of course as a mission organization moves toward operation—the routinization and utilization of a new technology—the structural decisions may be very different. This raises the obvious question of whether the two are mutually compatible and can co-exist in the same sponsor or agency. But such considerations would take us back to the issues explored in Chapter 7, and all development efforts should seek to maintain their forward momentum.

BUILDING
THE PROJECT
ORGANIZATION

NINE

In the preceding chapter we dealt with some of the major management-structure decisions which must be made by a large, advanced-technology organization that seeks both to maintain a strong research base and to guide the implementation of complex development programs. We wish to continue looking at structure by moving from those loftier issues of top-management design to the structuring of individual projects.

□ It is clearly unrealistic in any but the smallest projects to conceive of neatly autonomous project groups containing all the necessary manpower, skills, and physical resources. As we have noted frequently, advanced technologies usually require the collaboration of outside organizations (which we have subsumed under the generic title of contractor). In addition, both within the sponsor's own organization and each of the contractor's organizations there are a multiplicity of divisions and subdivisions, each possessing their own unique expertise and having some function to perform in the total project.

□ All these units will have to evolve reasonably predictable, routine ways of dealing with one another if the hundreds of thousands of questions that come up are to have any chance of being answered. (The point has been made before, but is worth making again, that a painful characteristic of these technologies is the number of unknowns and unanticipated problems.) There is going to have to be rather a great deal of contact among these various units both within and among the many organizations that make up the total federation.

□ In examining the structure of individual projects, we shall move from the more static to the more dynamic administrative patterns. At the outset the sponsor's top management, with or without the collaboration of the project manager, probably makes some tentative decisions about the size and comprehensiveness of the project staff as compared to the *nonprojectized* or functional or line staff. Similar, but not necessarily parallel, decisions will have to be made by the various contractors who are going to be part of the project. Even these decisions do not fully determine the relationship of the project office to each of the functional groups, and that is also a choice we shall wish to examine.

□ At a more dynamic level, once the external form of the project has been decided, a viable pattern of communication and coordination that keeps the parts functioning in concert must still be evolved. Three distinct patterns or styles are observable: integration, dispersion, and redundancy. Interestingly, and perhaps paradoxically, these represent almost directly opposite or mutually contradictory techniques, and yet they frequently are used simultaneously and in a mutually supporting fashion.

THE POSITION OF THE PROJECT OFFICE

In the Sponsor's House

□ A project office is established with a very explicit goal and an implicit life span, the time needed to complete the mission. The projects we have been concerned with in this book are development efforts whose product is typically a new aircraft or spacecraft or some other embodiment of advanced technology. It is the responsibility of the project office (more precisely, of its manager) to accomplish the project goals within the usual constraints of time and money.

□ The project will have its own internal staff of functional specialists reporting directly to the project manager. The specialists may be in engineering or scientific disciplines like guidance or propulsion, electronics or biology. There may also be administrative specialists in fields like finance, scheduling, quality control, and testing. These are the "assistants" who will help the project manager monitor and advise the groups performing the actual engineering work. Some of these groups may be directly under the project manager's jurisdiction as well—professional personnel who have been "centralized" into the project office.[1]

---

[1] Advanced technology appears to require a multiplicity of cross-cutting management positions. While in traditional business organization it is sometimes assumed that management will make a choice, for example, between product- and function-based organizational divisions, advanced technologies will have both. In the Washington and center program offices for NASA's Apollo activities, managers are divided functionally: design, quality control, schedule, etc. However, within the centers there are managers responsible for the key components, systems, and subsystems (in a sense "product" managers).

□ Of course, in addition, each of these is responsible *both* to the center management and to the Apollo Program Office management.

☐ Within the project manager's own company or government development center there will be parallel functional departments who will back up the work of the project group by doing special studies, design work, and even fabrication or testing. Some of these personnel and facilities will temporarily be placed in project groupings within the functional department. Thus the "electronic-components-design department" may have a project group made up of some of its permanent staff.

☐ There may also be central-project-office people co-located in the functional departments; their dual status allows them to utilize the equipment and the skills of these groups while also reporting to the project manager.

☐ In most cases, some form of *matrix management* is involved; that is, employees are expected to be responsive to the requests of both the project office and the functional-department head. The "most" responsive will be the co-located personnel; those in special project groups located within the functional areas will be somewhat less so, and the functional department members who are assigned project work by their regular superiors but who are not part of any special groupings will, of course, be the least responsive.

☐ The kind of authority exercised by the functional manager thus varies broadly, even ignoring such factors as personality and temperament. There is also in these complex endeavors a wide and interesting variety of forms of shared authority. No longer is a boss simply a boss. He is surrounded, both figuratively and literally, with a multiplicity of other managers controlling scarce resources and professional talent with whom he must negotiate a viable sharing of power.

In the Contractor's House

☐ Of course, the same patterns as those in the sponsor's organization apply to contractors. At least on larger projects they will have a centralized project office, which is supported by functional departments with various degrees of responsibility and power. The same can hold true for subcontractors.

☐ The sponsor's project manager hopes that the project-functional boundary in the contractor's house will be a readily permeable one, that the contractor has in-depth technical strength that can be called upon should major problems emerge. A "good contractor" does not allow the formalities of the original project organization to deter him from making

changes when schedule and performance milestones are endangered. (There have been times when the sponsor has supplemented the contractor's functional support group with reinforcements from his own internal functional forces.)
□ The diagram below should clarify this relationship between project office and functional departments in the sponsor and contractor organizations.

Project Office		Functional Departments		
Project manager	Functional & administrative specialists	Staff assigned to project	Project-office co-located personnel	Nonproject personnel available for support activities

Contractors and Other Affiliated Organizations

Project Office		Functional Departments		
Project manager	Functional & administrative specialists	Staff assigned to project	Project office	Nonproject personnel

Subcontractors

Project Office	Functional Departments
(same as above)	(same as above)

Figure 1. Sponsor with prime responsibility for the project.

PROJECT VS. FUNCTIONAL ORGANIZATION

□ Any project may appear to have a comparative advantage if all the resources it requires are directly under the immediate control of the project head. At first glance the ideal appears to be simple: Give the manager the resources he needs and thus minimize the number of interfaces he must handle, the number of external groups (that is, external to himself) who must be policed, cajoled, and negotiated with. But the real world is not that simple, and there are many good reasons why development organizations can reject building large, all-inclusive project groups encompassing the necessary disciplines and functions.
□ To be sure, reasonably autonomous project groups give visibility and emphasis to the project, but they also tend to narrow the training of, and increase the difficulty of moving,

personnel. In organizations where function, or "line," identifications are very weak, individual managers or technical
personnel who are shifted back and forth among project
managers can feel isolated and rootless.[2] Most career lines
are by specialized function. Also, all-inclusive project groups
conflict with the organization's desire to build up a tech-

Table 1
Summary of Relative Advantages of Project Organizations Versus
Functional Organizations

Project Organizations	Functional Organizations
Advantages	*Disadvantages*
• Full-time attention of personnel to the project	• Part-time attention to any one project
• Single focal point for sponsor and contractor for all project matters	• No single focal point for a given multidiscipline job
• Project visibility	• Poor visibility of a given job
• Cradle-to-grave responsibility for a given job	• Diffused responsibility for a given job
• Flexible level of reporting for project	• Department reporting level relatively fixed
• Tailor-made to fit the job	• Must accommodate full range of interests for each specialist
Disadvantages	*Advantages*
• Personnel experience limited to project requirements	• Reservoir of personnel skilled in a given functional area
• Little interchange with similar functions outside the project; tendency to "reinvent the wheel"	• Automatic interchange of ideas and solutions in a given functional area (prevents "reinventing the wheel")
• Massive requirements for facilities for short periods	• Amortizes large facilities over extended time
• Fluctuating manpower levels and skills mix	• Work base spread over many projects; therefore, relatively stable manpower level
• Job performance very sensitive to organizational structures as well as skills and ability of personnel	• Overall performance relatively insensitive to structure—largely dependent on quality of personnel

[2] See Joan Woodward, *Industrial Organization,* New York, Oxford Univ.
Press, 1965, p. 121.

nological and scientific base that allows a variety of projects to be conducted concurrently and over time.

☐ A strong functional group can act as a conscience, imposing standards of technical performance upon the project group. A conscience usually includes a memory. With one-of-a-kind development projects, the project team can be ignorant of the relevant solutions and innovations of other projects. When the earlier work was accomplished by a relatively durable functional department, its experience is stored, ready to be recalled by the next project.[3] This can also be a limitation because such standards can be excessively confining or even inappropriate to a given project. Functional groups can become ingrown and shortsighted, as well as being sources of accumulated wisdom.

Roles of the Functional Manager

☐ It is instructive to move from a gross to a more "micro" structural level in examining the division of labor between project and functional groups. Therefore we shall look more closely at alternative roles for the functional manager.

☐ At one extreme the functional manager may be little more than a landlord "renting out" physical facilities and/or personnel. While it is his job to maintain their potential and capabilities, the actual direction of their utilization and, of course, the responsibility for the results of their use is entirely in the hands of project-office personnel, either co-located or in the project office itself. Obviously this arrangement recommends itself where there are expensive facilities (such as atomic piles, computers, wind tunnels, or towing tanks) that have to be shared by a number of programs and projects.

☐ But frequently, there is pressure from the project office for a more involved relationship. The project office seeks to force "power" (or responsibility, depending on your point of view) on the functional manager. The project manager is willing to trade away control—the ease with which he can get the functional people to respond to his centralized direction—in return for greater motivation and commitment. He wants the functional manager to take full responsibility for the ideas, decisions, and work generated in his area rather than simply making recommendations. In the bargain the

---

[3] Effective project managers substitute in part for the memory of a functional group by spending time with key groups who participated in earlier, comparable projects. They devote substantial time to personal visits, recognizing that documents and publications rarely encompass all the technical experiences of previous projects.

functional head also takes responsibility for costs, schedules, and performance. (Then, of course, he becomes very much like an outside contractor, demanding reasonable autonomy and fixed specifications if he is to get his work done within the constraints that have been agreed upon.)
□ Within the sponsor's own house, the project office can behave like a functional department. This occurs in rather complex projects requiring the collaboration of several NASA centers. Each may have its own area of expertise, its functional contribution. Typically one center is more expert in booster design, another in spacecraft engineering, and so on. Each has its own supporting contractors, of course, and each project office also depends upon the functional departments within its own "shop" for a good deal of operational work.
□ The parallel center structure is illustrated below.

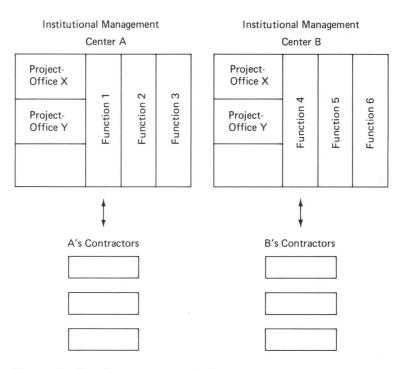

Figure 2. Parallel center organization.

□ Some centers will be more equal than others. To facilitate coordination, a "leader" is chosen; this "lead" center has significantly greater responsibility for the total effort than the others and acts as the primary source of direction and control. (Its project-office staff accordingly will be larger.)

The Role of Institutional Management

☐ Where other centers (really outside organizations for our purposes here) are involved, the project manager usually must negotiate with the institutional head of those centers when serious problems emerge requiring changes in the work to be done by them.[4] The other center heads must be convinced of the need for, and concur with, these changes, although, as we shall see later in our discussion of "dispersion," in effective projects there is a good deal of direct contact among working groups that bypasses the institutional heads.

☐ In a sense there are three types of managers involved in every organization that is tied into the project:

1. project managers,
2. functional-specialist managers, and
3. institutional managers.

All co-exist within the same center or company:

Table 2
Three Types of Managers

Center A	Center B
Institutional Management A	Institutional Management B
Project Offices A	Project Offices B
Functional Support Groups A	Functional Support Groups B

A project-office manager maintains relationships with his own institutional management, with his own functional managers, and with their counterparts in any other organizations that are tied into the project.

THE PROJECT AS PART OF A LARGER PROGRAM

☐ In a large, complex institution, any given project may well be part of a larger effort to accomplish a more major objective. For instance, a group of development projects can serve to establish the competency of a company in some

---

[4] We use the term *institutional management* to refer to high-level line managers and their supporting staffs responsible for the operations of a given organization *qua* organization as distinct from project or functional managers, who have more specialized responsibilities.

new technology, or they may be part of a government agency seeking to carve out a new jurisdiction. The individual projects are supposed to "add up" to some total new accomplishment.

☐ Of course, this means that another hierarchical level must be introduced to "coordinate" the individual projects so that they do in fact complement and supplement one another. However, given the taxing demands on the project manager and his need for leeway in dealing with a variety of unanticipated crises, it is too much to expect a great deal of joint decision-making between these two levels. What seems to work best is a lateral division of labor. The program manager handles the "external-to-the-project" interfaces. Many of these involve maintaining the sponsor's enthusiasm and support for the project during its "dark days" and informing and reassuring the outsiders who need to know about its progress and pitfalls. The project manager handles the internal interfaces, and the two keep each other informed in advance of problem build-ups that are likely to have serious implications (e.g., an unresolved technical difficulty that is likely to affect schedules or a coming financial stringency in the larger organization that may affect the project).

☐ The actual formal organizational system for a large project appears, on paper at least, to be almost unmanageable. There are just too many managers, in too many organizations with multiple responsibilities and identifications, and too many levels to expect timely coordination. But the remarkable thing is that such projects do work! Surely this represents a major human achievement, although it is one that cannot be appreciated without some comprehension of the problem.

☐ Remember that there is, in each organizational unit, a mix of institutional managers, project managers, and functional managers (and there may also be project offices within the more critical functional groupings). These *three* types of management, with their distinct professional interests and points of view, are often replicated at contractor and even subcontractor levels. They may also exist, for very large projects, at the headquarters of the sponsoring agency, where projects are grouped in coherent programs that are monitored by program managers and by high-level institutional managers. Added to this, in the case of programs like those undertaken by NASA, are principal investigators and outside, university-based experimenters.

☐ All this must then be multiplied by the number of parallel centers involved, each of which can have its retinue of internally specialized offices, plus contractors, subcontractors, and experimenters. In more user-oriented projects there will be another set of managers and specialists in the one or several user organizations. These too must be coordinated with and integrated into the management system.

□ Thus the total array of specialists encompassing the total system coordinated by the sponsor of a development program looks like Table 3, using NASA as our model.

□ Another way to grasp the organizational complexity of some of these high-technology projects is to look within the NASA system at a single stage of the work flow. To simplify the structure to be described, we shall examine the organizational units that work together in an unmanned-rocket launching. (Needless to say, the launching of a manned spacecraft brings together many more different groups.)

□ For our example, we shall restrict ourselves to just one element of the total work flow involved in planning and executing a mission, the actual launch organization.

□ During launch preparations and the launch itself a number of contractors who service the Cape Kennedy complex are involved. They handle a variety of support activities connected with security, communications, fueling, and the like. In addition there are civil-service personnel who are part of the NASA managerial and technical teams permanently based at the Cape. Air Force personnel and Air Force contractors who have responsibility for operations of the Eastern Test Range also participate in a wide variety of meetings and decisions concerning the launch. There are Air Force and NASA tracking and data-acquisition personnel whose work and plans must be tightly integrated since they will handle the first few moments of flight. These diverse groups, however, are only a small part of the total.

□ Aside from these more permanent contributors to the launch stage there are also the specialists who have been involved in the development of the specific hardware that hopefully is about to become operational. These more temporary participants include:

the launch-vehicle (rocket) contractor's launch team;

engineers from the NASA center responsible for the procurement of and monitoring of this particular rocket;

engineers from the launch-vehicle contractor's home site involved in the design and production of the rocket, who are on-call to help interpret and remedy any malfunctions;

the spacecraft contractor's launch team;

Table 3

Sponsoring Agency
Headquarters Management
Program Management
Project X Management
Project Y Management
Functional or Discipline Specialists

Center A	**Center B**	**User C**
Institutional Management	Institutional Management	• • •
Project X Management Office	Project X Management Office	• • • •
Project Y Management Office	Project Y Management Office	• • • •
Functional Support Groups 1	Functional Support Groups 4	• • • •
2	5	
3	6	

Center A Contractor or Contractors
Institutional Management
  Project X Management Office
  Project Y Management Office
    Functional Support Groups 1
    2
    3

Center B Contractor or Contractors
Institutional Management
  Project X Management Office
  Project Y Management Office
    Functional Support Groups 4
    5
    6

Contractor Subcontractors   **Contractor Subcontractors**

Center A Experimenters and Principal Investigators   **Center B Experimenters and Principal Investigators**

Contractors for Experimenters and P.I.'s[a]   **Contractors for Experimenters and P.I.'s**

[a] P.I.'s (professional investigators) are discussed in detail in Chapter 11. They are responsible for the design of experiments that will be flown on a spacecraft.

engineers from the NASA center responsible for the procurement and monitoring of this spacecraft;

engineers from the spacecraft contractor's laboratory and factory who worked on this spacecraft and, like the rocket-development people are on call;

the principal investigators and experimenters;

the experiment manufacturers; and

engineers from the NASA center responsible for total project management and perhaps their Washington counterparts.

☐ In addition there may be subcontractors representing the manufacturers of the rocket motors and the more sophisticated guidance systems and their electronic components. There could also be representatives of some present or future "user" organizations that are seeking an operational version of this particular spacecraft.

☐ Thus it would not be unusual to find several dozen departments or divisions of half as many different business and governmental institutions collaborating at just this one final stage of the development cycle.

☐ Of course, to cope with such an array of organizational units which must communicate, arrive at mutually supportive decisions, and provide one another with advice and warnings, many communications and coordination techniques are required. We shall turn to these now.

MANAGERIAL TECHNIQUES TO FACILITATE PROJECT COORDINATION

☐ We have endeavored to identify and categorize the organizational units that participate in a typical project. These include the one or more project offices internal to the sponsor and sponsor's offices. The same type of structuring is found among contractors. After we have seen how these groups interact, we shall examine some managerial devices to facilitate effective patterns of interaction.

☐ Here is a not-too-unusual scenario. A systems-test manager in Contractor A's organization has been monitoring a series of tests being conducted by the company's quality-control group. One particular component is not performing as desired. The engineers in A's organization (in another functional department) who designed the part are called in, and they assert that the test is not adequate for this particular unique design. The sponsor's project office is called and also the sponsor's functional department that originally worked with the contractor's engineers in designing the part. Contractor B also gets involved, since the component is part of a subsystem that has to be delivered to it in the very near future in order to be mated with some B subsystems to undergo another series of tests. Eventually the sponsor's project office calls in technical personnel from other functional departments and from other contractors who have had prior experience with this kind of work to assess whether the current design is critical or could be modified. The sponsor's chief of testing, another functional department, also gets involved.

□ Not surprisingly it turns out that there are a number of interrelated problems and a number of trade-offs involved. A slightly modified component will not affect most of the systems; it will have one deleterious effect, on power requirements. Delays in redesign and fabrication will affect Contractor B, but the costs will be minimal. However, delays in B can begin to affect Contractors C and D, and so on. At some points in this decision process information needs to be exchanged; at others it is simply a matter of helping to maintain confidence and enthusiasm. Some groups should be working closely to solve this question; others ought to be kept apart.

□ In the kinds of technologies we are dealing with uncertainties persist, suboptimization is a continual threat to systemwide optimization, expert opinion often diverges rather than converges, routinization is not possible or impedes improvisation, and enormous quantities of information must be disseminated. There is the constant threat of omission, of a crucial detail that "falls through the cracks." Policies, like control data, are often outdated by the time they are promulgated, and so on. Coherence, coordination, quickness, and control are the underlying requirements.

□ It is the organization of these exchanges to which we now turn. We shall describe three organizational tactics used by project managers to facilitate these exchanges: multiple intermediaries that act as focal points, widely dispersed exchange channels, and redundancies in the division of labor.

Intermediaries for Integration

Institutional Foci

□ Given the enormous number of exchanges that must take place, the project office can easily be overwhelmed. As a result, larger projects are likely to establish a number of *intermediate* "foci" that can integrate trade-offs, interconnections, and exchanges through which working plans are updated and technical barriers overcome.

At Cape Kennedy, a "launch operations office" is available to supplement the efforts of any project office intending to launch an unmanned satellite. On pp. 190–192, we provided some indication of the number of different NASA center and contractor groups whose work has to be coordinated to check out, fuel, and launch a rocket. Their experience in integrating the needs of experimenters, on-site tests and loading, personnel, spacecraft and booster engineers, and their NASA "monitors" can be passed on from one project to another (in much the same way that a functional department provides a project with historical perspective).

Most satellite projects having scientific missions to perform have a "project scientist" attached. He serves as an intermediary between the scientists (those who are experimenters on the mission as well as those who are advisers) and the engineers. The scientists will have needs and specific requests that have to be communicated to the project engineers, and the latter in turn will have requirements and modifications they wish to impose on the scientists.[5]

Foreign space-research teams wishing to use NASA's expertise or facilities are directed to a special office (part of a launch-vehicle group) at one NASA center which accumulates data, techniques, and sources of supply and which will facilitate their mission as much as possible and will introduce them to the procedures and facilities of Cape Kennedy's launch operations.

On large programs like Apollo, of course, there are a multitude of intercenter "panels" and interface "boards" that bring together all the parties interested in a specific problem.

☐ These structural devices, of course, are typical of advanced engineering applications where the total systems implications of design changes must be simultaneously evaluated by all those who may be affected and whose concurrence must be obtained.

Functional Integration at a Lower Level

☐ Another integration activity takes place lower in the structure, within a supporting functional group itself. At least three structural arrangements are possible:

1. Several project-office specialists or managers interact with each key functional specialist or manager. He, in turn, within his own subsection, serves as an integrator.
2. These same project-office specialists are required to go through the head office of the functional group, which integrates and makes the trade-offs.
3. Same as (2), except that integration is handled by the project office within the functional department.

[5] The functions of the project scientist are detailed in Chapter 11.

☐ Thus, the integration function is *not* limited to a project office; there are many foci. Project offices, outside integration contractors, and interface "boards" may all integrate the same activities.[6]

☐ Another way of viewing this process is to think of large projects as having several layers, with widely dispersed divisions of labor refocused at alternate layers by these integration groups.

Dispersion

☐ In traditional management theory, a great deal of attention is paid to the concept of delegation: the breadth of decision-making of the subordinate relative to his superior. We believe that the analog to this in a systems organization is the frequency of contact and subjects dealt with *outside the integration channels.*[7] The total volume of relationships is so extensive and the technical detail so intensive that the system requires a great number of alternative channels for processing information. Also, the time requirements can be so demanding that there is not time to input questions and information to these integration centers, allow them to be interpreted and transmitted to appropriate other points, receive responses, and reverse the process. In a sense point-to-point communication channels, as distinct from direct broadcasting from central stations, are required. Without them a single problem would be vulnerable to the costs (in time and in mission distortion) of an extended chain like this one, assuming the problem emerged at the subcontractor level:

Subcontractor	Functional or line technical group
	↓
	Project coordinator
	↓
Contractor	Functional or line group
	↓
	Project coordinator
	↓
Center A	Project office (and line office)
	↓
Center B and/or	Project office
sponsor headquarters	↓
	Program office

[6] For a discussion of integration contractors, see Chapter 12.

[7] The integration structures previously discussed are analogous to superior authorities; except in systems organization, such hierarchical concepts are somewhat misleading.

□ The needs for channels bypassing the formal hierarchy also reflect the obvious advantage of personal contacts over written reports, requests, and memoranda. The latter both require and produce relatively routine, conservative, and even self-protective reactions. More inspired problem-solving depends on less formal and more improvised give-and-take and the stimulus of face-to-face contact and divergent views. Also there frequently is the need for "off the record," trial-and-error type discussions where questions such as, "What would happen if we did have to change this mode?" and "What would your reaction be?" can be asked.
□ Below are some examples of the direct channels that connect elements of the organizational system.

Project engineers deal directly with functional engineers without going through the functional project office.

Project engineers go directly to a subcontractor without the contractor being present.

Contractor engineers deal directly with other contract engineers (both when they both work for the same center as well as when they work for different centers) without going through project engineers.

Functional engineers or functional project engineers deal directly with contractors without going through project-office engineers.

Project engineers from one center deal directly with functional engineers from another center without going through the second center's project office.

Functional engineers from two different centers deal directly with each other without the intervention of the project officers. The project office from one center deals with a contractor of another center without going through the second center's project office.

Project or functional engineers deal with the principal investigator's contractor without his being present.

□ Unfortunately one still finds substantial emphasis on prohibiting the use of these direct channels, an emphasis that grows out of the project manager's fears of groups "ganging up" and collusion (e.g., two contractors finding a way to blame a third party—perhaps the sponsor—for malfunctioning equipment) and concern about lack of proper clearance, consistency, and checking with centralized monitors.
□ By preventing some people from talking to each other, at least with any regularity, the project manager seeks to avoid the development of "unfavorable" sentiments or coalitions. Apparently the assumption is that those who talk together

may act together. The manager seeks to avoid being confronted with a solid bloc of opinion or pressure by keeping the parties with whom he must deal partially fractionated.

On one project requiring unusually precise and complex tracking, NASA tracking personnel were supplemented by an operational contractor. Another contractor handled the systems engineering for the tracking stations. The two groups were kept apart for fear they would "gang up on the project and blame any operating difficulties on badly designed or malfunctioning equipment." Such a consensus nicely eliminates either contractor as a source of the problem or a source of the solution. Keeping them apart keeps open a kind of mutual check on each other—on the operating procedures and the underlying system design—and it may, in fact, pit one against the other.

☐ This practice has a number of drawbacks. Effort is wasted hiding these contacts, some necessary contacts are avoided, and general demoralization may even result as those involved in the project begin to perceive a gap between management principles and practice.

Direct Contacts Between Research and Development

☐ The importance of convenient, direct, and often informal links between researchers "upstream" in the development process and "downstream" engineers closer to the hardware is understood by many experienced project managers. An administrator at the Bell Laboratories, in fact, concludes that they are careful that *either* geographic proximity or common organizational membership encourages this kind of relationship, and they never allow both factors to be absent.[8]

☐ The same requirement for dispersed, frequent contact was observed by Burns and Stalker in reviewing the contrasting records of wartime radar development in England and Germany. In Britain the development engineering was handled by the Telecommunications Research Establishment (TRE), and leading figures from this group met weekly in an informal session with high-ranking Air Force officers:

Differences in rank were obscured or ignored. A particular type of equipment or an operational problem would be selected, and the division leaders and group leaders on the TRE side would be there to discuss it. There was thus a very intimate, personal

[8] Jack Morton, "From Research to Technology," in David Allison, ed., *The R&D Game,* Cambridge, Mass., M.I.T. Press, 1969, pp. 213–235.

connection between the people who had the operational knowledge and the problems to face [and] the people who . . . had an intimate knowledge of the scientific techniques and their scope. The result of this was that the laboratory workers got an immediate emotional as well as intellectual appreciation of the pressing operational difficulties, needs, and problems. . . . Equally important, the operational people began to acquire notions of the potentialities of the techniques [from] the people who had originated them.[9]

☐ The Germans, on the other hand, appointed a czar (a Plenipotentiary for High Frequency Techniques), whose job it was to receive specifications of Air Force needs (from his Air Force counterpart) and reduce them to equipment needs. These in turn were assigned by the Plenipotentiary to one or another of the research institutes or laboratories (apparently using availability as the criterion of selection).

The laboratory would thereupon make an equipment [*sic*] designed without any real knowledge of the operational needs and therefore, in many cases, not meeting them adequately. But . . . most of the possibilities were not realized anyway, because the operational people could not envisage the potentialities of the techniques available, nor could the technical people appreciate the problems of the men who were flying machines.[10]

Autonomy vs. Shared Control

☐ Many elements within the total project sphere seek to reduce the frequency with which they must engage in either these "dispersed" (i.e., direct) contacts and negotiations with other units or "integrated" contacts with project or program offices. Their tactic is a very old, tried-and-true management technique: full control of resources.
☐ For purposes of simplicity and quick response, most units want to control as many of their own resources as possible. Over time these demands increase. For example, in one large post-Apollo project a key center attempted to obtain its own "mission control" function that would enable it to check out directly its hardware at the Cape. At the same time other organizational units were seeking to prevent outsiders from having any direct contact with (and perhaps thereby direct influence on) their jurisdictions. Thus one

[9] Tom Burns and G. M. Stalker, *The Management of Innovation,* London, Tavistock Publications, 1961, pp. 40–41.

[10] *Ibid.,* p. 41.

applications-spacecraft project insisted that no outsiders (i.e., no one outside the project office) be allowed into any of the tracking stations used by its flights. Each functional group seeks to obtain this independence.

□ But usually the technology requires a sharing of control. The Cape Kennedy people had controlled a number of testing facilities and procedures that would be used by this post-Apollo project, and gradually the center obtained the right to have some voice in these processes without always getting Kennedy's approval.

□ A balance in these opposing trends is necessary. Increased internal elaboration and self-sufficiency should be balanced by increased *shared* authority. As one unit adds complementary and support activities to "round out" its functions, it should be simultaneously giving up sole control over some of its resources so that outsiders can obtain quick responses from their personnel. Without growing autonomy, the number of interfaces can overwhelm organizational procedures and lead to costly duplication and inadequate integration.

How Much Dispersion?

□ From a control point of view, one needs to ask what is the anticipated frequency of these dispersed contacts, what channels need to be opened that do not now exist, and which are overused and damaging the integration function. Obviously these widely dispersed relationships can be destructive of system integrity unless there is a reasonably infallible system for recording any changes introduced that affect only the two participants and reviewing proposed changes that have a wider impact.

□ Like bypassing in traditional organizations, dispersion can be overdone. For the project manager to keep the project in phase (ensure that adequate attention is paid to all relevant variables, maintain parameters including time, etc.), great numbers of inputs to his office are required.

□ Thus one hears (when direct channels are used):

We want to be able to go directly to X without Y feeling that we are taking over, undercutting them, or reducing their responsibility for the end result.

When we do undertake direct contact, we are careful not to give them orders. However, we do need to give them some understanding of what we are doing and learn from them some of the things they are going to be doing that will eventually affect us.

Redundancy

☐ Traditional thinking about specialization and the division of labor breaks down in these high-technology organizations as the same function or task is performed by more than one group. Thus one finds design specialists on the project staff sharing the same skills with their counterparts in the functional groupings within a center. Such redundancy has several advantages:

1. Communications and exchanges between the project office and the functional group are facilitated.

2. There is a somewhat greater likelihood that nothing will be overlooked as both sides stimulate and check each other. As we noted in the preceding chapter, such independent centers of competence provide technically expert and legitimate analyses that can serve as a wholesome check on internal project enthusiasms and biases.

3. Within each group a balance of skills and interests facilitates certain efforts where quick systemwide assessments, calculations, or decisions are necessary.

☐ Successful managers know that no specification is ever complete; there will always be mistakes or omissions. An individual or group may find it hard to check their own work. What are highly useful human characteristics, adaptability and perceptual accommodation, also are the source of costly oversights. Emerging trends are not seen. Having made a decision or concurred with one, it is easy for a specialist to take the next step and say that it must be right; in any event, he is unlikely to challenge its validity or completeness.

☐ These threats justify redundancy, for example, in the control area. Testing, quality control, and systems checks are performed by functional quality-control groups, by project specialists, and often by outside contractors. (Headquarters management has even, on occasion, urged centers to serve as checks on one another.) Everyone, in some measure, becomes his brother's keeper. Also, an advancing technology does not stay within neat boundaries; professionals and their departments elaborate their skills and interests to become more "well-rounded," and the ramifications of most decisions cross jurisdictional lines. This inevitable overlap can be made functional and contained by proper ongoing patterns of exchange between "adjacent" jobs, functions, and specialities. Further, the overlap and blurred boundary provide a legitimate cross-check, stimulus, and continuing critique which is useful in the context of uncertainty within which most projects operate.

☐ Any idea, change, or design is thus evaluated, criticized, and probed by a whole series of groups and individuals, in the hope that these redundant procedures will guarantee that sins of omission or commission will be detected before lasting damage is done.

☐ In practice redundancy also means a deluge of information scattered broadside through the organization, communications that spill over what in more traditional organizations might be conceived of as appropriate jurisdictions or boundaries:

The key to making the NASA structure work rests upon creating an effective network of formal and informal communications. . . . To be on the safe side, NASA may err in over-communicating upward, laterally, and downward. It engulfs anyone who can conceivably influence or implement the decision. It establishes various "management councils" composed of co-equal associates to share progress and problems on a frequent basis. In an unending effort to exchange information in real-time, it uses telephone, hot lines, executive aircraft, datafax, long distance conference hook-ups by voice and data display and computer data transmissions.[11]

☐ Thus a distinctive characteristic of project management is that the organization *cannot* compartmentalize its activities into the neat boxes the chartists and consultants envision. In any organization faced with the problems of both innovation and the management of large numbers of details, this redundancy can be useful, although very costly. For example, it provides the kind of professional critique and stimulus that helps produce more original proposals and designs. Responsibilities too clearly compartmentalized can lead to stultification. The gradual accretions of habit, perceptual bias, and conditioning that lead to neglect and smugness are reduced by fresh approaches and questions, often from unanticipated sources.[12]

[11] Albert Siepert, "NASA's Management of the Civilian Space Program," speech prepared for presentation to The Institute for Management Science meeting, March 28, 1969, mimeo.

[12] Thus in NASA's early history space flight was associated with streamlining. Numerous designers, in the ballistic-missile tradition, were designing more and more streamlined spacecraft. Harvey Allen's blunt-nosed ablation shield represented a major departure. Similarly, Houboldt's lunar-rendezvous mission profile was a departure from the thinking of other

☐ Internal balance also may help to avoid the build-up of needlessly strong "party lines" within a professional group. In the academic world one frequently observes the tendency for a department or professional school to adopt a single popular approach to its subject when most of its members have common backgrounds. Inserting members of other disciplines who do not accept the "obvious" programmatic approach to the work at hand serves to maintain a desirable amount of disequilibrium in the system. In newer fields particularly it can be fallacious to assume that the correct approach is known and only the details of implementation deserve attention.

☐ Traditional organizations, doing repetitive work, increase the effectiveness of managers by drawing clear jurisdictional lines and issuing broad policy statements. Both serve to let individual managers know (1) who should or can make a decision and (2) the precise limits—or even the specific dimensions—of the decision. Where either is in doubt there is usually an appeal upward that results in the jurisdiction or the applicability of the policy being clarified.

☐ Project organizations lack these advantages. Not only is the work usually unique (being done for the first time), so that precedents and policies are somewhat irrelevant, but it is difficult to draw neat jurisdictional lines.[13]

SUMMARY AND CONCLUSIONS

☐ Project organization can be deceptive. On paper, the neat charts suggest the structure of a traditional organization, but such is not the case. Problems and answers both can come from unexpected and nonlegitimate sources. An electrical specialist can spot a mechanical problem, perhaps in part because he does not know the conventional wisdom, and a bright engineer working in an apparently unrelated field can come up with a solution to a problem that has been frustrating the functional specialists.

☐ To allow these insights and bits of information to receive proper attention, once one accepts the need for *redundancy,* there must be both integrative mechanisms—the intermediaries we have described—and allowance for direct

---

parts of NASA who favored other ways of getting to the moon. Significant departures and innovations are often associated with individuals and groups working apart from those with primary responsibility.

[13] See John Stewart, "Making Project Management Work," *Business Horizons,* Fall, 1965.

access among specialists through *dispersed* contact patterns.

☐ Traditional organizations can assume that they know all the problems and the methods. They therefore can assign expertise to a single specialist or compartmentalized, functional group. They also can assume that they know all the interrelationships; thus lateral contacts can be limited to those who have a "need to know." And, of course, this enormously simplifies the structure, and all, or nearly all, the *integration* can take place through the hierarchical "focal points," that is, the line managers.

☐ Advanced technologies are unfortunately implemented through complex social networks, which lack the neatness, the sparsity, and the lock-step precision that their formal flow charts imply. The project office and its offshoots in the functional support groups must carry an enormous burden of liaison and communication if effective integration and coordination is to take place. Much depends, as we have seen, on the skill, energy, and perseverance of these unique administrators, project managers, and their staffs; but the structuring of the total system can facilitate their work. The technological-human system must allow for iterations, perturbations, and all the "devious" channels we have been describing. The pattern is very different from that shown on the flow charts prepared by systems analysts who see communications in mechanical terms. Thus the need for dispersed contacts, multiple integrative mechanisms, and redundancy.

THE PROJECT MANAGER: ORGANIZATIONAL METRONOME

TEN

The key executive position in any development organization is that of project manager. As the administrator responsible for pushing a project through to completion, he occupies a unique position in the managerial world. Unlike most managers, he is largely dependent on outsiders to get his work done. Although he is given some staff of his own to assist him in dealing with these outsiders, for the most part the real work of the project is performed by personnel who report not to him but to other managers in various technical, functional, and professional groups scattered throughout the parent institution and, often, the contractor companies as well.

□ It would be a mistake, however, to neglect the growing social significance of project management. Whenever an organization—or community or agency—seeks to get a new job done *without* changing the basic structure (or division of labor) of the organization, that is, without creating new jobs and lines of authority, it typically establishes a project task force or working group which operates for the life of the project. This is in sharp distinction to traditional managerial thought. For scientific management, having a job to do meant creating specific organizational slots under the direct control of a boss who would thus have authority and resources commensurate with the responsibility given to him. The project and the project manager go off in a very different direction: Clear responsibilities are assigned to get some critical task accomplished, but most of the resources are left where they are—in other people's departments.

□ The project manager thus has a very different supervisory challenge: getting work done through outsiders. As we shall see, this requires rather different skills and a different "theory of management" than traditional supervision. The emphasis is on *monitoring* and *influencing decisions,* not order-giving and decision-making in the usual meaning of those terms. The project manager has overwhelmingly more responsibility than he has authority. The groups and employees he will be dealing with not only work for other departments to which they give their primary loyalties, but such groups have standards of performance—of what is a good job—built up over many years that are consistent with these affiliations and which may be inconsistent with the special needs of a project with a limited life. The project manager's job is to find ways of making consistent the standards of performance of the outsider and the needs of the project in regard to cost, schedule, and performance standards.

□ While there are obvious and taxing problems associated with pulling together a "team" of outsiders, the difficulties should not be exaggerated. There are also strong positive human sentiments associated with membership in what have been called "temporary societies."[1] A good deal of zest, spontaneity, and even pleasure can be derived by the participants, who can develop surprising degrees of "involvement, engagement, 'engrossment' in the system's goals."[2] Of course such positive sentiments are difficult to sustain over long periods, particularly since many crises may occur in which there are conflicting pulls between the participant's permanent and temporary homes, pulls that the social scientist labels simply *role conflict*.

Start-up Patterns

□ Most projects begin when upper management creates the project office and assigns the project manager and gives him a budget that allows him to purchase "contributions" from these outside departments. Even with this budget, the project manager may still have to woo and win reluctant line managers who will question whether they should assign their better people or resources to the project, particularly if there are other project managers in the market for these human and technical resources and the line manager is skeptical about the feasibility and prestige of this one:

I tried to keep most of our people off [Project X] even though it was reasonably well funded. I knew it was the kind of project that headquarters could cut off tomorrow and then we would have all those disappointed engineers to reassign who had just gotten all excited about the work and now were going to have to do something else. This creates serious morale problems and I try

[1] An excellent summary of a wide-ranging series of studies on such nonpermanent organizations is provided by Matthew B. Miles, "On Temporary Systems," in M. B. Miles, ed., *Innovation in Education,* New York, Bureau of Publications, Teachers College, Columbia Univ., 1964, pp. 435–490.

[2] *Ibid.,* p. 472.

to get my people projects that have a real chance of going down to the wire.

☐ The critical skills for project inception can best be viewed in situations where upper management has not yet decided to endorse a new project and is allowing lower levels of management to take the initiative. Under these circumstances, the projects that will be funded and that "will fly" depend upon the selling ability of the would-be project managers. The ones who are successful in this entrepreneurial-like function (really in getting a new business started, albeit one with a finite life expectancy) are those who can generate enthusiasm and confidence on the part of other managers who can give the nascent project political and economic support. Here is how one successful project manager described the start-up function:

I had gotten the green light from my boss to try to get support for a special computer project which would develop a technique for letting our large computer handle a great deal of the test work we now do manually. First I got every department head or his deputy to come to a meeting. There my function was to first get everyone to agree we had a problem with our current test procedures and secondly on the kind of procedure that would cope with these problems. I then tried to generate enthusiasm for the solution: this computerization project. This meant showing people that they would be in heaven if we could pull it off and that everyone would benefit. Of course, I wasn't above a little log-rolling either, indicating I would back them on some things they needed. I also tried to play up the losses for those who stayed out. You find after awhile, when you keep talking something like this up, the enthusiasm can become contagious, and they'll convince one another.

☐ Often these charismatic entrepreneurs who get new projects off the ground are almost like evangelists. They have so much faith in this special project, its workability and its long run value, that they can convince doubting Thomases, almost like a good "pitchman" of old. It is not unusual for zealots to be hard on subordinates. They are loathe to delegate authority, and keep making all the technical decisions themselves, perhaps, in part, because in the early stages they are the only ones who see the "big picture," the grand design or conception.

☐ But such single-minded conviction, and reluctance to delegate anything is inconsistent with the needs of an established and funded project. It is the managerial skills that come into play *after* the promoter or major organizational supporter has won the battle of getting the project accepted that are our primary interest in this chapter.

What Kind of Executive Is the Project Manager?

☐ We have already observed the significant contrast between the clear, single-minded "objectives" of a program and their more subjective, ambiguous "ends" or purposes. The former can easily be represented, and even, in part, implemented, by computer models and a rather easy consensus based on rational thinking by rational men. The latter inevitably involves political considerations, vested interests, and the human skills of negotiation, timing, and execution.

☐ Efforts to extend the experience of large-scale, advanced-technology programs to social and community problems can be deterred by the mistaken belief that one represents the rational world of science and technology and the other, the irrational world of people and politics. Such a conclusion is in no way discouraged by the emphasis on mechanical planning and control systems.[3]

☐ The same contrasting emphases can be observed in the functions of the project manager, the key executive in development programs. His job involves a great deal of executive-political skill, as we shall see; and the computerized records, print-outs, and models are like the visible tip of an iceberg.

☐ While there are a number of new terms and phrases associated with the role of project manager, there has been little attention paid to its underlying organizational significance. We have sought to examine the relationship of this manager to the other ongoing components of the technological system. The view we have obtained is best described by the analogy to a metronome, a time-keeping mechanism which is designed to keep a number of diverse elements responsive to a central "beat" or common rhythm.

☐ Of course, this is symbolized in the fast-paced climax of a space development program: the test and final launch countdowns, in which the term "conductor" is actually used, and the participants refer to him as "beating a drum." Our concern, however, is with the somewhat slower-paced elements that still must be responsive to a common "beat."

[3] A recent Congressional effort to wring out the potential managerial applications of the Apollo Program to social problems concentrates almost entirely on these mechanical systems. See *Apollo Program Management,* Staff Study for the Subcommittee on NASA Oversight, Committee on Science and Astronautics, Washington, D.C., Government Printing Office, July, 1969.

KEEPING TIME BEHAVIORALLY

☐ Although it is rarely stated this way, the project manager is primarily dealing with rates (of time) and organizational process, not technical variables. He cannot easily second-guess the technical prowess of his line-support groups. Obviously he and his staff may often try to, but in the long run he is dependent upon both the support and the technical judgment of the outside groups.

☐ What he can and must do, however, is control their organizational participation, as distinct from their technical contribution. This means making sure that "line" or functional people do such things as:

1. Give problems their "proper" weight and context: for instance, the line departments may want to engage in an extensive study of some problem to arrive at an optimal solution, but the delay in making the decision may be much more costly than any increase in return generated by the improved decision. Of course, the opposite may be true; the program manager may want to encourage longer study of some issue that has profound "downstream" significance beyond the particular line manager's field of vision.

2. Tackle problems in the right sequence and at the right time. The line manager may be willing to countenance (perhaps because of his own budget) a certain problem build-up—schedule delays or deteriorating labor relations—that could be disastrous for the program. The program manager pressures him to be adequately responsive to these "out-of-limit" situations and give them a priority based on program needs—even though this may be inconsistent with the management style or managerial judgment of the line manager.

3. Shift the decision criterion. It may be very costly (and appear foolishly so) to carry an excessive inventory of a particular component for a production operation, but if a stoppage should be intolerable because of other considerations, the program manager's job is to shift the decision criteria the production manager uses to reflect these out-of-sight costs.

☐ It is this balancing act, by which technical decisions are made to reflect multiple considerations, that takes most of the project manager's time. A nice example is furnished by one small aspect of a large aerospace project.

In one installation, fire-prevention equipment was being installed and the safety and equipment people were intending to use their usual criteria in design and installation. Traditionally every effort was made to design a system that was *sure* to function in an emergency. From the project management's point of view, in this particular location it was more important that the prime criterion for design and installation be that the system *not* function unless there was an emergency. Of course, even such a subtle difference in purpose has a major influence on how and where redundancy is provided in electronic circuits and other fail-safe components.

□ The project manager acts the role of a *marginalist.* He widens or narrows limits, adds or subtracts weights where trade-offs are to be made, speeds up or slows down actions, increases the emphasis on some activities and decreases the emphasis on others. He cannot make very many of the decisions himself because of the time factor, and because he is not empowered to do so—that power resides in the line and functional groups in most cases. Further, he would not want to; he usually cannot know as much about the incident or the problems as some other man closer to the work level. What he wants to do is be sure that the decision is made at the proper time, within the proper framework of knowledge and concern, and by the proper people.

□ Of course, there are key times and places in which the project manager must make the decision:

One of the key decisions in a spacecraft project is the so-called "launch window": the time period during which the rocket must be launched if it is to achieve the desired trajectory, orbit, or target. The more narrowly this "window" is specified, the less fuel must be provided for course adjustments and the fewer tracking facilities may be needed. Of course a narrow window is also more difficult to achieve because everything must be ready at precisely the correct time.

The project manager in space projects insists on making these critical decisions because he is the only one who has all the necessary inputs for making the trade-offs and also at times because he does not want the various subparts of the project to know how narrowly the launch window has been defined. If it can be a very narrow window, many of the managers of these subparts might relax concerning the weight of the components they are designing since hardware weight can be traded off for fuel weight (saved by the narrow window). The project manager knows that weight tends to grow in any hardware development effort, and he would rather keep the pressure on to hold the line on the weight each manager has committed himself to in order to preserve an additional safety factor.

Overcoming Resistance to Change

☐ A challenging aspect of the project manager's work can be seen when activities are being transferred from one organizational unit to another. There are strong pressures, growing out of the complexities and uncertainties of the technology, on the management of the transferred function to retain the identical work rules, constraints, work practices, and the like so that existing relationships will not be disturbed.

A key group on the operations side of NASA that worked closely with many of the research-oriented centers was transferred "organizationally" to the jurisdiction of another operations group that handled development projects. While, in theory, this allowed a consolidation and centralization of similar functions, in fact, it did not. A rather formal agreement was negotiated prior to the organizational change guaranteeing that existing practices and relationships would not be changed.

A similar event occurred when a testing group was shifted from the jurisdiction of a development center to the jurisdiction of another NASA center that had more broadly based quality-control responsibilities. In return for allowing the move to go unchallenged, the original center insisted that there be no changes in procedures.

☐ This rigidity is part of an understandable reluctance to change anything which might upset the already tenuous balance in a highly uncertain, threatening environment. (One can even observe this phenomenon in agencywide management, where a number of pressing organizational problems were ignored prior to the success of Apollo 11 for fear of somehow inadvertently changing something that could further complicate the total process.)

☐ But the project manager must often seek to counter this inherent conservatism, particularly when "playing it safe" by one manager increases the risk for the total effort. A manager may wish to build only familiar hardware, use familiar components or traditional standards, or "gold plate" his contribution, any one of which actions may be harmful in terms of time, dollars, or performance to others.

☐ The project manager functions as a giant metronome that enables the diverse parts of a large program—parts that would normally be responsive to an internal group rhythm—to respond to the same "beat." To do this he forces people to see the consequences of their actions (through visual and conceptual tools like critical path scheduling) and through verbal and written inputs forces other managers to make commitments and decisions by affecting their trade-offs (e.g., schedule vs. costs) and priorities. In shaping the response of his "team" to this centralized "beat," he may also seek to change the resonance characteristics of the system. Requiring a shift in organizational relationships (so that group A now reports to Division B instead of Division A or gets consulted earlier, or more frequently, or now must give its consent before x, y, and z occur) changes the character of response of the system.

□ The project manager may discover that a particular function being performed by one group neglects the needs of another group and, in fact, that the latter's requirements are too dynamic to be simply specified for the first group to meet. This can require a jurisdictional shift of an activity from one side of an interface to another. In other instances the organizational-process problem can be solved by an administrative (as distinct from a structural) change. The second group can be brought into design or design-review meetings, or they may be given "sign off" authority—meaning that the first group must submit final plans to them for their approval.

Managing a Vulnerable Mission

□ Engineers like to talk about fail-safe procedures involving the identification of critical elements which can abort the mission and the provision of redundancies and other safeguards to guarantee their operations. Unfortunately the organizational interfaces of a large project cannot be similarly protected.

NASA's launching procedure for Apollo allows more than one hundred engineers and technicians to stop the countdown if they observe some malfunctioning in the systems or subsystems under their surveillance.

□ The typical large program has an analogous number of people who can call a halt and upon whose concurrence the program depends. This can be seen easily in urban-redevelopment programs. In one instance, because one department store changed its mind about moving from an area to be torn down into a new shopping center, the total redevelopment plan was halted. In another case the reluctance of one faculty in an urban university to offer consulting assistance to a set of potential new tenants (who were to be attracted partially on the basis of the availability of high-quality technical support) caused the early demise of an imaginative "university park" type of redevelopment program.

☐ The gross numbers of discrete organizational components who must be kept "in line," who must be persuaded, cajoled, and satisfied, comprise a significant element of the project manager's workload.

DEPARTURES FROM TRADITIONAL MANAGEMENT

☐ All this represents a major departure from the tenets of human relations and traditional management. To the latter there is introduced the heresy of multiple bosses, ambiguity—frequently clear orders are not given but the balance of pressure or influence is changed—and staff groups with clout. Managers with human relations oriented bosses are supposed to be left alone to sink or swim—as long as they appear to be motivated to meet their established-through-participation objectives. In contradistinction, the project manager must constantly seek to penetrate the organizations upon which he is dependent but which he does not directly supervise. He must often get into the minutiae of decision processes to judge whether the desired system is being maintained, for example whether adequate weight is being given to factor x, adequate consultation is taken with group A, the sign-offs are procured on time from group B, and the appropriate appeal channels and conflict-resolution procedures are being used when stalemates occur. *Time* is of the essence and constant *monitoring* is the rule: *Knowing whom to contact, when, and how* is crucial.

☐ Thus project management is not a curious blend of the old and the not-so-old; it calls for a new set of skills and procedures. It is dealing laterally, but not in the informal-group, informal-organization sense. It requires a capacity on the part of the manager to put together an organizational mechanism within which timely and relevant decisions are likely to be reached (as distinct from individual decision-making), a conceptual scheme for "working" interfaces and for predicting where structural changes should be introduced if the response is inadequate, untimely, or insubstantial. This is a highly dynamic, interactive, iterative, and intellectually challenging concept of the managerial role.

☐ Most of his contribution is at two administrative extremes. First, he seeks to establish an organizational structure which will be relatively self-maintaining. And second, he seeks to facilitate the operations of the structure by appropriately timed pushes and pulls. But, for the most part, he does not operate the structure; operations are handled by a variety of functional, line, technical, and contractor groups.

DEALING WITH COMPLEXITY

Is This Computerized Management?

□ Unfortunately, most discussions of the functions of project management stress the painstakingly logical activities: making sure that specifications are clear, that no step is omitted, that only authorized changes are made, that responsibility is clearly allocated and compartmentalized, and that appropriate measures are constructed to monitor every significant aspect of the program (costs, performance, schedules, weight, etc.). In many ways these are computer-like functions: Reality is checked against a preprogrammed "inner logic," and where the former is found wanting, a bell rings or a light flashes. And, in fact, in very complex programs, such as Apollo, computers are handling a larger portion of this paper-control function.

□ It is easy to be deceived about the functions of the project manager because these computerized controls appear to play such a crucial role. In fact, their operation is largely the responsibility of staff personnel within the project office. The project manager is more likely to want to see raw data, original correspondence, and the actual people who must make and carry out the development decisions.[4] It will be his personal energy, powers of influence, and quickness that will be crucial in keeping things moving, avoiding holdups, and resolving seemingly unresolvable problems.

□ As one observes these managers, they seem to be engaged in a ceaseless round of "political" give-and-take. They appear to be seeking, by weight of a variety of influence techniques, to counter the frictional forces and fatal drift in the human systems. There is always a tendency toward suboptimization: a tendency for disciplinary or subsystem logics to prevail over larger program interests, for existing practices and comfortable routines to remain unchanged, for protective "safety" factors to inflate time and

---

[4] In fact, there is evidence that there is some decrease in the use of techniques like PERT and some reversion to much simpler and more primitive visual techniques such as bar charts. See *ibid.,* p. 46 (reviewing Grumman's experience with the lunar module).

cost estimates. Where this constant contact is lacking, these programs tend to slip back from the weight of technical and organizational complexities.

☐ What we learn by watching project managers is that words seldom mean what they seem to, that agreements can easily be misunderstood or ambiguous, that no agreement covers every contingency, that a variety of temptations can lure committed people to take chances which they would be less likely to take under less pressure or with less provocation, and so on ad infinitum.

Categories of Managerial Behavior

☐ We have endeavored to review the behavior of project managers we observed. While management texts traditionally talk about planning, directing, controlling, and so on, the behavior in our data seems to fall into these other categories:

bargaining,
coaching or cajoling,
confrontation,
intervention, and
order-giving.

Bargaining

☐ Managers prefer to spend a great deal of time negotiating. In part this is due to the continuing appearance of unanticipated problems or opportunities—"What will it cost us to avoid this or take advantage of that?" Some of it is due to inevitable differences in judgment—"I don't care what the tests show, I am sure we can get by with the extra five pounds; or at least that's what I am going to try to get approved." There are individual differences in objectives. A subcontractor wants to use a manufacturing method in which it has a proprietary interest, and the prime contractor is fearful that this may adversely affect an already tight schedule.

☐ In addition, there are the foibles of organizational life. Estimates, specifications, and requests tend to have fat in them, because everyone knows they are going to get less than they asked for.

We spent 18 months convincing NASA and the prime contractor that the test standards were just too high on this stress resistance factor. We knew we couldn't complete the fabrication if that figure stood, and we also knew that it was unrealistic. You see, NASA managers jack up the requirements they place on the prime and he in turn amplifies things when he deals with us. It takes a lot of talking to get it reduced again.

☐ Whatever the source, managers know there is often not a precise, rational solution to most questions; rather, the answer is a product of flexible give-and-take.

Coaching

☐ In many ways project managers are more like *coaches* than supervisors; they exhort, urge on, cajole, browbeat, and pressure. By their very presence, their personal intervention and force of personality—through talking and pleading and demanding—they seek to counteract the various frictions that would slow down or misdirect the activities of other groups, particularly the primary contractors and functional groups.

☐ As in life itself, complex projects produce a variety of oppressive frustrations as well as destructive temptations. When parts shortages occur or facilities are not available or parallel activities (under the control of others) are slowed down, there is a tendency to let down, to wait, to take a somewhat easier way out.

☐ Like an ever-present conscience, an effective project manager keeps urging the key people on whom the work depends to keep fighting a recalcitrant Mother Nature, to keep pushing against time, to pretend that everyone else will be on time, to seek equally satisfactory alternatives when the original plans are no longer feasible.

☐ This pressuring includes keeping people from falling back into old familiar routines and ways of doing business. The project requires nonstandardized approaches that may be inconsistent with the habitual patterns and least-cost methods of a particular organization or functional group. "We never do it this way" has to be a call to arms for project managers. The tempos of work of a university laboratory and an industrial fabrication shop start out "miles apart." The project manager has the job of getting these incompatible habitual patterns into more congruent form.

☐ Sometimes the problem will be that the functional group wants to "gold-plate" something, to overprotect or overtest or include too much redundancy. Obviously the opposite is more frequently the case in space hardware: the temptation to take shortcuts, to do inadequate testing.

☐ In so many walks of life there is a type of Gresham's Law

operating in which the easier, or more clear-cut, drives out the harder or more ambiguous. The project manager must constantly add the weight of his intervention to the side of that objective or interest which is most likely to get slighted to counteract the inevitable temptations.

□ Thus it is often easier to concentrate on engineering requirements than scientific requirements, as we have seen. The project manager strives constantly to keep an appropriate balance in relative effort for what are always somewhat conflicting objectives and to avoid the usual degradations by which high hopes are dashed on the rocks of "realistic solutions."

Confrontation

□ One of the techniques most often used to deter backsliding is deceptively simple and direct. The project manager raises questions; he confronts and challenges:

"What makes you think that those bearings are comparable to the ones we discussed last week?"

"What is your evidence that this redesign is likely to solve the problem? Prove it to me."

"Have you checked all the sources of stray magnetism?"

"What have you done to correct the malfunctioning that showed up on the special test we agreed upon?"

"How can you expect to catch up on the lost time when you haven't authorized overtime and there is no additional staffing?"

□ The project people are in the position of endeavoring to get the others to justify their present courses of action, their decisions and choices. It is one thing to do something that seems reasonable under the circumstances; it is another to have to try to prove or rationalize the action in front of an inquiring, reasonably well-informed, and potentially critical observer or interested party. This process forces people to face up to unpleasant realities by constant reminders and the stimulus of a friendly critic who will demand answers to a somewhat unpredictable set of potentially embarrassing questions. Telephone calls, visits, and regular meetings are all used for this purpose.

□ The process thus becomes a kind of continuous test of the perspicacity, alertness, and omniscience of those engaged in the project. As such it provides very useful feedback to the manager, perhaps much more useful than the data provided by traditional appraisal mechanisms which focus on a preestablished set of abstract criteria. As sophisticated managers know and many research studies suggest, conformity to these can often be "fudged"; and even when the data are accurate, conformity can lead to serious distortions in patterns of coordination.

☐ The constant interchange demonstrates to everyone that the project manager is vitally interested and alert and that everything is open to question. This is essential in view of the unusual potential for problems in complex endeavors with hundreds, if not thousands, of interdependent variables. One can always be sure there will be problems, although one can never be sure where and how they will appear.

☐ In the words of one of the highest ranking managers in the Apollo Program, "these reviews involve excruciating attention to detail and patient probing to insure that weaknesses are discovered and corrected."[5] Management by embarrassment (no one wants to be identified as the holdup), a "goldfish bowl atmosphere" (you're "in the open" for all to see), constant challenges by devil's advocates, and "needling" take the place of direct orders.[6]

☐ The cocksureness and the self-deception that any professional group evolves is offset by the outside interrogation and the need to justify to one's organizational, but not professional, peers.[7] Hopefully human error, biased judgment, and omissions will be "smoked out" in this intensive interchange.

Intervention

☐ Many of the behavioral patterns we have been describing have both a before-the-fact and an after-the-fact quality. The project manager is seeking to avoid problems or solve prob-

[5] Address by Lt. Gen. Sam Phillips to the National Conference on Public Administration, Miami, Florida, May 20, 1969.

[6] See *Fortune*'s description of Apollo management, June, 1969.

[7] Even with this intensive, costly, and time-consuming organizational process, serious mistakes get through the system, particularly when the engineering system comprises tens of thousands of parts. A NASA Review Board, formed to find the cause of the near-fatal Apollo 13 explosion, found that the thermostatic switches installed inside an oxygen tank had maximum voltage specifications that were different from the maximum voltages specified in the launch-readiness and test procedures. As a result, higher voltages were used during an oxygen-purging procedure; this welded the switches permanently closed, making them inoperable as a safety device. *New York Times,* June 16, 1970, p. 1.

lems. There is a more immediate, real-time role he plays as well.

□ In working to maintain a forward momentum, the manager seeks to avoid stalemates, polarization of issues, entrenchment of vested interests. Fluidity and movement, accommodation, solving problems rather than assessing blame, all these are part of the distinctive point of view of program management.

□ To demonstrate his concern as well as to get a feel for what is happening and the many facets that cannot be documented or transmitted in either verbal or written reports, he appears on the scene. During crucial tests, for example, many project managers want to be present to observe as much as possible themselves.

□ The project manager also has the job of keeping things moving, by maintaining a consensus, "jelling" decisions, and resolving holdups when those immediately involved are unwilling or unable to do so.

□ As we have described elsewhere, the primary function of any manager is probably to maintain regularity and continuity in the flow of work.[8] He often faces conflicting technical judgments. Deciding who among a group of conscientious experts is right is a difficult task. While a manager realistically may suffer through this kind of choice, it is not realistic under most circumstances to endeavor to prove who is right. It is more important that a decision be reached so that forward momentum can be resumed. Insecure, risk-fearing managers fret and fume over such decisions, until, regardless of who is right, it is too late to avoid grievous schedule losses.

□ Thus the project manager wants to force a choice. His own dispassionate position, somewhat removed from the battlefront, may help in resolving the issue, as does his prestige and force of personality. Intervention is also a means of gaining familiarity, a "feel" for the real situation, and keeping in touch with technical realities.

Order-Giving

□ There is rather little direct ordering in the relationship between project managers and the outside groups and individuals they seek to influence. There are many reasons for this aside from the fact that many groups are not immediate subordinates.

[8] See Leonard Sayles, *Managerial Behavior,* New York, McGraw-Hill, 1964, p. 47.

☐ Orders raise legalistic questions: "Is this a change in our original commitment?" "Who is to pay for the change?" They also encourage this reaction: "No, we can't do it; this is our only choice under the present circumstances."

☐ Further, the project manager often does not know the answer; he is never as close to the situation as the individual immediately responsible, although he may have available a much better view of the total system.

DEALING WITH CHANGE

Developing a Quick-Response Capability

☐ The heart of the matter in both intervention and decision-making is quickness of response, the focusing of collective energies toward the solution of a critical problem. Given the large number of unanticipated barriers to following the original plans, the interdependencies that multiply the impact of any holdup, and the ever-present schedule problems, the manager must be capable of rapid adaptation after normal sequences and procedures are ignored or bypassed. The legitimizing takes place after the fact, to changed circumstances.

☐ In fact, many effective managers insist that the manager cannot wait for a problem to make itself known officially. (Thus the well-publicized computerized schedule control techniques, such as PERT networks, are often well behind the action.) Anticipating trouble requires very close contact, keeping in touch with the thinking and planned next moves of the key participants. Thus daily or twice-daily calls, weekly visits and bimonthly meetings are par for the course.

☐ Another penalty for waiting is that in a good many situations corrective action is possible only during a brief "window" (space jargon for the permissible time limits to launch).

Within an hour the support crews at the pad would be going home. The manager had minutes to decide whether he should plan to de-mate the spacecraft and the launch vehicle or whether to allow the normal working hours to be preserved.

The effort to improve on the functioning of a major subsystem in a key NASA program was thwarted when the contractor rushed to reassign personnel to other projects when it appeared as though the program was successful.

☐ There are at least two quite different types of adaptation required. The first is the more obvious and well-recognized.

An unanticipated technical problem or opportunity for gain presents itself. Major relief or return can be obtained only by a rapid mobilization of resources and improvisation involving a tremendous number of contacts and synchronized relationships conducted in a very short space of time.

In an early NASA flight project a last-minute problem was solved by erecting a special scaffolding on the pad which permitted the launch vehicle to be disassembled and rebuilt over a relatively short period of time. The mission "window" was a brief one, and normally this type of difficulty would have been handled by shipping the rocket back to the manufacturer.

OSO-II "developed an unexpected eccentricity which was threatening its life in space . . . it had somehow acquired a new magnetic field which was being attracted by the earth's magnetic field. This torque caused the craft to pitch up and down . . . The danger was the craft was attempting to correct every pitch motion with its gas jets, and would exhaust its gas supply prematurely. [An aide to the project manager proposed:] Why not cut off the automatic gas system and let him pilot the craft on a real-time basis? [This] extended OSO-II's life for an extra three months."[9]

☐ Sometimes the problem results simply from an oversight, a significant parameter neglected in the earlier planning.

In designing the film system for a photographic mission the implications of a flight through the Van Allen Belt had been ignored. When this was noted, specifications for film shielding in the spacecraft required major modification of the system.

☐ In all these examples everything is speeded up, and the frequency of contact increases rapidly. Rather than waiting days or weeks for a response (e.g., for test results or a technical judgment), the project people expect a support group to respond in a matter of hours (if a test must be performed) or minutes (if technical advice is needed). Individuals who formerly saw each other only a few times a week or a month must work closely together for hours and days at a time to improvise a solution.

Reevaluating Basic Parameters

☐ A somewhat slower-paced response is required by a more subtle, but perhaps more drastic, type of unanticipated

[9] Alfred Bester, *The Life and Death of a Satellite,* Boston, Little, Brown, 1966, pp. 205–206. (Also see the examples cited in Chapter 11.)

problem. In large-scale endeavors there are always a number of basic parameters taken as givens. These often include some of the major objectives, some of the basic resources, and some of the basic constraints. But over a long-lived program these, too, become variables.

NASA managers have often been hit with what they would call a change in the "rules" by which the game is to be played. In midstream many projects discovered that a previously accepted percentage component-failure level was now unacceptable; close to 100-percent performance was required. This meant a whole new approach to component and subsystem reliability.

A major program "discovered" in midstream that the new launch vehicle would not "lift" the weight originally contemplated and a drastic cutback in spacecraft weight would be required.

☐ Changed parameters require project changes all the way down the line. Organizationally, this means replanning, renegotiation, and reanalysis of many decisions reached with internal functional groups and external contractors.

REMAINING AN OUTSIDER

Knowing When to Wait

☐ Perhaps the hardest thing the manager must do is nothing. It takes restraint to see a problem and sit tight: "It's up to the [vehicle-contracting center] group to come up with a 'fix' on the rocket and I am sure they will. That's their job."
☐ An experienced, astute manager knows when to let the other party work through the difficulty and when it is necessary to intervene, urge reinforcements or a different approach, and the like. Not only is moving in too early costly and disrupting, it is also wasteful of the special capabilities of the contractor or support group handling the problem.
☐ Staying out for an appropriate period of time also provides perspective, which can be lost when one is personally involved in the emotional effort of endeavoring to solve recalcitrant problems. Many of the costly mistakes in any large program are the result of rather obvious negative trends being overlooked.
☐ In a sense the project manager wants to play both sides of the street, to be an outsider as well as an insider, a dispassionate observer and an accepted member of the team.

Providing Assistance

□ The project manager is not just a goad, a timing mechanism, a conductor. He also has a set of more supportive relationships that can balance off his more pressureful relationships, particularly from the point of view of those being pressured.

□ He can aid them in providing priority access to scarce external resources (in effect, by acting as an expediter), or at least resources beyond the organizational reach of the line or functional manager. He can serve as an "honest broker," bringing together conflicting groups or factions. He can act as a *buffer* between project groups and external auditors or controllers who might interfere with their internal work relationships or tempo of operations.[10] He is also responsible for getting adequate financial support, dealing with outside critics (such as Congressional committees, in the case of NASA), and perhaps negotiating with user organizations who might wish to exercise greater control over various developmental stages.

□ It is particularly important for the project manager to protect the line managers from outsiders whose time constraints and internal work tempos are most likely to diverge from those the project is seeking to maintain—outside legal authorities, for example, or scientific bodies.

□ The relevance of providing assistance can also be observed in the division of labor worked out between the headquarters level of program management and the field level of project management. The headquarters often musters resources, answers internal and external critics, and protects the activity from interference. On the other hand, the field level is able to provide advance warning of problems, evidence of effectiveness, and other reassurances that can be passed on to headquarters to bolster the position of the program. Where this reciprocity is fully developed, the relationship between the two is both effective and cordial; where one or the other fails to reciprocate, we observe animosity or distrust.

USING MEETINGS TO COORDINATE AND MOTIVATE

□ Evidence of the importance of human contact and exchange is the widespread use of meetings by project management. Some occur at predictable milestones (e.g., prior

[10] In nuclear reactor production, for example, the project manager handles the large number of inspectors representing the customer, his government, the insurers, and other international control authorities.

to commitment to hardware production); others are in response to crises. Many are regularly scheduled to deal with the approval (or rejection) of proposed changes.

☐ Some meetings are useful for the same reason that managers prefer to confront subordinates directly rather than using the mail or phone. Where groups are interdependent and risks are substantial, it is hoped that face-to-face questioning will dispel doubts and answer nagging worries. Thus contractors, support groups, interdependent center work groups, and others get together to seek reassurance that the other fellow is doing his work in a way that will not adversely affect one's own costs, schedule, or performance. For example, a project manager coordinating the vehicle procurement and launch preparations for a non-NASA customer said:

Even though the spacecraft team has met with us here we are going over there to meet with a much wider group of people who want to ask us a series of questions. I know they want some reassurances concerning the launch vehicle itself after some of these recent problems. But they are also worried about the trajectory, the unusually long coast and reignition of the engine, and we shall be trying to convince them that the data upon which we're working is good and that everything is likely to go well.

☐ Clearly, even among like-minded professionals who share a common language and respect for technical approaches, the data report does not speak for itself. There will always be innumerable ambiguities, questions that cannot be answered definitively, instances where only confrontation and playing devil's advocate can impart trust and confidence. Such encounters are also useful in reassuring everyone involved that highly responsible people have left no stone unturned in seeking to come up with the best answers available.

☐ Such meetings also impart a sense of personal participation, of comprehending the situation with your own senses rather than through intermediaries. They tend to dispel the fear, which arises in any hierarchical system where artificial barriers separate people, that information or unpleasant facts are being "hidden." Thus managers frequently invite nervous "dependents" to come and view hardware, tests, and work methods with their own eyes, to prove "we're not keeping anything from them."

☐ Being personally involved and allowed to hear firsthand progress reports, status reviews, and debates concerning alternative engineering approaches demonstrates that one is an accepted member of the team. Contrariwise, being ex-

cluded from these get-togethers suggests lesser status: "They only call on us when there are troubles, when we've done something wrong or they're looking for a scapegoat."
☐ Meetings also allow for the continuous updating of milestones, plans, and procedures. New data, financial problems, or other factors may require a decision to drop certain tests or eliminate certain steps or hardware. Similarly time pressures may encourage shifting from sequential to parallel production and projections may have to be changed. Contrariwise, additional steps, more redundancy, or less parallelism may be in order.
☐ The meetings give individual functional specialists a chance to express both their concern and anxiety about various aspects of the project, and this in itself is important. One hears comments like "I want to reemphasize our very real concern that the existing reinforcing may be inadequate," or "While I know you are doing all you can to speed things up, we want to underline how important an earlier delivery date would be to our schedule problems." Many times the same underlying problem is probed with a wide variety of questions in an attempt to make sure that things really are going well.
☐ Those who espouse the present course of action respond to these anxieties, as we have indicated, by recapitulating the underlying logic of the existing decision, describing the reasoning behind it, the safeguards, and even exhibiting or offering for exhibit the raw data, test results, or calculations by which the present decision was reached.
☐ Such solving of innumerable simultaneous equations through a process of give-and-take serves to legitimize the decisions reached and produce the emotional commitments needed to effectuate them.

ADMINISTRATIVE RESPONSE TO COMPLEX ENDEAVORS:
CONCLUSIONS

☐ One managerial response to the type of world we have been describing, where technological hindrances, intimidating size, and organizational complexity challenge traditional management thinking and methods, is the effort to do things more precisely, more systematically, more rationally. Scientific management, the effort to impose systematic, rational order in human affairs as a replacement for whim, passion, and ignorance—or indifference, has a long and honorable history. However, such techniques would convert the development program into something more closely resembling a traditional production operation.

□ One hears such recommendations as the following:

Don't use any really new technology, or at the most, accept one new thing. Everything tried and true is a good motto; the combination of these is enough newness.

Make sure the interfaces [between subsystems] are clean, that is, that each subsystem manager can do his job pretty much on his own without being concerned with, or dependent upon, the problems other managers are having.

Clarify responsibility and authority. . . .

□ At least some of the meticulous planning and laying out of schedules, costs, and performance criteria may be more than force of habit or a mistaken belief that a large development project is nothing more than the sum total of a number of relatively routine, production-like efforts. Managers may soothe their own doubts or those of their external or internal supporters by giving the impression that the knowns far outweigh the unknowns.

□ In the extreme case, as Hirschman argues, if the true scope of the problem and the attendant costs were known, the endeavor might never be started.[11] Thus the effort to make the program look like applying some finishing touches on a known process or transferring a successful technique from one usage to another may have a rational basis.

□ There is a sharp contrast between the precision of specification and record-keeping in high-technology projects and the managerial process associated with their effective pursuit. The latter is characterized by a highly fluid, iterative, and seemingly imprecise series of activities that require a high degree of personal interaction.

□ At least two underlying reasons explain the apparent paradox that precise coordination must be attained by repetitive, personal, and diffuse administrative techniques. The first is the inability to define unambiguously what constitutes satisfactory progress in accomplishing requirements, designs, and all aspects of performance. Thus wide-ranging and continuous inquiries and assessments and a pooling of judgment are required.

□ Second, the extent of interdependency is such that cor-

[11] Albert Hirschman, *Development Projects Observed*, Brookings Institution, Washington, D.C., 1967, p. 12.

recting even rather minor problems or instabilities involves a large number of complementary or corresponding readjustments. The working through of these mutually compatible recommitments requires an enormous quantity of unprogrammed interchange and negotiation.

☐ Aside from the administrative requirements for monitoring and managing change through confrontation and face-to-face interaction, these managerial jobs require widespread contacts with individuals and groups representing adjacent stages of the work flow, with diverse functional and institutional interests, with broader programmatic interests, with potential users and basic knowledge sources.

THE PROJECT MANAGER'S
INTERFACE
WITH SCIENTISTS

ELEVEN

"A mission is either a scientific triumph or an engineering failure."

In advanced technologies the project manager must coordinate scientists and their work. Most such projects use outside technical experts as consultants and experimenters. These may be the self-same prestigious professionals, university or "think tank" based, whom we described in Chapter 3. While the sponsor as a whole may be concerned with how much relative weight to give the interests and voice of the scientific community in establishing its objectives, the project manager must be concerned with the more mundane but critical task of integrating these outsiders, as well as their work, into an ongoing development effort.

□ Few outside scientists care to serve on NASA advisory boards or attend planning conferences out of any love of administrative work. Their service is offered primarily because they can help the cause of space science in general, and help themselves and their field of specialization in particular. As advisors they can promote missions and experiments in which they can participate in hopes of advancing their professional careers. No other agency can offer the rockets, launching facilities, and communications network necessary for research in space.

□ NASA requires research investigators (or principal investigators—P.I.'s—as they are called) for two overlapping, reinforcing purposes. The first is to gather and develop *operational information* about the space environment. Operational missions such as placing communication satellites in orbit and maintaining them, launching earth-orbiting spacecraft for lengthy surveillance of oceans, croplands, and weather, and orbiting and servicing manned laboratories require a detailed, thorough knowledge of the effect both of the emptiness of space and of the matter and energy that pervade it. The second purpose is to gather *scientific knowledge of space for its own sake,* a purpose designated by the President and approved by Congress. In 1958, when President Eisenhower proposed that NASA have responsibility for civilian space science and authority to conduct research in its own facilities or by contract,[1] he made it clear that space should be primarily an area for scientific exploration and that NASA should do all that it could to further this objective. President Kennedy, four years later in 1962, reiterated the nation's purposes in sponsoring scientific experimentation in space:

We set sail on this new sea because there is new knowledge to be gained and new rights to be won, and they must be won and used for the progress of all people. For space science, like nuclear science and all technology, has no conscience of its own. Whether it becomes a force for good or ill depends on us, and only if the United States occupies a position of preeminence can we help decide whether this new ocean will be a sea of peace or a new, terrifying theatre of war.[2]

□ The scientist as experimenter is both inside *and* outside the organization. There is rather substantial ground for what might be called "role strain" here. As an outsider (and often an honored and sought-after participant in the space program), he receives the deference and special treatment due a distinguished academician. He often has contacts with, or can rather easily find the means to reach, the ear of very highly placed NASA administrators or Congressional leaders, any one of whom can overrule operating-level management. But as an insider he is subjected to rules, constraints, base lines, and a variety of pressures to modify his experiment (e.g., by reducing the power requirements), to meet deadlines, to attend meetings, to effectively monitor a contractor, and so on. Some academicians are not able to meet the contradictory requirements; they do not have the flexibility to shift from an advisory role to one of a participant. What is required to make this adjustment?

SCIENCE AND ENGINEERING: THE PROBLEMS

□ To attract capable scientists to work in the demanding field of space science, NASA managers have encouraged P.I.'s to take full responsibility for their experiments. It has been traditional in the university laboratories for each researcher to invent his own experiment, design or even build

[1] Eugene M. Emme, *Aeronautics and Astronautics, 1915–1960,* Washington, D.C., NASA, 1961, p. 97.

[2] Lloyd Swenson, Jr., James Grimwood, and Charles Alexander, *This New Ocean; A History of Project Mercury,* Washington, D.C., NASA, 1966, p. 470.

the apparatus, and analyze his own data. The complexity of modern science, however, has forced the principal scientist in an experiment to surround himself with helpers and assistants of all kinds, from junior colleagues and graduate students to technicians and skilled workmen. Scientific journals also provide evidence of a change from the old single-researcher approach. Nowadays one often finds articles reporting the latest findings with anywhere from two to six authors. The old scientific practices and the demands of modern research diverge widely; traditional research, with its promise of individual freedom and flexibility, and the traditions of the university pull the investigator one way, while the technological and organizational demands of modern research pull him in an opposite direction.

□ Dr. Hugh Dryden, then NASA's Deputy Administrator, averred in 1962 that, though the organization's managers appreciated "the importance of the creative activity of the individual working in the [space] program," the usual relatively simple procedures for conducting research were not possible in satellite and probe missions—for, he added:

Satellite launching requires large rockets, special launch sites, a worldwide tracking and data-acquisition network, sharing by many experimenters in a single flight, and a large team of co-operating specialists. The scientist becomes involved in scheduling his work to meet a flight date, once that date is set. His apparatus must be engineered to meet severe environmental requirements of vibration, temperature, exposure to radiation and charged particles, and so forth. . . . The role of the university scientists often reduces to [sic] concept of the experiment, development of laboratory prototypes of the equipment, analysis of data and publication, plus participation in a large team to design the actual satellite, launch it, and receive the data.[3]

□ NASA was hardly the first organization to encounter problems as a result of the conflicting viewpoints of scientists and engineers. Below is a description of these antipathies in the operation of the enormous proton synchrotron constructed for CERN (Conseil Européen pour la Recherche Nucléaire):

The user wants his experiment to be done as quickly as possible and under the best possible conditions. First, he wants to know

[3] "The Role of the University in Meeting National Goals in Space Exploration," *Proceedings of the NASA-University Conference on the Science and Technology of Space Exploration,* vol. I, Washington, D.C., NASA, 1962, p. 89.

the scientific results of his experiment as soon as possible. Second, his achievements are not expected to occur at regular intervals, but in spurts; therefore, it is easy for him to work at an unusual pace. Seen from the viewpoint of the machine personnel, things appear in an entirely different light. To the machine physicist or mechanic this experiment is simply one of many. He will be intent on ordering the different jobs in the proper sequence, and . . . will try to arrive at the maximum output with the greatest efficiency . . . he cannot afford to work at an abnormal pace.[4]

Jungk seeks to summarize the differences in attitude thusly:

[T]he nuclear scientists exhibit a kind of arrogance [and] are aware that they are the elite of the institute . . . They are reproached for not properly appreciating the arduous and highly creative work of the machine . . . engineers, electronic specialists, programmers. . . . "In their eyes we're only blacksmiths." . . . In the engineer's eyes, these physicists are fussy, irresponsible, and unrealistic pushers.[5]

□ But it is really useless to document these different perceptions; conflicting viewpoints divide groups in all organizations and are little different for production and marketing personnel than for these more sophisticated specialists. The administrative question is how to bring these groups close enough together to moderate the differences and encourage the necessary collaboration. Otherwise, the differences become exaggerated and destructive to the work system.
□ Any technology pushed hard by scientists and engineers into the unknown forces men of both specialties to work closely together. The scientist cannot conduct experiments to test theories or to provide data without understanding the limitations of the complicated, intricate equipment he must use; the engineer cannot prepare the equipment and maintain it without understanding what its functions are and the possibilities it is to test. Both must cooperate closely, guarding against misunderstanding and jointly contributing their specialized knowledge to the explorations. Two project managers' comments on their troubles in merging science and engineering are quoted below. The first, in charge of a major NASA science mission, reported:

I had never worked with scientists before I was put in charge of this program. I worked for [an industrial firm] before I came out

[4] Robert Jungk, *The Big Machine,* New York, Scribner's, 1968, pp. 134–135.

[5] *Ibid.,* pp. 136–137.

here. I've had to change my perspective completely since I've gotten involved in scientific work. When I was strictly an engineer, I thought the scientists were crazy men to have to deal with; they were always making what I took to be impossible demands of us. I didn't know then, but I've had to learn, that I'd better fight for them. I'm doing my best to protect them from the insatiable demands of the engineers.

☐ The second explained that he had had to learn on the job how to deal with scientific investigators:

We started out to impose a discipline on scientists to get them to tell us exactly what they want the engineers to do. It is hard to get them to spell out their specifications and the detailed requirements. But until they do, it is hard to produce a piece of equipment that can be integrated into the complex spacecraft and successfully withstand the launch and space conditions. Since it is the data they want, I have learned why they want to cycle and recycle through design to get the very best—the very most they can. But you can't tune a circuit forever; you can't stay in the conceptual stage too long. We have schedules and costs to worry about. They press us hard and we press them. I've learned, as have most of them, that we have to share ideas and technology among ourselves. We waste a lot of time until we learn this.

☐ Scientists and engineers meet each other on projects apparently completely unprepared to deal with a new perspective or language. Misunderstandings may arise because one group uses new concepts without informing the other group. In designing instruments to be deployed on the lunar surface, for example, scientists and managing engineers ran into difficult problems in working out thermal and power requirements. Since the instruments would be in shadow once every lunar day, the engineers had prepared a radio-active-isotope power generator as an energy source. Its working characteristics were quite different from those of conventional generators or the usual power source in space, solar-cells panels. The isotope generator worked best when it was having *peak power* drawn from it. Thus, instruments designed to use peak power all the time worked best with it. The scientists had been used to conventional power sources, whose capability was expressed in terms of *average power*. They either were not told about, or simply did not grasp, the implications of the different generating characteristics of the new power source. Nearly two months of mutual frustration passed as the two groups discussed equipment designs, simply because they were judging them by a different criterion.

☐ In another situation, an experiment failed because engineers and scientists assumed a knowledge of each other's requirements which neither in fact possessed. In a biosatellite experiment frogs' eggs were to be flown in space, then hatched on their return and tested for the effects of exposure to radiation and weightlessness. Unfortunately, the eggs died shortly after the spacecraft was sealed, and the experiment was never completed. A thorough examination later turned up no failure of the system to maintain life in the eggs nor any other reason for the failure. After a long, frustrating review of every detail of the experiment, the cause was finally found. An engineer had removed a small, defective part of the water pump and replaced it with a cadmium-coated part. The cadmium turned out to be exceedingly poisonous to the eggs. The engineer had not been familiar enough with biosupport systems even to question the use of cadmium in them, and the bioscientists had never considered the possibility that anyone would be so lacking in knowledge that a cadmium part might be used.

☐ If the search for new forms of life and research on the effects of space on known life forms becomes a large part of the science program, engineers and bioscientists will need to prepare themselves better than they have in the past to work together. Physicists and engineers have usually had more opportunities to work with each other and learn each other's peculiarities. A group of scientists from a discipline only just introducing itself to the rigors of space technology runs into especially severe problems as a result of misunderstanding and working at cross purposes. The instruments and equipment for life-support systems in satellites are perhaps even more interrelated than those typically used by physical scientists, while the bioscientists unfortunately are often unable to specify the exact engineering requirements for successful operation of them.

☐ At one NASA field center, for example, the managers had to resolve a nest of problems that grew out of the inexperience of bioscientists and engineers working together on a particular mission. The scientists proposed to fly a monkey in space for thirty days to conduct a series of experiments upon it testing the long-term effects of weightlessness upon body function and health. The monkey, of course, was to be kept in as good health as possible. To remove liquid contamination (sweat, spilled water, saliva, and condensation from its breath) from the cockpit, a wick was to absorb them and transmit them to a waste container; a catheter was used to carry the monkey's urine to the same container. The bioscientists specified a sterile system which would not introduce germs into the monkey.

□ The first problem arose in devising the urine transport system. A section manager explained what happened:

The specifications mentioned monkey urine but they indicated no special characteristics of it. The contractor in this case assumed that monkey urine is much like human urine. It probably was less involved and less costly to test with human urine. But it turned out they are not the same at all. Monkey urine is thicker, has more particles and other things in it than human urine. I guess any biologist might be aware of the difference, but the men working on the system didn't know because the specs weren't precise. It was that we had no engineering specification for the kind of liquid to be used.

□ The problems had just started, however. After the cockpit in which the monkey was to sit had been completed and the systems tested, the investigators became concerned because they noticed that the liquids from the cockpit and the urine would both drain into a common receptacle. They feared that in the course of a thirty-day mission germs from the cockpit liquids might enter the monkey's body through the catheter. Since the resulting possible infections could invalidate the experiments, they requested a change in design to allow two separate containers for the two liquids. The contractors estimated that the change at that late stage of development would cost about $500,000! Even after the safety-factor "padding" was removed from the estimate, the NASA managers realized that the change would add at least $200,000 to their already strained budget. The engineers suggested that a powerful disinfectant, something as simple as Drano, be introduced into the tank to kill all germs. Unfortunately, the investigators pointed out, it would not destroy the bacteria about which they were most concerned. Before insisting upon the change, the investigators ran tests to see what the probabilities were of bacteria entering a monkey's urinary system from the liquid-waste tank. The cost of the tests was considerably less than the cost of changes in the spacecraft.

□ The project manager concluded the illustration by saying:

We had two problems. The investigators thought they were being specific when they asked for a sterile system to conduct monkey urine. But the engineers didn't understand either the meaning of "sterile" or "monkey urine." We simply didn't understand each other. The engineers took sterile simply to mean "clean"—void of all obvious dirt and contamination. The one talked about a "sterile" system and the other nodded and assured them it was "clean." This problem has been bothering us for a year and I hate to think of the money we spent, and the difficulties we had in smoothing it out.

□ An old maxim of project management is to define interfaces explicitly as soon as possible. In practice it turns out that definition is a continuing process, not a single action. And the process often involves difficult problems of communication for technical personnel with different backgrounds, perceptions, and expectations.

In one critical program, the scientist-principal investigators defined the required spacecraft temperature as 70°–50°. The engineers didn't comprehend that the scientists were in fact saying that a *single* temperature (within those limits) had to be maintained unchanged throughout the entire mission and identically the same throughout the capsule's interior. This misinterpretation was very costly.

□ Just as frequently neither group is aware of its total requirements until preliminary data begin to accumulate and reflect in the operations of the system as a whole, or at least larger subsystems than any specification initially covers.

In the biosatellite program, it was discovered that the monkey's touching of noninsulated surfaces and nibbling of almost all surfaces disturbed both the electrical system and the monkey. Further, various elements contained in the spacecraft hardware "degassed" toxic substances affecting the monkey's biological well-being during flight. As more of these interactions were discovered, the specifications both changed and became more far-reaching.

□ On their part, the scientists always fear that the engineers are poised to delete from the mission whatever is the most difficult to engineer—regardless of its scientific merit. The engineers easily can grow impatient with what they perceive as the narrow loyalty of the scientists to their experiments and their indifference to the overall mission. This reaction is aggravated by the pride many academic scientists take in being uncommitted, or in carefully rationing their identifications.
□ It is unrealistic to ignore the existence of these preconceptions and the likelihood of conflict over *objectives*.

Further, as we have often noted, it is equally unrealistic to expect that meticulous engineering and scientific advance planning will make unlikely the kinds of omissions and commissions we have described above. What can be anticipated as managerial sophistication increases is a gradual reduction in the amplitude of the perturbations and increasing mutual understanding over the life of the project. But if this is to occur, certain managerial actions are required.

IMPROVING SCIENCE-ENGINEERING COORDINATION

Improving Communications

☐ One of the obvious ways of improving coordination among professionals relates to that classic subject, communications. Timely and complete exchange of information is vital. Since the two groups speak different "languages," tacit assumptions are often unexpressed, and long-standing biases go unrecognized. Scientists and engineers must be prepared to interact with each other over an extended period of time; it is only after frequent and extensive meetings that some of the small but critical misunderstandings or contradictions can be unearthed and "put on the table."

☐ Often the improvements can be quick and dramatic. As one investigator pointed out:

A large number of the engineering constraints that degrade experiments are not big and costly. They are only bothersome. That is, you have to think about them before you get the design set and into development. For example, keeping a spacecraft magnetically clean may simply mean putting in nonmagnetic nuts and bolts. If this is done early enough it causes no trouble for anyone, but if you wait, then any change becomes costly.

☐ Note that this is not a process of putting "everything" down on paper and making sure that everyone gets a copy. First, as we have already emphasized, what each party thinks is "everything" usually is not and differs depending upon whom you are talking to. Further, clarification of the respective needs of the experimenter, the spacecraft manager, the launch and tracking engineers, and everyone else involved in a project is a dynamic process. By confronting one another with their respective requirements and problems, they can often develop truly creative solutions.

☐ An investigator and a managing engineer who had worked on a magnetometer experiment separately told how their challenge to each other's demands led to a marked improvement in equipment performance. The project manager explained why he had to be hardboiled:

Scientists are impossible—they ask for it anyway. Have you ever dealt with a scientist? Well, they're nothing but trouble. This one fellow told me he had to have a 30-foot boom on which to put his magnetometer. Can you imagine the problems that would give us on this size spacecraft? We told him to drop dead. He wound up with a 13-inch boom he devised and he is getting back the best data that he has ever received.

The usefulness, if not the necessity, of long booms was apparent to all, however; thus the engineers explored ways of providing extended booms in space but packing them compactly for launch. The investigator who had had to settle for the short boom initially related how the engineers later helped him:

They knew we still faced a problem of magnetic contamination. By continuing to work together we developed this extended boom. I explained the problem to them, and they came up with this telescoping boom, twice as long as before. We also worked on the solar cell wiring and came up with a way to cancel the magnetic effect as the sheet of current flows across them to the base. Now this is something the engineering staff would not normally have thought about or been concerned with. They're interested in its being as efficient—that is, low weight and cost— as it can get. Working together we enlarged their view of efficient, with great gain to the experiment at small cost in engineering.

Using "Intermediaries"

☐ Another means of improving coordination is to establish special "intermediary" roles in which the major assignment is to "translate" the needs of each party into terms the other can understand.[6] Modern organizations, with their penchant for specialization, typically add numerous "intermediaries"

[6] Of course from one point of view, to wait until scientists and engineers are working on complex projects or missions before introducing them to their mutual interdependence is to delay too long. One would think that almost a generation after the group effort of physicists, chemists, mathematicians, and engineers produced nuclear power the graduate-science facilities of our universities would have made study and exploration of the specialties' interdependence in pushing technologies at the frontier a regular, routine, and important part of all curricula. That scientists and engineers still have to discover on the job, with surprise and amazement, the different assumptions and approaches of each is a serious

to their staffs. Their function is to maintain liaison with outsiders and facilitate the coordination of outsider interests. There are, among others, community-relations, labor-relations, and international-relations specialists, each of whom helps the insider to comprehend and predict the demands and perceptions of outside groups that will affect his work. In the same vein, advanced-technology projects are likely to have a project scientist and/or an experiments manager who facilitates the give-and-take between the outside scientist-experimenters and principal investigators and the inside engineers and project managers.

□ The intermediary acts as a point of contact to help the outsider get information, resources, and understanding and to aid the insider to communicate with and justify his needs to the outsider. As many have documented, the intermediary's success depends on his speaking both "languages," sharing some of the values of both sides, and maintaining his acceptability and legitimacy to both sides.[7]

□ The scientists themselves recognize this need for intermediaries, as the following policy statement of the National Academy's Space Science Board suggests:

During this period of preparation for flight, investigators must deal with various NASA, MSC [Manned Spacecraft Center] and industrial [contractor] personnel. Compromises between scientific requirements and engineering constraints are sometimes required. The appointment of an arbiter who understands the science involved and the spacecraft configurations is extremely important. It may be that a series of arbitration procedures are required,

---

indictment of the universities.

NASA administrator James E. Webb was well aware of the problem. Though he recognized that those involved directly in a project learned quickly the need for intergroup cooperation, he believed that earlier, prior exposure to the needs of modern scientific experimentation might provide a better basis of education. He said in 1967:

We wish we could find more ways on the campus to associate graduate and postgraduate engineering education and research with the advanced engineering required to prepare scientific experiments for space flight such as those now on Mariner. . . . In my view, too many space scientists at universities insist on doing too much of their own engineering, and too few engineering, education, and research leaders have found ways to help them and to help themselves at the same time.

See "NASA and the Universities," speech given at the dedication of the Coordinated Science Laboratory Building, University of Illinois, Urbana, October 17, 1967, p. 3f.

[7] See Paul Lawrence and Jay Lorsch, *Organization and Environment*, Boston, Mass., Harvard Graduate School of Business Administration, 1968.

such that for final decisions, "science representatives" may be necessary at the contractor's plant and at the Center as well as at NASA Headquarters.[8]

☐ Interesting to note in this statement is the recognition that exchanges and representation are required simultaneously at all levels in the system. Further, the board sees that compromise and negotiation are integral to this type of science.
☐ In space projects intermediaries must be men whose credentials are acceptable to the principal investigators and to the engineers alike. In one sense, they are teachers explaining the relevant requirements of both or all "sides"; but they also play a more active role as a catalyst, serving to change the situation. This was best expressed by one of the directors of a major NASA field center:

On every project we have to have help for the investigators—help from really knowledgeable men at the centers. They have to understand the science involved but they also have to know how a center operates and the technological problem of putting an experiment on top of a rocket. He doesn't have to be, and we wouldn't want, a man who simply fights for everything an investigator may first ask for. I've seen cases where an accuracy of 1/10,000ths was put in the specs though nothing like that was needed at all. A challenge to his specifications and a clear statement of the costs involved—the trade-offs of other gains—helps the scientist to devise better, more imaginative experiments.

☐ In the more successful face-to-face discussions with experimenters of their engineering requirements (for equipment accuracy, for power, for data collection, etc.), a number of results are possible:

1. The scientists may become convinced that their initial requirements were overstated, unrealistic, or incomplete. Substitutions, alternatives, and additional clarity may result from the discussions.

2. The engineers may come to understand the reasons for a very difficult or cumbersome requirement imposed by the scientists. If they do accept the rationale, they are more likely to seek energetically ways of meeting these more trying specifications.

3. Both "sides" may give a little.

☐ These negotiations try the patience and skill of engineering managers, project scientists, and the principal investigators. Fixed perceptions do not change at once, and it is

---

[8] National Academy of Science, Space Sciences Board, *Lunar Exploration, Strategy for Research 1969–1975,* Washington, D.C., NASA, 1969, p. 37.

easy for either "side" to freeze its position and think the other either ignorant of or indifferent to its technical needs.
□ As in labor relations, there will be times when group meetings will be best. These allow quick exchanges among all the interested parties so that the implications of changes can be quickly evaluated. However, there will also be times when such meetings will only harden opposing views and cause scientists to unite against engineers and vice versa. One engineering manager described this well:

If one of the scientists makes a point, the others will go along with total belief in what is being said. If one of them [the project management] is resisting us, they will all get behind him. . . . The scientists tend to open up more when we are dealing with them individually. Together, they forget their differences.

□ Of course this mutual respect can be used to advantage by the program office or engineer. If he can convince one of the scientists, this "convert" often will help convince his more recalcitrant colleagues:

The experiment engineers do not have Ph.D's. There is a tendency on the part of the Principal Investigators to want to be dealing with someone at the Ph.D. level. Status symbols are quite important and it takes us a long time to convince the scientists that we are capable of speaking their language and of helping them. To solve the problem we have developed some gimmicks to extract information out of the scientists without taking the frontal approach. Thus, for example, it might be necessary for us to derive some information from one of the Principal Investigators. Our question may be scientific in nature and we know we might get some resistance. So we select a scientist whom we have gotten to know on a personal basis. Informally over coffee in one of our meetings we will get this scientist aside, tell him of the information that we need from one of the other scientists, then let him carry the ball. Later on in the meeting we will notice that our contact will ask the scientist from whom we need information some pretty sharp questions. Our questions get answered indirectly. As a matter of fact, the scientists have gotten very sharp about asking questions of one another. It is often precisely these questions that we as engineers and as management people need answers to.

The Role of the P.I.

□ There are obviously substantial differences in the relative importance of scientific experiments and the scientist on various spacecraft. In some programs it is made clear to the scientist that he is simply a "passenger" who has been assigned an inflexible "seat" for his experiment which he must fit if the experiment is not to be rejected by the program manager.

□ At the other extreme, there are programs in which science is the major focus. In such cases the program people may insist that they go out of their way to communicate to the scientists that they, the scientists, are indeed in control and will make the crucial decisions. That relationship is well described by a project manager:

The Principal Investigator must feel he has control and be in control of the entire sequence of activities up to the Critical Design Review. He has to fully understand what is going on. So, for example, in defining the optical physics interface to meet the scientific requirements, the Principal Investigator had to be constantly telling the engineer what the end objectives were of the instrument itself. *It is this constant information about end objectives that permits the kind of fruitful exchange which is bound to result in success* [italics ours]. The engineers must know how the scientists' instrument is going to affect all of the supporting housing, structures, and electrical systems. It is the Principal Investigator's job to keep pounding hard on the scientific objectives.

Most of us here think that wise decisions were made thanks to the close collaboration. In the first place the Principal Investigator was given total freedom for the scientific objectives with the realization of the necessity for certain degrees of sophisticated management controls. We have a rule of never giving the Principal Investigator the impression that we are dictating. However, let's not forget that the Principal Investigator has the legal and moral contractual responsibility—the ultimate control device. We offer the help. We have to help them build the cameras, the T.V., all linked with the instruments. *Don't alienate the Principal Investigator. After all, he should be a friend.* He has a great deal of power as a respected member of the scientific community, and he has access to the top echelons of NASA and right up to the President's office. In short, he's a valued customer of ours. And we are also cognizant of the fact that the success that we have in winning over this customer could largely determine the future of all programs at this Center and NASA.

□ Even in projects such as that just described, the status of the scientist must constantly be reinforced by careful footwork. For example, the program engineers will have to be in contact with the contractor fabricating the P.I.'s experiment. Such direct contacts have to be handled in such a fashion that the P.I. does not feel that his control over the contractor has been endangered or his responsibility for the outcome reduced. Similarly the program people, in imposing budget and schedule and technical limitations, must do so in such a way that the scientist recognizes them as legitimate constraints rather than interference from above.

When Battles Occur

☐ Major design changes can profoundly affect budgets, schedules, and organizational relationships. Project and program managers seek to minimize such changes by having the parts "keep time," or move at relatively similar rates. In one instance the principal investigator went to the very top levels of the NASA organization to insist that a change be allowed; but the views of lower management prevailed— at least at the outset:

When our program began, Dr. X came up with a very complicated proposal for his particular equipment. He came to us and indicated that there was going to be some delay because there were still some highly scientific and technical problems that had not been worked out. But by this time the program all across the board with all of the experiments was running full steam. We on the project level saw that any further delay would interrupt the entire program. Therefore, Dr. X was persuaded to go to a simpler type of experiment configuration. [With] a simpler scientific concept we found that it was possible for us to stay on schedule. However, when, because of Congressional cutbacks, it was realized that the entire program was going to have to be stretched out, Dr. X seized on this opportunity to go back to his original proposal of a more complicated unit but one which he was convinced would do a far superior job. He also indicated that his laboratory support now had the scientific know-how to make the proper breakthrough.

FABRICATING EXPERIMENTS AND IMPLEMENTING DESIGNS

☐ Many times more difficult than the conceptual stage is the actual implementation, moving ideas into hardware. Space scientists not only have to produce handcrafted instruments but integrate them with as intricate an array of sophisticated mechanisms as men have ever put together. They are expected to take individual responsibility in conducting their experiments but at the same time to merge their work into a perplexingly involved group effort. Investigators are chosen on the basis of their specialized scientific competence, but they are required to master the skills of a financial manager, an administrator, a personnel director, and an engineer. The organizational processes within which investigators work and through which managers may help them are incomplete and often unsatisfactory. Their shortcomings arise not so much from a lack of attention to the investigator's problems as from the speed with which the advanced technology has compounded their complexity. Thus, helping university space scientists in their role as investigators is not easy, for they are confronted with a confusing set of contradictory obligations, overlaid with a web of inconsistent demands.

□ A scientist at one of NASA's field centers, describing the massive organizational support for scientific experimentation, declared:

People still think of government-sponsored research as something like sending Lewis and Clark out to map the Northwest. That kind of research is as obsolete as those two explorers are old. It's more like a battle now. We are part of an advancing army going into battle, supported and serviced by ten men for every one of us. The logistics and paperwork are as involved as that of a conquering army—and that is what we are.

□ The simile may be correct, but it does not emphasize the dependence upon individual initiative and responsibility of either a modern army, fighting wars with no fronts, or scientific missions.

□ Many scientist-experimenters are tempted to (and some do) turn over the fabrication of their experiments to a contractor and forget about the whole thing until the hardware is complete. Like other naive participants in complex technologies, they view the work-flow stages, design, manufacture, test, delivery to installation contractor or NASA center—as neatly compartmentalized and discrete.

□ University scientists and project managers alike stress the necessity for investigators to work on, or closely oversee, the construction of their instruments. So few of any given model or design are produced that the factories in which they are built resemble the craft shops of olden times rather than the assembly-line plants assumed to be characteristic of present-day industry. Production of a dozen space instruments can be considered a big run. More frequently, an investigator will prepare only a "breadboard" arrangement, an engineering model, a flight prototype for testing, and the experimental instrument itself, with one or two extras for spares. To complicate matters, the schedule may be so tight that the investigator will proceed with all the models at the same time, building them in parallel rather than in series.

☐ Two high-level center managers argued that, given the unknowns with which the scientists are dealing and the lack of guides or standards, investigators have to be deeply involved in the design and construction of their instruments. "It is different from anything else he will have worked with—the equipment, the spacecraft, and the environment. If he does not know it intimately, he simply will not be able to tell what the data mean." A young university investigator, who had worked through another center, agreed:

Given the extreme limitations on power, weight, size, and the stress to which it will be subjected, your instruments are pushing the state of the art. You have to get involved very deeply in engineering problems. You can't simply be concerned with theory and data, you have to know what the nuts and bolts do to your readings—what effects they produce. You have to see that the hardware meets the mission needs, and you have to know the hardware well enough so that you know what you are getting when you begin to interpret your data. Knowing the limitations and the requirements of the equipment we design and build is an integral part of the job. And every instrument I make for a new, different mission is different and better. So I never get a chance to consider theory alone; I am always involved with the equipment, too. I'm an experimenter, not a theorist, and that's what we all have to be.

☐ An experienced investigator, who had flown many instruments on both small and large rockets declared that scientists will have to be well-acquainted with the instruments for their experiments, familiar with every quirk and characteristic, "until we get some standard instruments. But that day is not coming quickly as long as we continue to press separate and unique experiments. We're always searching for new and unknown phenomena—there's nothing standard about that."

P.I. Contacts with the Project

☐ There is little question that communication and understanding are facilitated by the opportunity to speak frequently, informally, and spontaneously. Telephone conferences, formal meetings, and written memoranda often impede this type of easy-give-and-take relationship in which mutual problems can be explored and resolved. It is therefore not surprising to read the following recommendation from a high-level scientific advisory group:

A better communication between those familiar with the concept and objectives of an experiment and those persons within NASA who know environmental problems and instrument testing could perhaps be established by inviting PI's or their co-workers to work at NASA facilities during the initial stages of instrument development. During their stay they would have made available to them engineers on a consulting basis. . . .[9]

Design-Review Meetings

□ Often the formal mechanism for linking principal investigators with center personnel is a review meeting held every six to eight weeks. These meetings include the principal investigators, personnel from other centers, representatives of program management, and finally, the engineering groups from the laboratories. Those at one center spoke with considerable enthusiasm about the success of those meetings:

These meetings have proven very fruitful in generating a better interface and understanding. This is the real opportunity for those of us in operations to be in direct and close contact with our own experiments' engineers and with the scientists within the Center complex and the Principal Investigators. We try to hold many of these meetings where the Principal Investigators themselves are located. We rotate around at the various locations.

□ The substance of these experiment-coordination meetings is described below by a project manager:

The purpose of this coming meeting will be to tell what the latest cluster configuration can be. This will follow up a presentation on missions and operations so that the Principal Investigators will know all of the rules of the flight. It will tell them what the ground base support will be, the experiment sequence, and the experiment time lines. Also this meeting is going to be used for a special item. The Principal Investigators are very concerned about the use of a particular piece of equipment from one of the manufacturers. They feel that it will *not* be right. There will probably be thirty-five people at the meeting around the table plus another fifty or sixty in the audience. Careful notes will be made at the meeting with the chief points and agreements transmitted back to all of the interested parties.

□ Being deeply involved in building one's own instrument for a space experiment requires more than putting together a few wires, transistors, transformers, and resistors in the university laboratory with the assistance of a few graduate

[9] *Ibid.,* p. 31.

students. Unless an experiment is to fly on a smaller rocket probe, used by a single investigator, it will involve the scientist in a complex set of relationships with one or more contracting firms that supply designs and fabricated parts; with other investigators whose experiments will also be flown and their contract suppliers; with the firm that integrates all the experiments into a complete package; and with the NASA officers and centers that select the experiments, oversee the program, manage the spacecraft-rocket assembly, control the launch facilities, and collect the data. In many ways the P.I. will become a project manager himself!

□ A package of experiments to be flown in a spacecraft large enough to need a Saturn rocket may require the regular meeting over several years of at least fifty people representing the interests directly affected, who must coordinate their work so that all the instruments and parts will form an integrated package. One of the larger, more complex projects designed to land experiment packages on the lunar surface for deployment by astronauts has, according to the assistant program manager, "seventeen first-order interfaces, any one of which could cause a breakdown should it fail. That means at least thirty-four people who have to coordinate closely or we're in real trouble."

□ These people must meet constantly to keep one another informed of developments, particularly changes in the instruments or structural changes in the spacecraft itself. A manager at headquarters declared that his experiences in directing one of the most successful space programs convinced him that "it was informal contacts and word of mouth, face to face contacts that were most important. If you try to handle everything by documents, you simply get too many to read, and you lag too far behind what is going on."

Proliferating Relationships: A Case Example

□ An example of the complexities in which an investigator may become involved is given by those which engulfed the experiment to measure the flow of heat from the moon's interior to the lunar surface. The instrument is basically simple, a probe containing platinum resistance temperature sensors to be buried about 10 feet deep into the lunar surface to avoid the effects of diumbral temperature variations. To dig the holes for the probes the astronauts would need a drill capable of functioning effectively in the airless environment of the moon.

☐ The investigator found that he had to be concerned, to a lesser or greater degree, with the work of seven firms that contributed to the probe and the drill. When he proposed his experiment the drill was considered a tool, and thus not something for which he was responsible. As he worked on the probe, however, he realized that no development of the drill was taking place. Without an investigator to push it and to oversee its completion, the drill would never have been successfully completed. Thus, he had to concern himself with a much larger project and a more complex set of instruments than he had anticipated. Arthur D. Little of Cambridge, Massachusetts, designed the probe; the Rosemont Company of Minneapolis furnished the platinum sensor; Gulton Industries of Albuquerque prepared the electronic box for the probe, which automatically measured its responses and transformed them into signals for transmission to earth; Martin-Marietta of Baltimore supplied the drill motor; while Black and Decker of Hampstead, Maryland, furnished the drill stems. The LaTrobe Company of Chicago produced a special bit for the drill, and a Long Island firm manufactured batteries to power the drill motor. Another company, Bendix, in Ann Arbor, Michigan, has the contractual responsibility from the Manned Spacecraft Center to integrate the heat-flow probe with the other nine experiments to be flown during the life of the project. A NASA center oversees the integration of the experiment package into the spacecraft and coordinates the requirements of the experiments with limitations in the astronauts' capabilities to deploy them during their relatively short time on the lunar surface.

The Need for Continuing Involvement

☐ The investigator must watch closely the work of the various contractors and subcontractors to make sure (1) that none of the instruments are being degraded and (2) that he understands fully all the problems that arise and can contribute to their solution by bringing to bear his awareness of, and sensitivity to, the needs of his scientific specialty. An experienced investigator explained why he found it important to oversee the contractors:

It is very easy to get a problem built into an instrument. If you wait for the monitoring report about what went on, you'll find you've lost out. They are too slow . . . you have to have a man at the contractor's, someone you trust and who knows your needs, if it isn't yourself. He has to be living there, practically. You simply have to monitor, because you can't lay out all the specifications in advance. You're always moving into the unknown. Even if you are building the same instrument for a later spacecraft, you find that it's not really identical—you push it a bit further, sophisticate it more, and get it to bring back more data.

☐ Investigators can provide example after example of the difficulty in making changes or correcting errors once something has been built into an instrument or even incorporated into a design. They need to be in the shop, following the work of the engineers, to take remedial action immediately or to introduce a change at the earliest possible moment. One man who successfully developed a complex instrument with a high scientific priority said:

I worked principally with one contractor who built the instrument. We had to produce one that weighed ten pounds, with capability and sensitivity at least equal to the forty pound instrument that had been our smallest. Unless I spoke to [the instrument contractor] and to [the integration contractor], the man at NASA headquarters and at the Manned Spacecraft Center, not enough weight was given to my suggestions. I have to talk to them, and they need to hear from me directly. We all meet every five weeks. That involves not only me and my contractors, but the other investigators and their contractors, too . . . I have to attend and monitor management meetings at [the contractor's] plant and at [the integration contractor's]. One of the problems now is that [the integration contractor] is putting pressure on [the contractor] because they are running over their cost budget. This gets me into policing. I have to help check on [the contractor], asking them, Why did you do that? Sometimes I am bludgeoning them into changing a part they put in to save money, but at the risk of degrading the instrument. They put it in, of course, to save money since [the integrator] is saying the budget is too low. Each blames the other and I have to trace down the difficulty and see exactly what the trouble is. . . .

It takes a lot of time, and I could send my chief engineer to a lot of the meetings, for he knows all about the project. . . . Yet I realize that if I did not attend all the various meetings I might miss too much. At one meeting I learned that the spent Saturn IV-B rocket was going to be left in space. It suddenly occurred to me that if it were shot into the moon we would have an impact of known weight at a specific spot and known time—and the chance to calibrate our instrumentation on the moon. Now suppose that I had sent down one of my project engineers to attend the meeting. He would have heard about the rocket but he probably wouldn't have seen the link between it and the need to calibrate the instruments. He has his selective hearing, like each of us, and he would have paid attention to the engineering side and missed the scientific implication. This is one of the reasons, though I find it time-consuming, I feel I must attend all the various meetings.

☐ Another reason the investigators give for having to spend much time coordinating the work on their instruments and experiments is that prior specifications are hardly ever adequate. Changes in the weight and power constraints of the mission, unforeseen difficulties in working metals or miniaturizing components, and other problems of space research often require alterations in the work. These are both time-consuming and costly, even when made at a very early stage:

The technology allows you to do more things but it creates more problems, too. We like to—and we have to—keep changing our experiments as conditions change, but micro-circuitry makes change about impossible. It used to be that you could change a single tube or a single transistor. Now we have to plug in or pull out a whole experiment, since it may be completely integrated. Taking it apart becomes impractical, so you build another one, incorporating the change or avoiding the fault, you hope.

☐ Another investigator pointed out that the number of engineering drawings for his instrument came to 1200, and the complexity of the instrument required almost 300 special tools, though it would not weigh more than a dozen pounds. The specifications for his instrument, which included a digital filter, made a pile nearly a foot high.
☐ The increased need for exceedingly high reliability has forced investigators to reconsider their approach to experimentation. For manned missions NASA has established specific quantitative goals for the probability of success: 0.90 for the probability of complete success in accomplishing the mission and 0.999 for the probability of crew survival. When the reliability requirements are apportioned to the vast number of subsystems and on down to components, the reliability specified frequently runs to 0.9999999![10] This kind of almost incredible reliability creates an enormous amount of paperwork for the investigator. One scientist described the problem many investigators face with a reliability of only 0.99:

[10] *The Space Program in the Post-Apollo Period,* Joint Space Panels, President's Science Advisory Committee, Washington, D.C., Government Printing Office, 1967, p. 92.

For this instrument we are buying hundreds of thousands of dollars worth of integrated parts. Each one has to be burned in [thoroughly tested under operating power and other conditions from four to sixteen hours or more]. Each part has to be identified for tracing and accompanied by an IBM card. Will you follow up failures and analyze them, or will the company? Will you examine the quality control of the supplier? Well, the answer is that I have to; as the principal investigator I have to make sure that for that money we're getting quality parts. Now this instrument of mine has 80,000 welds in it. I have to know how those welds are being carried out and what kind of quality control [the contractor] is instituting.

You understand that this is one instrument for a spacecraft package that is twice as complicated as the Comsat satellites. I have to worry about the design and tests of the thermal controls. I have to follow through on the digital filter and I have to know how it is produced. I've gained enough engineering knowledge from my experience that, at least, I can make some noise when I recognize something out of line.

☐ The investigator in a major project must learn how to maneuver for position and influence within the confusing, involuted web of relationships; he must develop negotiating skills and become adept at threading his way through the warp and woof of organizational activities to protect his work and to promote his interest:

One investigator told how he had to negotiate to gain approval of a small change in a detector, which would allow it to measure protons and electrons at the same time. A technician and an engineer in the school's laboratory worked out the design, built, tested, and calibrated the additional part in about two days. But he spent most of four months petitioning the contractor to accept, the NASA field center managers to approve, and NASA headquarters people to insist upon the change. Though the added weight was only 15 grams, the final cost of the change was $30,000.

☐ The examples cited may give the impression that scientists are consistently virtuous in seeking to overcome the encumbrances of bureaucracy and stubborn Mother Nature. Often it is the scientist who stubbornly insists on using an unreliable contractor or underestimates consistently the amount and quality of engineering required to implement his designs. Many ignore scheduled review meetings or schedules altogether and frustrate their fellow scientists since experiments are interdependent at the integration stage.

The extreme deference and independence associated with a prestigious university post is not the best training for someone who has to work as part of a team and learn to accept organizational constraints.

□ To protect themselves against an investigator's financial irresponsibility or his poor management of an experiment and instrument contract, a center's project manager may step outside usual procedure to secure added protection for himself. A lower-level engineering manager on a large satellite program gave this example:

I have had a bad experience with [a certain scientist] on his last experiment. He caused a month-and-a-half delay which cost me $120,000. It is important that he gets his work in on time and that it be right. I told headquarters, informally, that I would prefer not to work with [him], but that did not do me any good. His instrument is being built by a subcontractor of the company integrating all the experiments into the $5 million satellite package. His trouble is that he delegates too much work and doesn't really oversee what is going on. Well, I have a little extra in my budget from [another, unrelated project], so I hired an engineer in [a large electrical equipment firm] that has a space science division to oversee [his] work. He has access to the plant where the work is going on and reports to me. I haven't told [my superiors] about this and I don't think I will.

CONCLUSION

□ Many people within NASA have questioned the ability of the university scientist, used to the autonomy and the easy schedules of the campus, to adapt to the demands of contract monitor. They would have the scientist do the early conceptual work and the data analysis and leave the rest to NASA personnel, who would then handle the contractor relationships and perhaps a good deal of the other coordinating work. However, such a suggestion suffers from the same shortcoming as any proposal that is based on compartmentalized functions. As we have seen, at many points along the way, from conception to flight, the scientific worth of an experiment will be threatened by the hard decisions that have to be made when plans, as they surely will, go astray. Further, there will always have to be trade-offs between experiments, between experiment design and spacecraft performance, and adaptation to unanticipated problems. The investigator's knowledge of what he is seeking to do and what he requires to do it is essential. But to apply this knowledge he must also be up to date on what has transpired, on the realities of engineering and launching and telemetering and flight. If he is not there or not prepared to respond at a crucial moment, the inexorable pressures for timely decision-making or the choices that get made without anyone announcing a formal decision will surely degrade performance.

□ On the other side, he must be an active participant to allow for the necessary adjustments. The early conceptions the scientist has are likely to be faulty, incomplete, or needlessly demanding on technology. If he is not actively involved, the engineers may find it more difficult to modify his experiments, and there certainly will not be the opportunity for the kind of creative interchanges among experimenters and between experimenters and engineers we have described.

□ Scientists, like any professionals caught up in the stringent demands of advanced technology, must not only be willing and able to communicate with other professionals, but they must learn related parts of other fields. In cases like those we have been describing, the scientists must learn something of the other disciplines whose experiments shared an interface with their own, as well as a good deal of engineering and management. But most of all they must learn perseverance and be willing to expend enormous quantities of energy on what will appear to be unprofessional, unproductive distractions; particularly negotiations.

□ Thus the intricate process of negotiation and interchange that characterizes the ongoing relationship of the project manager-engineer with the principal investigator-scientist is well worth examining in all its remarkable intricacy. It is a complicated process of continuous interaction kept within the constraints of time, money, and performance by skills of project management exercised by the scientist, the engineer, and also by special intermediaries who help to bridge the gap, in experience and values, separating the scientist and engineer.

□ It is difficult to differentiate that aspect of the process which represents the development of mutual confidence and that which represents the exchange of necessary technical information and the working through of technical problems. Both require carefully planned and executed interaction in which it is recognized that what appear to be objective facts can slither this way and that or change completely.

□ As we concluded in Chapter 10, the heart of project management is the influencing of outside organizational units to conduct their necessary (for you) activities in such a way that they integrate technically, financially, and time-wise with the other components of the project. It is particularly difficult to control at a distance the coordination of scientific experiments which are under the control of independent scientific investigators. Such men tend to consider indepen- dence from external authorities one of the canons of profes- sionalism and modern scientific method. Freedom and good science are presumed to always walk hand in hand.

☐ We have purposely explored the elaborate (and painfully demanding) detail of the relationship of scientist-experi- menters to development projects because we believe that this is not a unique relationship. Professionals of diverse backgrounds—lawyers, physicians, architects—all discover, when they become involved in project work, that enormous expenditures of effort are required to ensure that their professional contribution actually is used to full advantage. Unfortunately professional education and professional ex- perience often incline the talented expert to expect that his work will stand on its own; he is loathe to become an "administrator," feeling that such activities will degrade his professional status as well as detract from the time available for his professional "responsibilites." Our interdisciplinary world requires this kind of involvement, however, if these projects are to meet their goals and professional standards. One sees the same need for involvement and the same frequency of problem in a broad range of social and eco- nomic programs. But in these the sensitivities of minority groups which can flare into symbolically profound conflicts and destroy imaginative projects are the equivalent of the unanticipated technical barriers.

SYSTEMS INTEGRATION: ASSURING CONFIDENCE AND COMPATIBILITY

TWELVE

A recurring theme in advanced technologies is the need to make compatible what superficially appears to be incompatible. A key point of interest in this regard is the managerial problem created by the twin processes of integration and differentiation. Integration and differentiation are interacting, interdependent processes, but their organizational and behavioral requirements are quite different.

☐ *Differentiation* involves the evolution of change, the exploration of various alternatives. This function is performed by highly talented specialists, designing subsystems in a work environment that nurtures independence and the sovereignty or NIH (not invented here) factor. *Integration,* on the other hand, involves collaboration among the various specialist-designed subsystems. If integration is to proceed successfully, it must take place in conjunction with differentiation. The two are actually inverse processes. Changes in subsystems components must be made in light of the interaction between subsystems. With regard to organizational behavior, separatist NIH sentiments associated with differentiation must be moderated to achieve sufficient cooperation to produce compatible subsystems for an end product, such as a spacecraft, whose successful operation can be depended upon with a very high level of confidence.

☐ The processes of differentiation and integration should constitute an oscillating system in which each element continuously takes the other into account. It is not possible to have both a high degree of differentiation and extremely precise integration.[1] The gold-plating specialist may make rather trivial gains in the functioning of his subsystem, while creating intense problems in integration. Figure 1 indicates that marginal increments of differentiation, when the process is pushed to extremes, can occur only at a tremendous expense in terms of integration.

[1] Paul R. Lawrence and Jay W. Lorsch, *Organization and Environment,* Boston, Mass., Graduate School of Business Administration, Harvard Univ., 1967, Chap. 4.

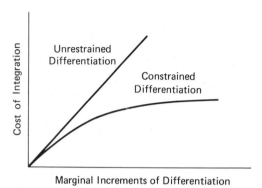

Figure 1. The cost of integration vs. marginal increments of differentiation.

□ We have briefly described the nature of the integration function and its relation to its counterpart, differentiation. In this chapter we shall view this function through the eyes of the systems-integration contractors. Of course there are such specialists on the project manager's in-house team, but in massive efforts such as the Apollo Program outside contractors may be brought in to do some of the work.

□ The experiences of these outsiders as they work through a sponsor's program office are especially revealing for those interested in the management process because these contractors must retrace past history and learn for the first time much of what is commonplace to the insiders in these offices. One obtains, then, an admirable view of the real—rather than the theoretical—world in which integration takes place, and one can learn a great deal about the nature of the skills needed to successfully perform this function. Superficially considered, integration might seem to involve largely "problem-solving" on the part of individuals who share the same goals and are basically agreed about the nature of the problem with which they are dealing. However, very real ideological differences can exist. There is no one right answer. Technological problems, like organizational and social problems, can have many solutions. Thus, as we shall see from the experiences of the contractors, integration actually requires different mixes of a variety of strategic approaches—notably, persuasion, bargaining, and politicking.[2]

[2] See James G. March and Herbert A. Simon, *Organizations,* New York, Wiley, 1958, p. 129.

THE SYSTEMS-INTEGRATION CONTRACTOR

☐ The following analysis is derived from a study of a number of systems-integration contractors as they conducted their activities in the field. Some entered at the beginning of a program; others were called in after an emergency developed. Most of them conducted sizable operations. Systems-integration contractors associated with the Apollo Program employed thousands. At one point one of these contractors had about 150 persons at the headquarters program office as well as groups of 500, 650, and 800 at three field centers. Before considering the functions performed by these contractors, we will examine some of the sponsor's reasons for employing them.

Organizational and Technical Reasons for Using Outsiders

☐ As integration is a core managerial function, tied closely to the ongoing flow of work, one may wonder why it ever is turned over to outsiders. As a matter of fact, the integration contractor's job and responsibilities are roughly those of the program manager, at least as this role is ideally conceived. Nevertheless, one finds that even in-house-oriented R & D-type sponsors contract out this function.

☐ Clearly, systems integration can be and is done with in-house personnel. Then why has the role of systems-integration contractor been created? The answer is not a simple one. Systems integration does not have the qualities of the ideal contractor assignment. It cannot be packed up and taken to one's own shop. It requires continuous interaction with, and penetration of, other organizations.

☐ From an organizational standpoint, the task is not always equally difficult. One manager, involved in contrasting integration work with two different sponsors, remarked:

In Sponsor A's organization there is some General who simply says, "This is what will be," but with Sponsor B we have this troika—headquarters and two unfriendly sub-units who also resent interference from headquarters. The huge size of B's program is another problem. It makes it hard to penetrate.

☐ Sponsors whose organizations are inherently difficult to penetrate—highly decentralized, with a number of competing in-house units in addition to a complex contractor structure—run a greater risk of getting poor results; and for them, bringing in an outsider to perform systems integration may be a mistake.

☐ However, despite these problems, some factors favor the use of a contractor. Systems evaluation and integration is a big job, demanding a wide range of technical skills and considerable manpower. Moreover, as this function generally is tied to the life of particular programs and projects, the workload and attendant manpower requirements fluctuate considerably over time. A large contractor may be better able than the sponsor to pull manpower from various ongoing projects as well as to find a place for these men when the assignment ends. When an emergency situation, such as the 1967 Apollo fire, demands an all-out systems-integration effort, the flexibility of the contractor may make his services the only reasonable alternative. One cannot argue with the statement of one top executive in a government agency that "if sufficient systems level capacity were available, we could do the integration job inhouse." However, this "if" is a big "if."

☐ Some sponsors have consistently employed profit-making industrial contractors for this function. One (NASA) has "fractionated" the responsibility among the space-systems divisions of a number of large industrial contractors such as General Electric, Boeing, and Chrysler. However, it is not surprising that others have turned to the single-structure "nonprofit" route, creating an "outsider" with a strong inhouse orientation. Thus, the Air Force replaced TRW's subsidiary, the profit-making STL (Space Technology Laboratories), with a specially created nonprofit organization, the Aerospace Corporation. The Air Force also uses the Massachusetts Institute of Technology's MITRE, another nonprofit organization, in much the same capacity. However, the shift to nonprofit groups did not represent a categorical rejection of the profit-makers; they continued to retain TRW in connection with work on its original assignment. A sponsor's decision to associate a dependency relationship with performance of this task reflects his recognition of its centrality to the management function as well as his recognition of the problems of acceptance faced by the complete outsider who assumes this role.

Role Problems

☐ The role of the outside contractor performing this function is admittedly a difficult one. In the first place, the basic structuring of the relationship is awkward, for one large company is placed in a position superior to that of its equals—and is potentially in a position to learn some of their business secrets. One integration contractor noted, "We can imagine what it would be like if the tables were reversed and 'X' was trying to tell us, 'Your design is no good.' We wouldn't stand for it. Most of the time I'm sure they'd like to tell us to 'get lost.' "

☐ It is difficult for the other contractors working on a program to regard the integration contractor as a neutral. They are more apt to view him as just another one of them, with a job to perform. And in one case the others regarded the integration contractor as a rather unfortunate fellow—of the various contractors belonging to the program, they felt him to be the one most in need of help!

☐ Surprisingly, the relationship of the integration contractor with units of the sponsor's own organization can be equally delicate, ambiguous, and frustrating. A case in point concerns the situation at one sponsor's field center where the heads of several functional areas "ran the show," while the program manager was pointedly ignored. His needs were regarded as strictly secondary. The systems-integration contractor who worked through the program office found himself in much the same position. His requests for data to facilitate the integration process were ignored, and important decisions regarding schedules and the like were made without informing him. Of course, in this case an in-house integration specialist would have been in an equally frustrating position.

THE INTEGRATION FUNCTION

☐ Integration is a systems-oriented activity: the integration contractor has the job of building confidence in a system's functioning, level by level. To accomplish this, he asks questions such as the following: What is functioning at a high level of confidence now? What needs improvement? What requirements are yet to be demonstrated? Are all significant subsystems interfaces identified and properly defined? In sum, the integrator determines what is needed for mission success. But he also is concerned with the possibility that the venture will fail, and he performs a "what if?" analysis to ascertain the protective measures needed in this event.

☐ To successfully complete his assignment, the integrator must comprehend the total system. All relevant data must be analyzed, particularly (1) engineering design changes and

(2) problems related to a given piece of hardware. What changes have been or are being made on, say, launch vehicle X? When did each change occur? What problems have been encountered on launch vehicle X? Have they been solved? One might assume that the requisite data are primarily technical, but in reality, management information constitutes roughly half the mixture.

☐ One observer expressed the feeling that integration was elevated to the status of a separate and distinct activity because sponsors had no effective administrative control mechanism for enforcing their directions to contractors performing design, development, and production functions. Actually, formal contractual agreements give sponsors and their program managers some rather impressive controls over their satellites, but these controls are apt to be legalistically rather than administratively oriented. There is no spirit of marginalism. Designed to reward or punish, these controls demand all or nothing: "If you don't do as we say, we will cancel your contract." Such a drastic action may satisfy the sponsor's need for authority, but it obviously can make no contribution to the success of a mission in which both sponsor and contractor have been heavily involved for a considerable period of time.

☐ Clearly, in advanced technologies integration is far from a simple process. It is not a matter of bringing together tried and tested parts. Instead, the integrator has to cope with unrecognized or ill-defined interfaces and the endless changes that have taken place in the specifications of the units in question. It is not surprising that those performing this function find that it has a high propensity to deteriorate into a "flesh-peddling" activity, with the integrator serving primarily as a labor broker, furnishing service personnel to the various divisions in the sponsor's organization. The integrator follows the human tendency to do what is readily acceptable and to avoid those activities that are resisted. The routine triumphs as the overall organizational function loses out to the day-to-day service needs of "differentiation-oriented" subsystems personnel seeking to "gold-plate" work on their particular part of the program.

☐ Achievement of excellence in the integration function is a matter of major concern. In view of the natural antagonism of subsystems personnel to this function, the integration contractor (or his in-house counterpart) must possess an unusual set of technical and managerial qualifications. Because he is conducting a fairly delicate relationship with other organizations, he needs a high degree of initial "acceptability," that is, he must be technically a peer. In addition, he must have the ability to realize that full acceptance—the development of trust on the part of other organizations—can come about only as positive results are achieved while the parties work together for an extended period of time. A manager at a sponsor's headquarters program office noted: "At first there was opposition to [the integration contractor]. People at [our field] sites were reluctant to go along. But they 'fell to' as the fruits of [the contractor's] efforts became known. Things were being done. [The contractor] showed some success. It was like insurance."

□ The top manager who is keenly aware of the significance of proper conduct of this function for mission success might well disagree with statements comparing it to insurance. But this comment illustrates the point that true converts are less common than coattail-riders—and that the basis for cooperation with an effort of this type often is something less than a sense of the vital importance of the function in question.

Authority: Assigned or Earned?

□ The amount of authority officially accorded the integration contractor varies a great deal. Some "integrators" have been given the authority to *direct* subsystems personnel in other organizations and some have not; they can only "advise and counsel." However, the possession of authority or its lack does not seem to be crucial. Those with authority seem to behave much the same in this role as those without it. A member of an armed-service's systems-integration unit with real potential for the exercise of power remarked, "Most of our technical direction is done by persuasion." Clearly, this is a world in which authority is apt to take the form of subtle pressures and counterpressures. Systems integrators find that they must use a variety of approaches to elicit the cooperation of others and let them see the goals of the project as more important than parochial concerns.

□ In some cases a problem-solving approach may be appropriate. However, as we noted above, problem-solving assumes shared goals and evaluative criteria. When these assumptions are not met, the integration contractor must use other strategies. If differences in goals and criteria exist, the integrator may resort to persuasion, like the unit cited above. However, persuasion assumes that objectives are shared at some level. If this is not the case and disagreement over goals is the appropriate assumption, then bargaining is called for—and perhaps politicking which treats the arena of bargaining as a variable, with the weaker party moving to obtain allies to reinforce his position.[3]

A Grass-Roots View of the Integration Process

☐ We can see how problem-solving, persuasion, bargaining, and politicking are intermingled in the integration process by examining the steps by which the integration contractor carries out his assignment in the field.

Gaining Entree

☐ To gain entree to organizations involved in a technologically complex endeavor, there seems to be no substitute for basic technical ability. As we noted above, the integration contractor needs high professional standing in the eyes of cooperating subsystems personnel, which means that he has both technical competence and a comprehensive knowledge of the field. At the same time he must avoid the appearance of being a "know-it-all," for in many respects he is engaged in a diplomatic mission.

☐ However, the task requires more than the diplomatic expression of sound technical mastery. It also demands high-caliber organizational skills, much like those of the program or project manager. One integration specialist reported: "There are more constraints in this. In part it is a political world. You are in the middle between the sponsor and [its satellite organizations]. The pressures are terrific." Clearly, the systems-integration contractor can be neither passive nor timid. He must be sufficiently aggressive to crack the protective outer shells of other organizations to determine what their subsystems people are doing and what they need in order to meet systems-integration requirements.

☐ One might assume that the integrator's problem is largely one of extracting data from sometimes unwilling "sovereign" units, but the situation is more complicated than this. In some cases the data the integrator needs will not be available. Then he must have the ability to move into another organization and persuade its members to take on the additional task of generating the data in question—a task that may seem unnecessary to them. Almost inevitably, the potential collaborator raises the chilling question, "Who's going to pay for this?"

[3] See *ibid.*, pp. 129–130.

Maintaining a Foothold:
Sales and Service

☐ Obviously it is not sufficient to obtain only the consent of top management in cooperating organizations. The new procedure must be "sold" to all relevant levels of the R & D organization in charge of a given subsystem. Upon hearing the integrator's "sales pitch," one potential customer was said to have replied warily: "Great, but show me. What's its use? Who needs a data bank to debug a circuit? Why does everybody have to know my problems? The top men have been looking for an excuse to reorganize us. This will give them the opening."

☐ Thus, data tend to get bottled up. Those selling R & D software functions often face this type of problem. The customer is buying an intangible product but requires assurance that he is obtaining some definite commodity. Performing a service for him often is one of the few ways of accomplishing this.

☐ To obtain cooperation, the integrator needs a bank of good will to fall back on, and thus he must be flexible with regard to the question of "sweetening the bargain" by providing various services. And while some services may be performed strictly "as a favor," others may give the integrator access to information that he would not have otherwise.

☐ One contractor put it this way: "We tap data we cannot get any other way, for instance, by working on the 'breadboard' at Site A."[4] Identifying the need for, and then providing, this type of service function need not be inconsistent with a general policy placing a near-embargo on such activity. Performing services can be reserved for situations in which sharp differences in goals necessitate bargains of this type.

☐ However, controlling the scope of his function is a very important part of the integrator's role because, in this field of increasing pressures, the customer's desire for services is literally insatiable and quickly outruns the limits of his own budget. A man coming to "sell" integration procedures is apt to be told that the buyer has more immediate needs. The seller will be welcome if he first meets these. One middle manager at a sponsor's field center greeted a systems-integration contractor with open arms because he was desper-

---

[4] "Breadboard" is a term used in the field of electronics to describe a spread-out version of a circuit in which the components can be changed easily in order to achieve the desired final form.

ately seeking a correspondence monitor (someone who sees that all communications are routed to the proper individuals)!

☐ Integration contractors vary a great deal in the extent to which they are accommodating in this respect. As one contractor put it, "Some are easily pulled by the fingers of the organization." They soon become submerged in the service role; others are tough and flatly refuse it. The more realistic "play it by ear," recognizing that, say, 10 percent of their effort may have to assume this form but nevertheless taking care to avoid softness in the face of demands for service. However, in geographically far-flung relationships, controlling the extent of this activity becomes difficult; and even those with a "tough" policy find they have soft spots with burgeoning service work: "We have held the line pretty well everywhere except at Site X. Our man there seems to be looking toward a more permanent connection." Thus goals apart from the immediate task may influence the integration contractor's behavior. In some instances, budget cuts have been almost welcomed because they provided an excuse for saying "no" to demands for expansion of their services.

Identification of Interfaces:
The Heart of the Integration Process

☐ More than one manager noted that the identification of interfaces lay at the very heart of the integration process.[5] Interestingly, this activity must be pursued in depth in one respect and limited in another. The need for depth stems from the basic fact that the integrator is dealing with a dynamic situation. There is very little that he can take as given. For instance, he cannot assume that all interfaces have been properly identified. One manager remarked that he was haunted by "the interfaces I may have failed to think of."

☐ At every step the integration specialist encounters the oversights and failures of others. He hardly can avoid reacting in a critical fashion, but he must never be an obvious critic, putting people on the defensive and encouraging "cover-up" reactions. In essence, he asks, How can I help you? What do you need? He has to become involved with subsystems personnel, identifying problems for them and helping to develop solutions.

---

[5] An interface is defined as the common boundary between two bodies, or subsystems. However, not all these common boundaries are readily apparent. Proper identification takes time and energy and involves the ability to overcome technical "blind spots."

☐ The need for a limitation on his activities now becomes apparent. The integrator's on-site work should stop at this point. If he actually begins to solve the problem, he loses his only-weakly-established value as an independent force and becomes a subsystem functionary. He must move on to other parts of the system to look for significant points of interrelation. For instance, if he notes a particular problem at Site A, he asks, How does this problem relate to one at Site B?

"Penetration, not Confrontation"

☐ In many ways the good integrator is like a good journalist or social-science researcher. He learns about the total system and on a selective basis becomes involved in it. This type of "aggressive" behavior is essential in organizational situations involving many unknowns. As we noted above, the skillful integrator must have the ability to "penetrate" other organizations. At the same time he cannot rely on the "confrontation" techniques so popular in complex systems management because confrontation by its very nature assumes only small ideological differences among the participants. (With these techniques, collaborators, such as a sponsor and a contractor, meet to engage in blunt face-to-face discussion of their relationship.)

Making the Facts Speak for Themselves

☐ We have been stressing the active (organizational-penetration) phase of the integration manager's role, but he also has another, more subtle, and indirect approach that he uses to induce cooperation. After taking note of important but neglected parts of the system, he proceeds to heighten their visibility. "Visibility" is almost a magic word in the complex systems-management field. The coercion of life in a goldfish bowl is substituted for more direct sources of pressure. Thus, a man is forced to cope with an unresolved interface problem because information about his dilemma is recorded on a computer print-out and distributed throughout the entire program. Everyone knows about it. It is no longer his private affair.

☐ The devices used in this approach include computers, data banks, and all the wonders of the electronic age, as well as a rather simple, old-fashioned procedure with a coercive twist—the persistent publication of reports (to the sponsor) about a problem that the integration specialist perceives. Hopefully the "offending" party—often a major contractor—will take action rather than endure this kind of

bad publicity. One manager described this process as follows: "You have to do what a journalist does. You keep
publishing and publishing until they finally clean up the
streets."

☐ The need to resort to journalistic methods reflects a serious problem in this field. A contractor's failure to respond to
the integrator's suggestions regarding such things as design
may seem to be pure intransigence, but it often is the result
of honest disagreement regarding the need for changes. The
facts simply do not always speak for themselves. However,
these are not mere academic debates. Especially in the case
of "hardware" projects, there is an inescapable moment of
truth—when the craft becomes operational—that finally
settles the argument. In reality, there are two such moments.
An earlier one occurs when the major components are
mated to one another in the final stages of testing. If the
various systems do not mesh at this point, the heretofore
neglected task of integration will force itself upon the
parties. One systems integrator noted that in some projects
most integration work seemed to take place at this stage in
the game!

DISPLACEMENT OF THE INTEGRATION FUNCTION: WHAT DID WE FLY?

☐ Obviously, before the hardware can become operational,
all interfaces must be effectively identified. However, in the
absence of a deliberate integrative effort, this procedure
may occur only late in the game. For example, a particular
spacecraft had two electric-power systems, one primary and
the other secondary. Three separate organizations were
responsible for the design function, and each one concentrated on his specific task. Responsibility for the interface
(the switching mechanism), because it was viewed by all
three as "the other fellow's job," was not clear. The task was
not done well; but this deficiency only came to light at the
operational center when the systems were being installed in
the spacecraft. Then it became obvious that things simply
did not fit. Moreover, the moment of truth was fast approach-
ing. Under this pressure the whole team pitched in and
tackled the postponed problem of systems integration.

☐ Situations of this type cause integration-management
skills to show up in unexpected quarters. One would be
justified in assuming that managers at operational sites take
no part in integration work, but the reverse has proved to be
true. Because these problems are virtually dumped in their

laps, they acquire a high degree of skill and an uncanny ability to resolve technical incompatibilities via "work-around" methods.

□ Work-around methods are far from being mysterious; they represent a distillation of experience combined with ingenuity. Still, their mastery is vital to the advanced program's ability to continue operations. Work-around procedures permit a complex system to function despite the failure of a particular component. For instance, if Component A ceases to give a signal, technicians will quickly put a signal generator into use to replace A's signal output. Then, despite the presence of a bad part, the system as a whole will be "go," and testing can proceed.

□ None of this experience, of course, is recorded in manuals or coded in computer programs. The system does not recognize its existence, and thus it tends to rest in a managerial limbo—another example of how people compensate for a system's failures and also of how, by introducing the element of personal and privately held skill, they render a system "unsystematic" at a vital point.

□ One observer described this ad hoc integration process as follows:

Those people at the launch site think the hardware delivered there is their own. They've had success. They know how to do things, but they drive other people wild. They have mastered the technology, the skills associated with the launch operation, taking the hardware and making it work and launching it. Some pieces don't fit. These people develop "work around" methods. They have lived with these problems for a number of years, but there's no documentation—data and information are not cranked back into the system. They are ingenious and skillful, but there is no configuration control. *What did we fly?* [Italics ours] But a substantial portion, maybe one-third, of the people there are absolutely dedicated and the success of the program ultimately will depend on them.

□ If integration "simply happens," as in the case above, responsibility for failure rests with the sponsor and a prime contractor or a group of associated contractors. Unhappily, the firm that accepts the integration function takes over much of this awesome responsibility. Since a highly differentiated, technologically advanced large-scale endeavor actually is quite resistant to integrative procedures, it is little wonder that the integration contractor seeks insurance by using impersonal methods such as data banks—methods that are not so dependent for their success on his organizational skills and that spread the responsibility, Japanese fashion, among all participants in a project. He places reliance on the coercive power of selected bits of widely disseminated and (hopefully) accurate information. The contractor can then focus his attention on the proper functioning of the *system* rather than the ultimate success or failure of the program—on the *process* rather than the eventual *results.*

FACILITATING THE INTEGRATION PROCESS

Information: The Key to Integration

Communications Aids

□ Systems-integration managers attempt to facilitate the process primarily in two ways. As a first step, they attempt to speed communications by using telecon, vudex, and hardcopy transfer equipment to bring people separated spatially and organizationally into contact with those whom they potentially can hurt. Those using telecon conferences report that the method is effective. The widely dispersed individuals participating in these interchanges are led to say more than they may have intended, and thus problems are brought into the open. In essence, all these methods overcome some of the geographic and organizational barriers blocking the oft-praised person-to-person route for technical information transfer. They are an important part of the third element in one integration manager's favorite formula: discreteness, firmness, and *good communications.*

Computer Information Systems

□ The second step is to try to develop computer systems to provide program managers with the information they need to run their programs. The limitations of such information systems often have been noted—the quality of the computer's output is directly related to the quality and relevance of the input data. One integration contractor gloried in the precision represented by outputs calculated to twelve places, but potential users reported they had little or no need for the information in question. One manager noted:

You have to give the manager information he can use. In one chart room there are 50 charts on 50 subjects. I read them in 15 minutes, but there is no information on points I am curious about. There is no information dealing with my steady job. How well are my people performing? Can I change X's behavior? Here we have:

1. Schedule Progress

2. Number of Test Failures

3. Number of Modifications

4. Number of Unsatisfactory Conditions

But how do you make a safety program work?

□ Thus, frequently, the type of information that can be quantified and supplied to a manager is only remotely related to the kinds of considerations that actually guide his decisions. Computer data also can be deceiving. The machine demands figures, and that is what people feed it— even though the data supplied may be more opinion than fact. The computer magically blesses them, and soon they are on their way to becoming gospel.

□ The computer also has a certain symbolic value. It provides a sense of security, and its aura of authority can serve as a first line of defense against potential critics. However, if one wishes to move away from symbolic values and the processing of useless data, one must seek out original sources and engage in the kind of backbreaking organizational spadework that everyone secretly tries to avoid.

Making the Information System Operational

Maintaining the Integrity of the Data

□ Integration specialists have found that there are *two key points* in the successful operation of an information system. The *first* is the integrity of the data. One has to go as close to the original source as possible. The effects of "translation" can be horrendous. A manager commented:

We had data going through 4 to 12 hands. Each one adds his interpretation, and no one is responsible. You wouldn't believe the number of versions you can get of hard factual data. You may wind up with 4 to 12 descriptions of a problem and its solution. Which set of data is right?

□ In part, disagreement occurs because normally more than one set of readings is taken. One man accepts a certain part of the data. Another decides these particular readings are not reliable. Then there is the matter of interpretation. One man examines some material and sees a significant reaction; another looks at the same material and reports a slight reaction. One concludes that there is a flaw in a piece of equipment; another feels that the equipment is working reasonably well. These "filters" are not dishonest men. In most cases they simply see the matter in question from their own specialty's point of view.

☐ Somehow, one has to move behind these filters. Going to the ultimate source is a major strategy in developing a *single* reliable information system as a base for effective systems integration.

Motivating Follow-Through

☐ A *second* and related point involves motivation of the people at the source. These are the members of the integration staff who uncover a problem and document its "unfiltered" state. The staff specialist who is working to eliminate filters must not act as one himself: "We encourage them to put down anything they think may be a problem, even if it's only a subject heading. We say, 'Don't wait for complete data.' " Since the ultimate goal is a successful mission, mere detection of problems is not enough. There must be sufficient motivation to follow through until a solution is reached, and this is no simple matter. In some cases, incentive to persist is provided by giving the man visibility: "His name is put on the material, and it is looked at by all levels of management."

Smoothing the Process of Change

☐ It has been noted many times that change is a way of life in advanced technologies, but people working in these fields actually have no more toleration of certain kinds of change than the classic blue-collar factory worker. Both become extremely upset when their work routines are overturned. One integration manager remarked:

I didn't expect it here. Change is what our business is all about. But people resist change. I didn't realize how much. They hate to adopt something new. An engineer who is designing a revolutionary process will react that way. He likes to see *other people* make changes.

Thus, even with the "now or never" time pressures introduced by an important mission's schedule, the systems "doctor" finds that he has to follow conservative procedures. He cannot use the "emergency" argument as a device for continually pushing changes. As one man noted:

Actually, the basic concept hasn't changed, we've stuck to that. We made one major design change and that was it. This is one place where we've made friends. At the operational sites many wanted all sorts of changes, but we said, "Hold to the system of Craft A; then make a block change." Constant change appeals to technicians and computer specialists, but if you want people to accept something, you can't give a new set of instructions every week.

Dealing with Zero Visibility

□ The problems encountered in introducing changes are not surprising; in fact, one's main reaction might be disappointment that such awe-inspiring enterprises suffer the same organizational ills as more mundane businesses. More surprising is the fact that achieving visibility for vital information is not just a matter of teasing it from hidden nooks and crannies. Organizations vary in their degree of stability, but all seem to have real breaking points. Pushing too hard, even for significant data, may entail more cost in terms of induced instability than the structure can withstand. The tremors generated may bring the organization down once and for all. So, like the ingenious operational-site craftsmen that he wants so badly to reform, the integration specialist must develop work-around procedures and skills:

Sometimes we feel we can't bear it, but we don't try to fight the system. We work with the system. If you can't get data, you work around them. Some data people refuse aren't essential. If you really feel you have to have them, you might try going to higher-ups—see if that will work, but you have to be careful. If you do much of that, it can kill you dead.

□ The problem of zero visibility raises interesting questions regarding the matter of *responsibility* for success or failure of the mission in question. Is the sponsor responsible if defects in his organization close windows to the integration contractor? Or is part of the contracted-for skill a toughness and ingenuity that will be able to overcome organizational roadblocks in any and all forms? Obviously, the contractor favors a positive answer to the first question, and the sponsor, to the second. But in the final analysis zero visibility is a problem that must be treated with organizational, rather than guilt-assigning, legalistic remedies.

CONCLUSION

□ Systems integration is a core function of the organization engaged in developing advanced technologies. Popular texts on project management generally maintain that processes such as systems integration should be planned well in advance; that they should be initiated at the very beginning of a program; and that they should be strategically located (e.g., in the program manager's office) where they will have appropriate visibility and where they will constitute a major activity. One cannot argue with these points, but they seem to be irrelevant in terms of many of the phenomena observed in our field research.

□ This research certainly shows that the systems integrator's life is not an easy one. The road is rough because organizations are not designed for the primary purpose of smoothing the way for this function. In fact, sometimes the reverse seems closer to the truth. Moreover, people with limited time and budgets will continue to push activities connected with tasks of this type to the side under the pressure of more immediate problems.

□ The chief satisfactions of his job are the challenge it provides and the unparalleled opportunity it gives him to learn about organizations and systems. But few systems integrators are able to bask in glory, and few sponsors hold celebrations in their honor. In fact, the very nature of the relationship tends to produce at least a slight souring and disillusionment as time goes on. As one integration specialist remarked, "The chances of recognition and success are remote. We won't come out heroes."

□ But while organizations may not facilitate the integration process, their internal structural defects should not serve to put roadblocks in its path. Integration procedures contain sufficient problems of their own and cannot easily bear the added burden of having to deal with matters that the sponsor has been either burying or ignoring.

□ To prepare itself for effective systems integration, the technologically advanced endeavor must seek ways to "surface" and confront problems of this type. Overemphasis on "peace at all costs" and not disturbing the status quo may only serve to perpetuate conditions designed to defeat the integration process. Of course, on the positive side, we have seen that such problems can be solved by the ingenious use of effective work-around procedures designed to circumvent the trouble spots. Our study of systems-integration programs underlines the observation of one informant, very experienced in this field: "You can never proceed on the assumption that you are moving into a completely rational situation, or anything approximating it."

□ There is a need for better understanding of the organizational implications of the integration process. Little consideration has been given to the impact of the integration process on the complex endeavor. Our observations seem to indicate that integration may serve as a kind of organizational insulator that causes a program to lose its susceptibility to external initiatives. The integrated system loses flexibility—much as the craft union whose members bargain internally to reach agreement about a given contract demand loses the ability to bargain with management. Having made its decision, the union will not budge. It tells management, "Take it or leave it. We've already bargained among ourselves."[6]

□ Interestingly enough, in the same manner systems-integration processes may serve to freeze a program into a given technical position. How then does one introduce needed changes? A fairly drastic step, such as reorganization, may be required to unlock the frozen positions. This may suggest in some cases a crucial role for the top administrator or some powerful external executive who must intervene to fulfill this function.

□ Finally, it should be noted that integration management is not a phenomenon unique to advanced technologies. It is part of the larger problem of exerting control and influence at a distance and without authority. Such problems are becoming increasingly typical of the modern social world, in which a high degree of interdependence is combined with demands for autonomy and organizational and professional freedom. Tasks analogous to the systems integration of advanced technologies are faced by a diverse group of enterprises, including the health and criminal-justice systems of any urban community.

[6] Margaret K. Chandler, "Craft Bargaining," in John T. Dunlop and Neil W. Chamberlain, eds., *Frontiers of Collective Bargaining,* New York, Harper & Row, 1967, p. 54.

TECHNICAL GOALS VS. BUSINESS REQUIREMENTS

THIRTEEN

We commonly recognize that stringent technical requirements in fields such as space and atomic energy have a potent influence on the management effort of all contributors to an advanced-technology program.[1] But there is another, equally potent factor, namely, the sponsor's way of doing business. It is a test of the contractor's managerial skills when, as often happens, these two major sources of influence exert conflicting pressures on the organization, pulling it simultaneously in opposite and inconsistent directions.

□ *Technical goals* are achieved via an "unprogrammed" process. Alternatives are left open, problems are unpredictable, and coordination takes place through feedback. *Business-system goals,* on the other hand, are achieved via a programmed process. Alternatives are closed, problems are predictable, and coordination is achieved by advance planning. Technical problems introduce a steady flow of changes and uncertainty, and thus they might be considered a "radical" or an unsettling force. On the other hand, the transactional bond tends to be a "conservative" force, requiring commitments, the spelling out of rights and responsibilities.

□ For the advanced-technology program, then, the business system represents an integrative process, while the technical system stresses differentiation. As we have noted elsewhere, integration and differentiation are interdependent processes.[2] The potential for performing one of these functions excellently is affected by the manner in which the other is conducted. Unrestrained pursuit of technical goals means sacrificing certain business-system goals. If the business system is treated as though it were a mere nuisance, tacked on to the end of a technically oriented program, it can become defensive and possibly even destructive. For these reasons the business and technical sides of an advanced-technology program need to be established as complementary halves of an oscillating system, in which each one is continuously taking the other into account.

[1] This analysis focuses on the sponsor-industrial-contractor relationship, but the findings are applicable to other situations involving technical and business systems goals. e.g., sponsor-university and contractor-contractor relationships.

[2] See Chapter 12.

□ The oscillations can be amplified or attentuated by the relationship between the business and technical systems. Much depends on the process of measurement. If the achievements of an advanced-technology program are measured, or judged, say, in terms of business-system excellence one month and in terms of technical excellence the next month, the detrimental oscillations will naturally be greater. On the other hand, if those making measurements and judgments are obliged to take the objectives of both these systems into account almost simultaneously—to consider multiple goals and trade-offs—then the oscillations, while still present, will be reduced to a tolerable level. In the upper portion of Figure 1 (Case 1), we see the adverse effect of violent swings in emphasis on business and technical goals; in the lower portion (Case 2), the business and technical goals almost balance one another, with consequently a much smaller impact.

□ However, in the real world this ideal balance is not always achieved. Relationships among participants in an advanced-technology program may very well founder when their treatment of one system creates problems for the other. It is very tempting to take an extreme position when conflict arises in a situation of this sort. There seem to be two basic reactions: Some style it a contest between two domains—business versus technology and science—and hold that all virtue lies with whichever side they favor; others naively deny the existence of a problem. Good management is good management, they insist, and if a program or project is properly managed, conflict between these two approaches will not occur.

□ From an analytical standpoint, another serious failing has been the tendency of those reporting on the business area to treat it normatively—to view contractual relations between the sponsor and the contractor in terms of "black" and "white," with "collusion" wearing the somber tones and competition clad in lily-white.

□ Both outsiders and insiders tend to concentrate on the *beginning* of a relationship (contract awards) and the *ending* (contract cancellations, lawsuits, Congressional hearings, etc.) and neglect the midsection. In part, this neglect may reflect the parties' own great uncertainty about control of this crucial part of the relationship, an attitude that is summed up in such plaintive words as, "We feel our way with our hands, day by day, hoping for the best."

□ In this chapter we turn our attention to the significance for program and project functioning of the coexistence of

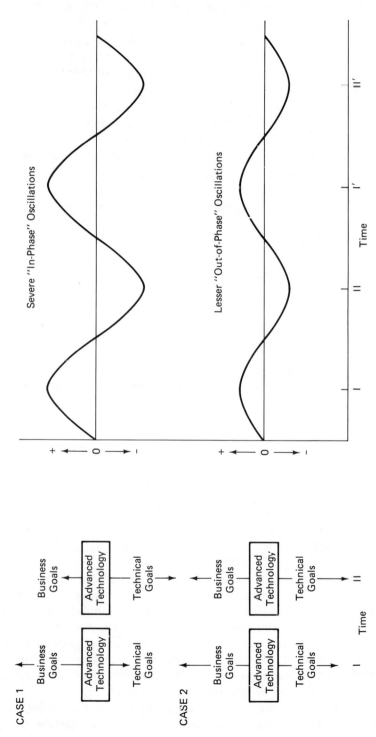

Figure 1. The adverse impact of conflicting business and technical goals on an advanced-technology program.

these two points of view, technical and business, both of which represent basic needs of the sponsor and its key collaborators. First we will look at patterns of interaction that affect the nature of relationships between the business and technical functions: the impact of initial negotiations, and the relationship between contracts and technical personnel. Then we will turn to the organizational effects of specific types of contracts, considering first their impact on dealings between the sponsor and contractor. Finally, we will examine problems in two key areas in which the business and technical forces frequently test one another out: the administration of incentive contracts and engineering-design changes.

□ It should be stressed that the technical and business points of view represent separate, but not completely divergent, interests. The technological side has its own accounting requirements concerning matters such as the mating of subsystems and the tracing of problems through an entire system (reporting and analyzing failures). Moreover, both groups are vitally interested in the management of problem areas such as engineering changes, but they do not share the same goals. One wants to control changes with the objective of successful technical performance; the other with the objective of successful fiscal management. This observation underlines the fact that we are not dealing with the familiar conflict between freedom and control. Both sides agree on the need for control systems and do in fact employ them. They differ in the nature of their objectives.

□ It should be noted, parenthetically, that not all the organizational instability coming from the business side is the result of problems within the sponsor's house. The apparently erratic approach of some sponsors to business is due, at least in part, to factors in the "environment." Government sponsors using public funds are especially vulnerable on this score: A program that has been under way for a year or so may be suddenly cut back if legislators decide that other national interests should be given priority.

□ A manager at a contractor-operated NASA facility noted that he had devoted the last five years to four projects, all of which had been cancelled. He laughingly described himself as "an expert at getting projects under way; not finishing them."

□ The vice-president of a medium-sized aerospace company remarked that during the course of one space project there were three design changes caused by unanticipated technical problems. These technically caused delays were aggravated by the fact that the space agency was in financial trouble because of budget cuts. Each time it asked the contractor to lay off project personnel. As a result the continuity of work in the contractor's part of the project was completely disrupted:

Half the time we were getting people off and the other half the time getting them on. When we needed people, they were no longer around. We wound up with inexperienced people, so many of the mistakes we made were ones we'd made before.

☐ Such comments reflect the existence of major sources of instability that cannot be corrected by better internal management of the business-technical interface. Problems of this kind require the top administrators to use their political skills to create greater support among crucial elements in society. There is no question that in periods when this support is forthcoming internal friction in the business-technical interface is considerably diminished.

THE BUSINESS-TECHNICAL INTERFACE:
PATTERNS OF INTERACTION

Setting the Stage for Future Conflict

☐ Generally speaking, the representatives of sponsors and contractors engaged in negotiating contracts are not greatly concerned with the building of relationships of trust and ensuring effective teamwork. This is not their problem, and that shoe is not yet hurting.

☐ For instance, a sponsor may be absorbed initially with stimulating competition in order to produce the lowest possible bid. In one case an aerospace firm believed that it had gotten a particular job. But although the contract had been signed and returned to the sponsor, the company lost out at the last minute in the course of the informal "reopening process" described below:

On Project X, the sponsor's people had Company A and Company B fighting tooth and nail. "A" signed and returned the contract, but it was awarded to "B." The sponsor played it down to the wire. He had "B" bid against the contract already signed by "A" and then awarded it to "B" as the lowest bidder!

☐ This action pleased neither A nor B. B, which was to undertake the assignment, felt pushed to the wall. Meanwhile A, although it was now eliminated from Project X, had other work with this same sponsor; but feeling "burned" by this experience, it was less inclined to be responsive to the sponsor's needs.

☐ In these initial dealings, the sponsor and contractor seem to be concerned primarily with driving a hard bargain from their respective parochial points of view. Each asks questions like these: (1) Is there an "out" in case we are unable to keep our part of the agreement? (2) Is it clear that the other side is to assume full responsibility for failure to perform satisfactorily? (3) Is the timing of the actual payment of funds to the other party favorable to our budgetary position? (4) Do we have final rights to everything they produce?

☐ In sum, *the formulation of the transactional bond—the legal, contractual definition of the relationship—places the parties in basically conflicting positions.* The legalistically formulated contractual bond that officially initiated the relationship can thrust itself upon the parties throughout its duration. This does not mean that conflict is inevitable; but "just in case," both sides are stocked with liberal amounts of ammunition.[3]

☐ There may also be a basic incongruity between the procedures involved in establishing the contractual bond and the organizational requirements of the technical work of the system. When technical emergencies create time pressures, a severe conflict may develop. In one hardware-based crisis a sponsor engaged a competent, well-respected contractor to undertake an urgent, as well as highly innovative, systems-integration-and-evaluation assignment. The task was a mammoth one: It involved an exceptionally large program, and it also had a fairly short "time fuse"—about one year. Initial efforts were begun on the basis of a letter of understanding; and thereafter, the official procurement process commenced. The harried contractor then found that he would have to tie up a substantial number of his people for eight months, trying to fulfill contractual requirements by *spelling out in advance, step by step,* exactly what this innovative crash program was to involve!

☐ There also can be excesses at the other extreme: sponsors who contribute to later technical crises by initially avoiding almost all contractual constraints and thereby appearing to be highly permissive. From the standpoint of the contractor, it may seem that this can only be desirable: the more flexibility, the better. But appearances can be deceiving.

☐ For instance, one sponsor simply delayed the formulation of a design specification for a major piece of hardware. The contractor, perhaps a bit naively, interpreted this delay as giving it "carte blanche" in carrying out the work in question. He discovered to his dismay, however, that the absence

---

[3] A perfect example is the case of Systems Engineering, Inc., discussed in Chapter 4.

of a design specification can be a proverbial Trojan horse. Specifications serve to bound and control the actions of both contractor *and* sponsor. Without this restriction, the sponsor was able to become deeply involved in every aspect of design and development. Thus, the apparent "carte blanche" was in reality a plan for meticulous monitoring.

☐ However, the contractor eventually gained something from the arrangement, for the long delay in writing up specifications gave him an unexpected source of bargaining power. By postponing action, the sponsor was able to exercise detailed control; but on the other hand, because specifications were being written at a late stage in the project, the contractor was able to be quite stubborn about their content. The sponsor had participated so fully in the design and development of the initially vaguely designated "end item" that he was equally responsible for the existing situation and hard-pressed to get the hardware he actually wanted. Moreover, he could not resort to his usual source of leverage, threatening to cancel the contract. After all, the contractor had been working for several years, and the sponsor was totally unable to develop an alternative program that could catch up in time to meet the mission's schedule.

☐ A sponsor's top manager described the total process as follows:

You know how this business is. You start with science and engineering, but a project, once it's decided on, has to be costed. You have to select contractors, get budgets approved, and get Congressional approval of funds. Then you turn to the companies working with you and write contracts that explicitly say you don't trust one another. What started out as a fine scientific dream becomes a mass of slippery eels.

The Relationship Between Business (Contracts)
and Technical Personnel

☐ Why does legalistic bickering continue to be a major component of interorganizational relations in advanced technological systems, a field in which such activity can be maximally harmful? Of course, there is no one simple reason for the perpetuation of problems of this type. One might surmise that this situation has arisen because "business types" play a dominant role in organizations in this field. However, the reverse actually is true, and this may be one of the sources of the problem.

☐ In complex technological systems, the sequencing of the decision process is such that administrators, scientists, and engineers make the essential decisions. The "business types," officials who are variously entitled "director of contracts," "director of material," or "contracts manager," are brought in to draw up contracts *after* this key point. Generally speaking, then, they are not the basic decision-makers. Moreover, business (contracts) people rarely advance to general-management positions in organizations devoted to advanced technological systems. The science and engineering emphasis works against them. Thus these men come to feel that the "administrative and scientific types" look down on them and that the total organization is not aware of the importance of their function.

□ It has been far from simple for the contracts men to shift their time of entry into negotiations to an earlier point, more favorable for developing an integrated technical-business system for a given project. Other managers may ignore rules stating that contracts personnel shall be included in initial discussions. This oversight is often difficult to challenge, especially when top administrators make the basic business agreement. As a result, some of those on the business side feel that they could gain recognition as an independent, co-equal force more easily if they were organizationally set apart from their technical brethren, even to the extent of being the equivalent of an outside contractor. As one of them put it: "If you're in the same organization with the technical people, they often place you in an inferior position."

□ When the contracts group is somehow external to the project organization—as it is in some international projects—it seems to be easier for these men to become an integral part of the negotiating group. Under these circumstances their status acquires a valuable ambiguity. In one instance the stage was well set from the standpoint of the business side:

The project asked us to do their contracting, so we told them what our work procedures were and that they'd have to abide by our rules. The fact that we were outside the project gave us strength. We said to them, "It's our rule that we sit in on initial negotiations," and they accepted that. Then, too, as outsiders we could insist on dealing only with the top man, the project director. It's all too easy for those below him to take our procedures and turn them around.

□ Pressures from outside sources also were used by contracts managers to overcome the resistance of technical personnel to procedures needed to keep track of changes in the specifications of a contracted-for item. In one aerospace company, the contracts officers were absolutely unable to get their more powerful technical staff to adopt the sponsor's "configuration-management" procedures, despite several embarrassing incidents resulting from the technical personnel's failure to notify collaborating firms of important changes. Therefore, the frustrated contracts men reacted with delight rather than indignation when an angry manager from one of the collaborating firms wrote a letter to the sponsor complaining that the delinquent company had failed to provide notification of changes it had made in the second stage of its rocket. (The complainant was responsible for the satellite sitting on top of this rocket!) The contracts section then proceeded to publicize the criticism in order to pressure the technical people to adopt systematic procedures.

□ The contracts officials' sense of low status and their limited hope for general advancement lead them to seek satisfaction by enlarging their own function, making it increasingly elaborate and, hopefully, increasingly impressive. Conscious of their lesser standing in the organization, they also are inclined to make every effort to cover themselves by creating highly involved legalistic frameworks designed to cover all eventualities.

□ Of course, contracts officials do not pursue their activities in a vacuum. "Administrative types," sensing some strategic value in all this legalistic paraphernalia, may on occasion even encourage it. In any event, an effort of this sort, once under way, becomes self-perpetuating. The business system is used because *it provides a common language for communications across enterprise boundaries,* and a contracts manager may find himself providing a convenient battlefield for those faced with technical disaster. When uncertainties and frustrations caused by technical difficulties begin to "unhinge" a relationship, the parties often turn to the language of the business system to justify their differences, as well as to fix blame and assign responsibility. As a result, the transactional side, in the form of conflict over change orders, battles over fees, and disagreements about incentive payments can dominate the relationship and set the entire tone. As the inevitable body of cases begins to accumulate, these then serve as precedents for future action, and the wheel is set in motion.

□ Top managers in the sponsor's house may find that activities associated with contract administration, such as the performance-review meetings, provide them with a means for opening a window on operations in their contractors' establishments. For the high-level administrator, business procedures can become a vehicle for achieving the system-wide visibility he needs. Especially in a country such as the United States, in which each company's private domain has traditionally been sacred territory, formal monitoring tools of this type assume great importance.

☐ Because it comes to serve a variety of unintended functions, the lower-status, static, predictable, but control-oriented business system may actually dominate the higher-status, dynamic, but less predictable technical elements. In commenting about his relationship with the sponsor, one contractor's technical vice-president noted, "Whenever a question arises, 'reread your contract' becomes a favorite response."

THE TYPE OF CONTRACT:
ITS EFFECT ON SPONSOR-CONTRACTOR RELATIONSHIPS

☐ To explore further the relationship between the business and technical sides of the advanced-technology endeavor, we shall look at the way in which basic contracts policies shape the relationship between sponsor and contractor. We shall then turn to the effects of specific business-system procedures on the sponsor's management of relations with contractors.

☐ Debate about the relative merits of various types of contracts frequently focuses on matters of principle and ignores the technological and organizational factors that may eventually cause a particular type to contribute to either project success or failure.

Incentive Contracts

☐ A case in point is the use of incentive contracts (cost-plus-incentive-fee) for R & D work.[4] To "energize" contractor performance, sponsors in the United States have become almost totally committed to the use of incentive systems. Incentive contracts are not harmful per se, but their effectiveness as an organizational-control device can be hampered by the tendency for business-system decision-

[4] The cost-plus-incentive-fee contract establishes target cost, schedule, and performance objectives. If the contractor fails to meet these, he is penalized; and conversely, he is rewarded for satisfying these criteria. Generally some upper percentage limit for earnings is set so that, say, in a given project, a contractor may be able to earn as much as $15 million in incentive fees. For relatively poor performance he may receive only $1 million.

makers to overlook the technical and managerial needs of a given program. Under pressure to improve cost estimation, a sponsor may adopt a policy dictating a substantial increase in the use of incentive contracts. Often a quota figure is set, say, 90 percent; and as a result almost all new contracts may take this form, whether or not it is actually appropriate in a particular case.

□ For instance, work that is pushing the state of the art, that involves many uncertainties, resists attempts to force it into the incentive mold. To set up relevant criteria, one has to be able to specify in detail precisely what is expected. Inevitably, for this kind of work, the incentive system is a superstructure built on a highly uncertain foundation. In addition, there is a real danger of a premature freezing of technical objectives, with only minimal evaluation of the potential alternatives. To fit contractual requirements, badly needed research may be sidestepped in favor of lesser efforts, more accurately described as design studies.

□ Moreover, incentive contracts may not "free up" the time of the manager in the sponsoring organization as fully as a cursory examination of these devices might seem to indicate. Rather, a major part of his effort is simply refocused on the early stages of the relationship, for these contracts require much definition of task and long, detailed negotiations.

Incentive vs. Cost-Plus-Fixed-Fee Contracts

□ Incentive contracts (CPIF) appeal to the sponsor because they are supposed to transfer to the contractor a greater share of the risk. By way of contrast, with *cost-plus-fixed-fee* (CPFF) arrangements, the sponsor is the big risk-taker, and he quite naturally then plays an active role in basic project decisions.[5] He may also protect his interests by close surveillance and monitoring of the contractor's operations. Some sponsors find it difficult to adapt to the less active style of administration that is appropriate for CPIF contracts. Those who have shifted from CPFF to incentive systems are especially apt to administer these as though they were still working under a CPFF arrangement. One contractor noted:

---

[5] Under cost-plus-fixed-fee contracts, the sponsor reimburses the contractor for his expenses and in addition provides a "profit" in the form of a negotiated percentage of the costs. The size of the fee is generally controlled by establishing an upper limit, such as 15 percent.

"There are so many of them and they are very keen on monitoring us. We say incentive or fixed price contracts are all right, but not if they examine us in detail because then our costs are bound to go up."

☐ In return for taking a greater share of the risk, the contractor wants a greater voice in the determination of project strategies concerning alternatives and trade-offs, and the sponsor often finds this difficult to accept.

Fixed-Price Contracts

☐ In contrast to some of the rather involved incentive structures, *fixed-price* contracts appear on the surface to be delightfully simple.[6] In a world replete with unknowns, these contracts specify a task to be performed for a definite, committed quantity of money. From the sponsoring organization's standpoint, it seems to settle the matter of expense once and for all. The contractor has agreed to receive a certain amount, and he is required to deliver at that figure.

☐ But the "hangup" comes in setting the proper price and remaining satisfied with the decision—a difficult task, given the uncertainties of advanced technologies. Agreement on an overly high figure defeats the whole purpose of a "fixed price," which is to hold down costs. Even if the figure set is "realistic," what can be done if the contractor apparently is efficient and turns out a good product, on schedule, for quite a bit less than the agreed-on figure? Should the sponsor then have cause to feel that he has overpaid and demand a return of some of the money?

☐ In the case of the British Bloodhound ground-to-air missile, for example, Ferranti produced a superb product, delivered it on time, and made an 82-percent profit to boot. However, this sizable profit proved to be the contractor's undoing. It became a national scandal, the subject of parliamentary investigations, and curdled this company's relationship with its most important customer. Previously, this same company had designed and developed the guidance-control system on Bloodhound I at a cost twenty times the original estimate. No unfavorable reaction ensued, although the decision to resort to a fixed-price contract was the result of this experience.

[6] With a fixed-price contract the contractor is reimbursed for the costs he specifies in his bid and is guaranteed a certain profit. In theory the contractor is stimulated to hold down costs because he can retain all his cost savings.

☐ Obviously the officials involved had not done a very good job of estimating; but the uncertain, open-ended nature of these technologies makes such a task rather difficult. It also seems that one side had considerably better information than the other. Because estimating is extremely time consuming, no price was fixed when the contract was first awarded; it was to be determined later by agreement. By that time, of course, the company had a fairly clear notion of what its actual costs would be! Thus the delay finally worked to the benefit of the contractor. The affair ended when the company finally settled on a 22-percent profit and returned the remainder of the money.[7]

☐ Ironically, the moral seems to be that if the firm's costs had equalled the agreed-on figure, there would have been no scandal. Going under, or over, the estimate creates problems; the bargain seems to require the contractor to defy the inherent nature of R & D work and give priority to sticking close to the amount specified in the contract.[8]

☐ It is clear that each type of contract described above produces its own characteristic style of sponsor-contractor relationship. Critics of the *"cost-plus"* system denounce it as "nothing more than a license to steal" and claim that it "leaves the sponsor with most of the risk as well as the major problem of controlling to insure that the contractor is performing in accord with the agreement." This contracting system establishes the traditional roles of *manager* and *managed.* No one pretends that it is easy to administer successfully. As one manager noted ruefully: "It is not hard to identify the beginning and end phases of our jobs at a contractor's shop, but it is very difficult to tell exactly where he is between times."

☐ Still, project officers in British government establishments, as well as others who have dealt with this system for

[7] J. F. Flower, "The Case of the Profitable Bloodhound," *Journal of Accounting Research,* vol. 4, no. 1, 1966, pp. 16–36.

[8] In the late 1960s the sponsoring agency's practice of recouping so-called excess profits was challenged by Grumman Aircraft, among others. Generally speaking, most companies "pay up" when the U.S. Renegotiation Board demands a "refund" of what it declares excessive gains, in part because the board also serves the reverse function of compensating firms for excessive losses. The board has not been obliged to substantiate its cases, although firms have argued that greater efficiency entitles them to higher profits. This viewpoint is represented in the Grumman action, which requests proof of the government's claim in the form of actual contrasts with other companies' data. (*Business Week,* March 21, 1970, p. 32.)

a number of years, do acquire contractor-monitoring skills that serve to make the cost-plus system quite workable.

☐ *Incentive and fixed-price systems* result in a more egalitarian relationship between contractor and sponsor. Because the contractor assumes greater risk and responsibility, one finds not manager and managed but two more nearly independent groups discussing what increasingly are seen as their "rights" and "interests." The issues debated and the manner of debate have much of the flavor of labor-management negotiations. In the case of incentive systems, the sponsor's actions tend to be judged solely on the basis of whether they hurt the contractor's chances of earning a larger incentive award. To reinforce a point about unfair treatment, a contractor may employ a slowdown tactic. On the other hand, the sponsor's representatives have been known to take a "You win, I lose" attitude toward the awarding of incentive fees. Contracts officials at one of a given sponsor's technically excellent R & D centers were "famous" for their long, legalistic battles with contractors over incentive payments.

☐ Clearly, the sponsor's managerial task varies considerably according to the system of contracting employed. Thus, changing one's system of contracting also involves a change in administrative approach. Incentive contracts cannot be handled in the same way as cost-plus contracts. But unfortunately, even with the best design, there is no easy way out. As an administrator in one sponsor's shop pointed out, there are no self-operating systems: "It is just a matter of where you want to apply your effort." In the final analysis it is most important to have achieved the proper match between the requirements of the system for contracting and the requirements of the technology in question.

ADMINISTERING INCENTIVE CONTRACTS AND ENGINEERING-DESIGN CHANGES

Evaluating Performance in Incentive Contracts

☐ Both business and technical managers in advanced-technology projects often spend as much time on one administrative area—incentive programs and awards—as on all others combined. This particular business-system contribution has a major effect on project management. The project manager sets performance standards, and especially in the United States this almost always implies a system of rewards for achieving them.

□ But do these rewards lead to the behavior desired? Business criteria, which set the rewards in the incentive system, tend to favor the risk-avoiding moderate, the man who is expert at holding to projected costs and schedules and who does not invest too much of himself in the enterprise. One might cynically add that business criteria also favor the man who saves his innovations and breakthroughs for noncontract work in order to have a clear title to a patent. The manager of a project universally regarded as one of the most successful cited "holding to original project objectives" as the key to his group's attainments. The unintended result of some incentive systems is the emergence of a new set of ground rules:

1. Be conservative.

2. Hew to your original plans.

3. Work only with known and tested systems.

4. Make few changes.

5. Save your sudden insights for the next project.

□ The uncertainties and lack of clear definition that plague the technical system also affect the process of evaluation that is part of every incentive contract. What finally constitutes good performance? If a contractor is hired to develop, say, a spacecraft capable of carrying out a certain mission, then the vehicle he produces obviously must be adequate to this task. But the sponsor may feel he is entitled to more than the bare minimum. Is actual completion of the mission sufficient, or does the sponsor have the right to demand that it be flawless?

□ In some cases spacecraft that functioned well enough to accomplish their mission did have some kind of operational difficulties (such as boom oscillations and the need for non-automatic operation of attitude-control systems). In one instance, members of the sponsor's establishment argued that because of such defects, the contractor should receive no incentive award. The contractor replied that this judgment was unjust. He felt that he was entitled to an award because despite the imperfections, the spacecraft in question produced more data than all the previous satellites combined! The contractor finally won his case, but the intervention of a high-level administrator in the sponsor's house was required.

☐ Some managers complain that in development efforts judgments are continually being fed into the evaluative system that represent assessments *after the fact,* rather than unequivocal assertions that specifications originally set forth have or have not been met. To put an end to the process of ex-post-facto shopping for criteria that affect incentive payments, the sponsor and contractor are obliged to settle on certain standards in advance. Such standards often are derived from the primary mission objectives. For instance, the contractor for the Lunar Orbiter received monetary rewards on the basis of the quality of the pictures returned to earth. The contractor for the Orbiting Geophysical Observatory (OGO) was given incentive payments based on the number of hours the satellite was in orbit. Secondary mission objectives—keeping to the schedule, controlling the weight, spacecraft's maintaining magnetic purity—are also used as the basis of awards.

☐ It is well known that incentives serve to distort behavior, and R & D contractors provide no exception to this rule. After examining the incentive system, the contractor often "clobbers his customer" with the most highly rewarded behavior. It also is well known that over time most incentives lose their potency and can cause the relationship to deteriorate. However, the parties tend to develop a dependency on the incentive approach to management, and when simple and easily measurable incentives have apparently failed, they may react by replacing them with impressive and complex three-dimensional systems designed to assess "total performance" at any given point in time, such as the *cost-plus-planned-interdependency method.* Such methods are supposed to permit real-time decision-making, but at least one contractor complained that: "If we want to make a decision with regard to our contract, we must run the computer to find where we are on this three dimensional surface. There is no question [that] it holds up decision-making, sometimes as much as two weeks."

☐ It seems clear that the development of perfect real-time incentive systems is highly improbable. The very nature of R & D work merely compounds the problems already encountered in incentivized routine production jobs, such as those found in steel mills and rubber tire plants.

☐ Apparently it is possible to operate acceptable advanced technological programs without the use of formally administered incentive awards. The British and Japanese have been much less enthusiastic about such devices. Instead, they have favored negative incentives—penalties for not meeting commitments! A famous Japanese project manager re-marked: "It is the Japanese idea you should hurry up and do something anyway. The worst danger is falling behind. Customers penalize you for that."

□ Traditionally, the Japanese culture has rejected U.S.-style incentive systems as an insult to the company, implying that excellent performance can be elicited only through the payment of money. Top-quality work is regarded as a matter of organizational pride. Recognition is gained via the award of a contract, the very fact of selection as a member of the sponsor's family of satellite companies. Those who are excluded frequently are very jealous of those who "made the grade." Strictly speaking, then, the Japanese do employ incentives of a less obvious, but nonetheless effective, form. Administrative problems encountered in the case of direct incentives may force a search for more indirect approaches in countries such as the United States.

Managing Engineering-Design Changes

Changes: The When and Why of Control

□ We have noted that in technologically advanced projects business and technical requirements converge on and clash over the management of engineering-design changes. How can one achieve an effective balance between the basic organizational needs these two points of view represent? This is the problem that absorbs management after the contracts have been handed out and the program is under way.

□ A continual flow of changes is endemic to complex technological systems, in part to accommodate fundamental improvements which become necessary as design and testing progress. If there were no money involved—and no schedules—there would be no problem; but virtually all changes take time and increase costs. Of course, in the case of small programs operating on a shoestring budget, the sponsor may declare that he has no funds for technical changes no matter how desirable they might be. (Although estimates vary, some credit the Japanese with having spent only $38 million for a ten-year space effort which culminated in a successful satellite launching in February, 1970.) A contractor working on a small program explained the situation with regard to changes:

Our customer is very hesitant to ask for a change. He has to request additional budget, and he hardly ever wants to do that. We keep to the original agreement. Industry people must compromise. You cannot oppose a government official. If you once best him, he will put your future requests at the bottom of his drawer.

☐ If such a contractor can manage a change within the limits of his own budget, he is welcome to make it, but the system gives him little encouragement to press for changes with budgetary implications. However, the matter is not as serious as one might imagine. Small programs typically are applications-oriented, working with previously developed systems, and therefore changes are not as crucial as they might be in larger, ground-breaking "U.S.-style" efforts.

☐ The more adequately supported, innovative program can afford what others regard as the luxury of giving a hearing to most potential changes. But even in these cases change, which in a romantic sense can be idealized as a continual striving for perfection, runs into the cash register. The age-old question, "Who's going to pay for it?" reflects the realities of organizational life. Outsiders seldom realize that a series of changes may cause the cost of a given piece of hardware to double or even triple.

☐ A change, then, is not just an abstract idea; it is a commodity. If the potential purchaser rejects the price, the change in question, no matter how desirable, will not materialize. A scientist from the sponsoring organization and an engineer on a contractor's staff may be engaged in a serious discussion about a potential change that will permit a piece of equipment to function more efficiently. The scientist remarks, "Why don't we try it?" And the engineer replies, "Fine, write me a change order." To this, the scientist responds, "But it's your company's responsibility to bear the cost. This change is within the scope of your contract." The enthusiasm of the engineer suddenly diminishes, and he replies, "There may be technical complications. I'll have to think about it." He then proceeds to forget the entire matter because he feels that if he is responsible for an increase in costs, he may be in trouble with his company.

☐ Changes are an especially persistent problem in complex systems because the customer is not ordering a standardized production item. The basic point of reference is vague, for the end product is at best ill-defined, and certainly does not meet the standard test of definition so precisely that it can be rebuilt.[9]

---

[9] Of course, no matter what the technology, there is no such thing as completely explicit specifications. Vagueness is inherent. Even the most detailed body of specifications excludes everything that is not specifically included!

☐ This lack of adequate definition in turn tends to generate situations that produce changes. For instance, the original bid price is affected by the uncertainty surrounding the nature of the item in question. It may not be obvious at the outset that a bid is unrealistically low, yet a tremendous volume of changes resulting in higher than anticipated costs may be inevitable. In other cases, a contractor might be fairly sure that the amount he has bid for producing the ill-defined item in question will not cover the final job, but he wants the contract and sets his price to get it. A case in point concerns allegations regarding what some described as Lockheed's "buy in, get well" approach to the C5A program, meaning that the company submitted an unrealistically low bid to obtain the business, with the hope of charging higher prices for future orders and thus showing an eventual profit. In this instance, a furor arose when it became evident that the first 58 planes would cost about $850 million more than the estimate.

☐ But even if the bidding procedure contributes no distortion, in the case of the ill-defined production item, an effective means of processing changes is crucial to good management. It determines whether the contractor will make any money—and whether the sponsor will get a well-engineered product at a reasonable price. The quality of the item in question may very well be threatened by a failure to make needed changes. Insistence on following early plans or a fixed trend has led to near disaster in several cases. The F-111 fighter-bomber is a notable example.

☐ During the life of the project a good portion of the interface activity involving the sponsor and contractor may be devoted to discussions and negotiations regarding changes. The sponsor does not initiate all the moves for a change; sometimes the contractor requests a change, and in the "ideal" case the change is the result of a mutual agreement between the sponsor and the contractor.

☐ Of course, not every change is the subject of interorganizational negotiations. If a sponsor orders a black box, he does not concern himself with changes the contractor makes inside the box. The contractor does not charge for these. But if the sponsor wants the power increased from 20 to 50 watts, the contractor may have to reprice the box because now more wire, diodes, transistors, and so on are required. The contractor then requests a change in specifications and the issuance of a change order, which will guarantee a higher price for the work.

☐ Although this procedure seems simple, problems may

develop. Budgetary worries may cause the sponsor to drag his heels in issuing the change order. In response, the contractor delays the work. He wants assurance that compensation will be forthcoming. Tension mounts. Each begins to feel the other is acting in bad faith.

☐ Because these dealings involve money and schedules, they quickly lose their informal character. The parties want protection, and they seek to obtain it by establishing a system for processing changes. Such systems are officially designated as a means for "smoothing the interface between sponsor and contractor." But they also serve as a very basic kind of control, designed to keep both sponsor and contractor from backing away from the original bargain—which is rather easy in the case of an ill-defined product.

Configuration Management

☐ One manager commented as follows on the need for controls: "In complex systems R & D you have to be able to reconstruct the crime." Government sponsors often require that techniques such as configuration management (CM) be employed for this purpose. In CM systems all items to be controlled are identified, and starting-point or baseline specifications are established. Each subsequent change and modification is then added to this record.

☐ Ironically, the system can be used to the disadvantage of the sponsor who initially insisted upon it. If the sponsor complains about the functioning of one of his black boxes, the CM record may be produced to show that this is indeed just what he ordered. And in negotiations, the contractor will price the CM program at, say, an additional three months of project time, $1 million in costs plus new capital expenditures for file cabinets, and so on. The CM program also serves as a ready excuse for the contractor, when pressed for delivery of a component, to snap, "I'm tied up in red tape."

☐ In the end the sponsor may not have the precise CM accounting system that he had envisioned because many projects involve a sizable group of outside contractors and their subcontractors. Introducing a CM program may cause problems in a major contractor's own organization, but its extension through several tiers of subcontractors multiplies the difficulties. A CM manager in a large firm noted:

When we tell our own people about CM we sometimes have to say, "Don't faint when you first hear it." But with the subs it's a magnified proposition. The sub says, "So you're X Company's program manager. I don't need you telling me how to run my business. If you want CM, you will have to pay for it." At first we specified CM for our subcontracts, but now we just insert some pages describing but not naming it to minimize the impact on the dollar.

☐ However, CM does have real value for the sponsor. Some of its proponents even assert that the Germans might have won World War II if they had used this management technique. As it was, when one of their rockets failed, they had no systematic record of the various components that would serve to pinpoint possible causes.

☐ The CM record permits the exercise of *systematic control.* It contributes to the development of what one contractor called "a management environment." Of course, organizational size is an important factor in determining the need for such a tool. For very large programs, some such procedure seems to be essential. Given a clear history of each item, the control of changes can be systematized by placing it in the hands of a neutral body in the contractor's house, a change review board, which frequently is a small core unit manned by a company officer with a staff of one or two assistants. When the group needs information, it calls on the functional divisions for help. This group basically serves to separate the crucial trade-offs regarding a given engineering change from those reflecting the parochial interests of the managers immediately concerned. The engineering manager is hard pressed to justify his stand before the board because the experience of most companies shows that the greater proportion of proposed changes are nonmandatory.

☐ In one case an engineering-design change was proposed by a group in Company Y because it would have served to make Y's production unit independent of that of Company X, a fellow subsystem contractor. The question of cost and the effect on other subsystems were not important to the local group, who were mainly anxious to cut out the unwanted interface. Processing the request through the change review board in Company Y served to broaden the basis for judgment and to clarify the full range of trade-offs. Not unexpectedly, the proposed design change was rejected.

☐ If the board accepts a change, this acceptance involves a change in role, for the board then becomes an advocate of the change and presents a solid front to the sponsor. The sponsor then passes the request on to his own change review board, which has the final authority to accept or reject it.

☐ The manager of the CM office in a major contractor's establishment remarked, surprisingly, that although seemingly dull and dry on the surface, CM was a "highly emotionally charged subject":

The engineer doesn't care about the drawings. He wants to get his hands on the hardware. We are the bad guys. We stifle their creativity. They blame us for all the delays. They tell us no one has time to go through all those drawings. It is just wasted effort.

☐ Another CM official noted that although his key function was resented to some extent, he was able to survive in the organization because:

For everybody CM is a communications tool. For instance, it opens up communications and brings problems to the level where the program manager can see them. For the task manager, it gives visibility to the relationships he engages in.

☐ Although the change-processing system is intended to regulate life in the organization as a whole, it also has very different meanings for the various functional units. One company manager observed, "When we started out, we assumed that we all agreed on CM, but when we had our meetings we found it was something different to everybody concerned":

1. To the materiel (equipment and supplies) group, it is a matter of cost and delivery—preventing overruns and schedule slips.

2. To the logistics man it is retrofitting (installing new elements in) the kits in the field.

3. To the reliability people, it is the definition of the "as built" configuration.

4. To engineering staff members, it is the definition of a product, so precisely stated that the item can be rebuilt on this basis.

5. To field-test operations personnel, it is a document prescribing tests of total systems and operations to determine if the paperwork matches the actual hardware.

☐ The fact that the change-processing system seems to offer something to everyone concerned is one reason for its acceptance. How it affects the way managers think and behave is another matter. CM systems are designed as management tools—devices to help people do their jobs. But when such a system is introduced, it also serves to alter the management process and to redefine the job in the manager's mind. It tells him that change cannot be a way of life, that it must be the exception and not the rule. The new watchwords are: "Hold to the specifications." "Apply rigid controls." "Keep an eye on your costs." *And, above all, "Make no changes unless they are absolutely necessary."* One manager commented, "People fight it, but there's no other way to make money in this business."

☐ Both the business and technical sides of the organization are vitally interested in the monitoring and control of changes. Nevertheless, CM has become a controversial topic. Like other business-system procedures, it has come to serve many functions, some intended, some unintended. It has become a jousting ground for technical men and business- and management-systems experts, for contractors and sponsors fighting to ascertain, through this elaborate machinery, who is responsible for a particular design change. In this role, it can become another source of the sometimes violent oscillations that wrench the advanced-technology program.

CONCLUSION

☐ The achievement of an optimal balance between the advanced technological system's business and technical requirements clearly is no simple matter. We have raised a number of questions that experts in this field have been struggling to answer.

☐ 1. *Can initial negotiations be conducted in a manner that avoids setting the stage for later conflict?* Although it would not resolve the basic problem, there seems little doubt that these negotiations would lose some of their unnecessarily legalistic flavor if contracts personnel were removed from their second-stage, defensive position and brought in at the very beginning so that the major objectives of the new relationship could be integrated into the business systems designed to govern it.

☐ The basic problem is more difficult to solve, especially when the sponsor is a government agency living under the threat of Congressional investigations and loss of public support. There is no question that these factors serve to perpetuate the drive to appear to be a hard-as-nails bargainer, getting the best deal and protecting the taxpayer's dollar at all costs. Large and powerful sponsors always have these invisible third parties sitting at the negotiating table, and their presence stimulates a push for a highly definitive, legalistic agreement. Removing the deleterious effects of this presence can be achieved primarily through long-term efforts by the sponsor to develop increased "institutional credibility."

☐ 2. *Can business-system concepts and methods be devised to stimulate maximum contractor performance in advanced technologies?* We have noted that incentive-award systems aimed at eliciting excellent contractor performance are a part of our way of life, although other countries seem to have been able to get along without them or to rely only on negative controls (punishing failures). Thus we are faced with the problem of making these systems work—no simple task in the case of R & D projects because the reward system, no matter how elaborate, is a superstructure built on a highly uncertain foundation. The answer would seem to lie in developing a pattern of business concepts that complement the technical side of the organization—dynamic, rather than static, systems-oriented incentive structures.

☐ We also must become more fully conscious of the need to tailor the incentive system and its administration to the technical objectives of the program. In addition, we must face the fact that incentive systems are inappropriate for programs or for certain parts of particular programs which clearly push the state of the art and are closer, then, to research than to development. In general, programs, or parts of programs, in which there is a lack of clear definition and a need to remain maximally flexible probably should be excluded from incentive contracts. Major policy shifts in the contracts area often tend to dominate program considerations. One way to counteract this tendency may be to change the kinds of decision criteria emphasized in this field, namely, those based on performance, cost, schedule, and mission objectives. In many cases these have gained acceptance simply because they are easily measurable elements. Achievement of the requisite degree of organizational flexibility is an example of the type of less easily quantifiable performance that could be accorded equal prominence.

☐ 3. *How can the advanced technological system achieve optimal management of one of its crucial elements, the processing of changes?* As we have noted, both the business and technical sides of the organization are vitally interested in the monitoring and control of changes. The mission-oriented engineer has to be able to trace the cause of a failure. The contracts man has to be able to assign costs and responsibility in the interest of good financial management.

☐ Moreover, in a creative R & D organization, the technical side is constantly initiating proposals for changes. However, it is clear that if all potential changes were attempted, the system would collapse under the weight of the effort. The organization needs a stabilizing element in order to be able to determine and to cope with those changes that are absolutely necessary.

☐ Thus the real problems in this area arise in connection with the different objectives of these two interest groups within the organization. And again, the corrective route is similar to that for the incentive-award structures—it lies in developing dynamic, rather than static, systems-oriented change-processing procedures.

☐ There is no question that sponsors have been powerfully motivated to develop effective business systems. The normal desire to produce good results has been reinforced by the sponsor's frequently being a government agency, needing public support for its costly efforts, and requiring answers to searching inquiries by Congressmen or members of Parliament or the Diet.

☐ Certainly, under these circumstances the complex, detailed system with fairly involved procedures has substantial appeal. The very existence of such an apparatus provides the basis for a good defense. It is not surprising that such control systems have been developed most fully in the United States, which has the largest and most far-flung programs, really impossible to manage via face-to-face monitoring. But the American effort has had, and will have, an impact far beyond its own boundaries as pressures for more precise accounting and control lead program managers in other countries to consider adopting or adapting these ready-made systems.

☐ Some of these controls—phased project planning, systems integration, data banks, and so on—have been examined in previous chapters. Some of them are "soft" indirect controls; some, such as phased project planning, are aimed at linking two basic processes: planning and negotiation. In this chapter we have examined "hard" controls, such as cost-plus-incentive-fee contracts and configuration management, designed to govern work relations, especially those peculiar to advanced technologies. As usual, the sponsor faces the formidable task of getting first its own people, then its contractors, and eventually the various levels of subcontractors to accept these controls.

☐ It has not been our intention to focus undue attention on conflict between business and technical goals. The instability and uncertainty of work in advanced-technology programs has served to aggravate normal tensions and to emphasize the differences in these two approaches. On the other hand, a stabilizing element is desperately needed in an environment almost totally dedicated to the encouragement of change. It is to their credit that business and technical personnel have learned to work together under these far from optimal conditions. But the marriage between these two groups is still far from ideal. For one thing, the pecking order in these technically oriented enterprises assigns to the contracts and business personnel a secondary, or "pecked" status, and they then respond with defensive, legalistic control paraphernalia. Key personnel never should be forced into this kind of position. Such developments are especially apt to occur in large advanced-technology programs with no user-customer in the loop. It may be that further integration of these two approaches will have to await developments in more fully applications- and market-oriented programs.

☐ Because of the precise coordination required among the various parts of an advanced-technology program, there is an even greater than usual need for the technical and business systems to operate in concert. However, because of their mission orientation, they present a rather uncongenial environment for the business system, especially as it is traditionally conceived. One is very apt to find business and technical systems operating in ways that aggravate one another. It is delusory to think that each system can be allowed to independently optimize its particular goals without regard for the other.

☐ We have noted in this chapter a number of sources of the severe oscillations caused by violent swings between business and technical goals. These oscillations can be amplified or attenuated by the relationship that exists between the business and technical sides of the complex endeavor. As these are multiorganizational, federally organized structures, subject to pressures from diverse sources, an oscillation-free situation is a near impossibility. But if those making judgments take the objectives of these systems into account almost simultaneously, considering multiple goals and trade-offs, the oscillations, while still present, will be reduced to the tolerable level depicted in Case 2 of Figure 1. Then the business and technical sides of the advanced technology can be established as complementary oscillating systems, each of which continuously takes the other into account.

MOTIVATING
SYSTEMS
RESPONSIBILITY

FOURTEEN

If one seeks to learn the source of program success simply by asking program managers what they do, the chances are good that one will hear something like the following:

The most important key to success is making sure that there is clear assignment of responsibility to individuals so that each manager knows what he will be held accountable for and that he alone is responsible for that assignment.

Given the strong emotion associated with such pronounce-ments, it might be inferred that this is, partially at least, a *moral* belief. There must be an unambiguous assignment of accountability so that there can be punishment should there be failure; the right culprit can be identified and, of course, the correct heroes as well.

☐ Motivational elements are also implicit—the belief that there is more commitment, more follow-through, when the manager knows he is clearly and solely responsible. And there is the psychological reassurance for higher manage-ment that there is someone to turn to when problems arise or failures occur, someone to whom the blame can be at-tached. (Provision for such targets is even made in com-puter data banks, where submissions must have the names of their sponsors attached.) For a workable responsibility system, students of management normally would insist that the manager be given a precisely defined task and a fixed time to do it. These requirements then would be matched with an allocation of resources and authority adequate to fulfill his commitments.

THE REALITY OF A SYSTEMS ORGANIZATION

☐ For the most part these requirements are *not* met in a systems organization designed to implement advanced tech-nologies. As we have seen in previous chapters, there is too much overlap in the scope of problems and competencies. Interfaces, unfortunately, even with all the effort devoted to their explicit definition, tend to blur. Managers are constantly being asked to make timely adjustments in the tasks for which they are responsible, to assist others who are in trouble, to share resources, and to live up to schedule, performance, and cost commitments despite a wide variety of externally generated complications.

Defensive Reactions

□ We have seen managers who do resist all outside "interference" from clients, from other stages in the work flow, from project offices for whom they are doing support work, and from scientific experimenters. To try to minimize the risk of failing in their responsibilities, they assume a highly rigid posture. They brook no interference in the form of suggestions for change or modification, they provide zero visibility to outsiders who may be seeking to facilitate systems integration, and they will share neither resources nor information:[1]

We thought we could help get our equipment effectively integrated in the next stage, help the guys who had to use it by showing them things about it they couldn't learn for themselves very easily and in addition pick up some information on their operation that would help us do our work better. But we had to fight to get in. The managers there didn't want our engineers having any contact whatsoever with their personnel. They, in effect, said that when the hardware left our shop, we had to let go, too.

□ It was this same phenomenon that caused some project managers to insist on sole control over tracking and telemetering facilities, and even launch operations, because only then could they ensure the success of the mission for which they were responsible.[2] Obviously such unitary control is incompatible with the need for sharing limited resources and making use of the specialized skills of other cooperating organizations that are part of the general operating requirements of a matrix organization.
□ This same point of view is expressed by those who look forward to the day when a spacecraft will be a standardized "bus" into which experiments are assigned "seats," the day when engineers will no longer need to engage in agonizing give and take with scientists. University consortia also want

[1] See Chapter 12.

[2] See Chapter 9.

the sponsoring agency to give them the money, set the goal, and leave them alone so that they can take "full responsibility" for the operation of some facility or some program.

□ Unfortunately, once this process of establishing semi-independent fiefdoms has progressed a certain distance, it is most difficult to reverse. Systems-integration managers seeking valid information about work being done "inside the gates" of these well-protected domains sometimes become desperate. It may take an enormous quantity of time and energy to penetrate them, and in some cases subterfuge may even be necessary. Moreover, these efforts are not always successful, and important managerial decisions must sometimes be made without adequate or reliable data.

□ Systems management has evolved a number of procedures to maintain the fiction that authority is equal to responsibility. Change Procedures for initiating changes, particularly the requirements for personal "sign-offs," are designed so that a manager will not be affected by changes of which he has not approved. Both internal and external review boards seek to restrict the number of changes and to assure their legitimacy and acceptability. Obviously there must be a procedure for systematically processing necessary readjustments, although the elaborateness of the procedure, which sometimes smacks of ritualism, in some cases seems designed more to allay anxiety and reassure harried managers than anything else.

□ Almost endless negotiation is another type of "work-around" procedure used by managers to accommodate the conflicting requirements of a systems organization and the pressures to assume individual responsibility. These negotiations often are far from friendly, for they are aimed at determining who is responsible, who should pay for a change or suffer for a mistake. A large percentage of the energy and time of key executives can be spent in trying to prove that blame lies with "the other guy":

One thing we knew was that we weren't going to open up that [subsystem] shipped to us by the sub-contractor. Once we started fiddling with it, if it didn't work, it would be our responsibility, or at least they would try to shift the blame to us. We were pretty sure we were in trouble with this [subsystem], but we didn't dare do anything about it at that point. We just decided to wait until it failed during a formal test.

□ In the example just cited, an earlier and more complete investigation of the "black box" received by the contractor could have prevented the serious delays that did ensue. But a legalistic point of view, aimed at providing adequate ammunition for future negotiations to determine responsibility, took precedence.[3] Using our earlier terminology, this is another example of business-system logic prevailing over the logics of the technical system.

□ "Involvement" is a popular concept today, but it is simply a source of trouble if one wants to maintain clearly defined lines of jurisdiction. The client who likes "to get his hands dirty" in the contractor's shop is at the same time polluting the stream of responsibility. As one aerospace manager noted:

Client B has a large group of technically competent people. They want to get involved in the design and they do get deeply involved. Still, they expect their contractors to operate as though they were independently responsible.

One cannot anticipate breakdowns, or insert oneself into another organization to provide an early warning system or assistance, without blurring the lines of responsibility.

□ Undoubtedly, a variety of unanticipated negative consequences flow from a legalistic view of responsibility. The quality of the product, for example, may be diminished:

Aerospace companies' executives may begin to manage their operation more with an eye to satisfying customer-designed management system requirements than to producing a product they think will perform best in a manner that they feel is most expeditious and most technically fruitful. This reorientation of management attention is more than just a matter of "stifling creativity." It places the right and responsibility for critical management decisions with the Air Force rather than with the contractor. If a wrong decision is made, a forceful argument can be presented that the Air Force had the right of technical review and disapproval and that, in not disapproving, it did, in fact, give tacit approval to the decision in question. This raises a disturbing question of legal liability for payment by the Air Force, even when performance of an end item is not according to prescribed specifications.[4]

[3] An example from the community is the problem of the good samaritan who seeks to help an accident victim and risks a lawsuit for being inadequately attentive or meticulous in the care he proffers.

[4] Edward Morrison, "Defense Systems Management: The 375 Series," *California Management Review,* vol. IX, no. 4, Summer, 1967.

☐ The examples we have cited concern sponsor-contractor relationships, for the most part. The implementation of advanced technologies often requires the close collaboration of a relatively sophisticated technical (R & D) organization with a user (operations-oriented) organization. Traditional management theory and interorganizational practice tells executives to hew to a clearly defined line of demarcation that separates the jurisdiction (and responsibilities) of one group from another. The result can be the kind of problem described by the manager of one joint R & D and user project, who worked for the R & D organization:

Our top management told us not to jump the interface. We saw that their equipment was not up to the job assigned, and I am sure we could have identified the trouble, but we stayed on our side of the line. Sure it was easier that way, our budget was limited, we had been given a narrow job to do, and we played it that way.

☐ Yet, as we described in some detail in Chapter 7, getting new technologies implemented requires, beyond any question, an enormous amount of give-and-take between the developer and the user. The former in particular has to get inside the potential or actual user's organization to assess its needs, methods, and capabilities. (Of course, the user must learn something of the developer too.) If there is not this rather intimate exchange and constant border-crossing, if the new techniques are simply left at the threshold of the user, there is almost no likelihood that there will be adequate psychological or physical preparation for their effective use.

How Managers Take Responsibility

☐ Fortunately, the temptations to sin greatly outnumber the actual transgressions. In fact, one sees only a minimal amount of this kind of maneuvering. It is remarkable how many managers maintain a high level of effort and commitment even when they have ready at hand a number of sound legal "outs":

They never called us in when they were designing the [key element of the spacecraft] and thus we have great difficulty with our part of the operation. We could complain that the standards we are being held to for that operation are totally unrealistic given the way the [element] was designed, but what good would that do?

☐ However, few managers seem to take the point of view, which some project heads have expressed, that any restriction on their freedom to do the job as they see fit releases them from responsibility for making the final product work.[5] Project managers and heads of functional or discipline groups do work together without either one concluding that the other is now solely in charge or that one or the other can simply abdicate responsibility.

☐ In this same vein it is interesting to note that a confrontation over the matter of responsibility actually may serve to draw client and contractor closer together. After a disastrous failure in a major program, a contractor reported that his relationship with his client seemed to be nearing the breaking point:

After [the incident] we nearly fell apart over the matter of blame. They seemed determined to hang it all on us. After all, it was their program. They had managers working on it too. But they seemed to forget about that. Oddly enough, after it all was over, our relationship improved.

☐ Thus, disaster can open the door on the constraints that normally lead the parties to avoid confrontations over the matter of responsibility. Under the pressures engendered by failure, an embarrassed client can gain momentary satisfaction by heaping bitter accusations on his contractor. But in the final analysis, a problem of this type only serves to underline their joint guilt and responsibility. Thus, if such a confrontation does not totally disrupt a relationship—and it certainly can do that—it may very well lead to a marked improvement in it. As they reflect on their joint failure, both parties may come to recognize the futility of attempting to hide behind artificial and meaningless boundary lines.

A SYSTEMS VIEW OF RESPONSIBILITY

☐ Perhaps what one is left with, and this has obvious limitations, is a kind of "best performance" criterion for assessing responsibility. An overemphasis on results leads to the types of rigidities and sophistries we have described: building walls, shifting blame, extended negotiating over who is at fault, pretending that all interfaces are clean and unchanging. It is a Solomon-like task to try to fix responsibility when

[5] George Steiner and William Ryan, *Industrial Project Management,* New York, Macmillan, 1968, p. 22.

a product or an effort is undergoing the rapid and interdependent changes so typical of advanced technologies.

□ On the other hand, managers can be held accountable if
they fail to live up to the constraints of the organization, for
example, if they are unresponsive to the demands of groups
with whom they must collaborate and build walls to isolate
their operations, if they do not improvise and adapt quickly
and effectively when continuous monitoring indicates that
current efforts are falling short or that complications are
imminent, if they fail to show initiative and perseverance in
solving problems. Many times a particular manager may
have to allow his own budget or schedule to be hurt so that
some larger goal will be fulfilled.

□ In traditional management thinking there is a clear line
separating that which is delegated and that which is not, that
which is in the jurisdiction of one manager and that which
falls into the jurisdiction of an adjacent manager.[6] In systems organizations, unfortunately, such compartmentalization breaks down, and with it goes the possibility of neatly
pinpointing faults or assigning blame. To avoid the needless
defensive tactics designed to provide ammunition for managerial "trials" and the endless negotiations over who was at
fault and to encourage responsible project-manager accommodations, managers need to be evaluated on their methods
as well as their results.

□ It is clear that individual responsibilities and authority are
often associated with the rigidities of organizational life.
Students of bureaucracy and informal organization have
long observed the inevitable, steady accretion of norms,
rules, and informal understandings that defend the jurisdictions and working methods of a group. Thus, over time
habits and vested interests accumulate that resist adapting
to new problems and new circumstances. It is well known
that in the bureaucratic world everyone protects himself
against the possibility that he will be accused of failure by
living up to the letter of established custom and precedence
regardless of whether these practices are consistent with
the overall needs of the situation.

□ The absence of such clearly defined practices, rules, and
jurisdictions is in many ways a distinct advantage of project
and program management. Rapid improvisation and adaptation that, of necessity, must violate past practice and past
expectations become the new rule. The *problem* is the focal
point for the group, not the legal responsibility. Managers

---

[6] See the discussion in Chapter 9 of redundancy in specialization.

don't ask, "Who is at fault?" or "Whose responsibility is it?" but rather, "What can be done to remedy the situation as quickly and efficaciously as possible?"

□ A recent, and as yet unpublished, study of thirty-eight R & D projects in a variety of organizations (conducted at M.I.T. under the direction of Professor Donald Marquis) confirms this fact. The study also notes that the real "authority" of the project manager on successful projects is indeterminate; he shares with a number of functional managers an ambiguously defined authority over the technical personnel, who, in turn, must come to accept a situation in which they have more than one boss and thus ambiguous responsibilities.[7]

□ Universities themselves are rather good examples of institutions in which key professionals are motivated to emphasize jurisdiction over almost anything else. Interdisciplinary, problem-oriented programs often fail because faculty members are rewarded not for collaboration and contributing to an overall goal, but for maintaining the absolute integrity of their specialty. Promotions are largely a function of peer-group evaluations of one's loyalty to discipline demarcations and contemporary discipline definitions of sound theory and methodology.

Dispersed vs. Jurisdictional Responsibility

□ However, evaluation of performance rather than results is only a partial answer to the problem of administering responsibility. Even with this improved basis for evaluation, the individual is still the focus of concern, and the potential for divisive fault-finding continues to exist. Individual responsibility for bad performance is substituted for individual responsibility for bad results. In the final analysis, a drastic reorientation to the question of responsibility is needed. We have noted that many managers refuse to be ensnared in legalism, and this is precisely the kind of behavioral approach that needs to be encouraged.

□ Presently, the administrator is forced to manage responsibility on the assumption that the lines are crystal clear, even though he knows that they are not. Instead of pretending that the matter is clear, one can deliberately proceed to make it even less clear than it presently is. Forsaking the individual, one can take the project group, broadly considered, as the basic unit.

[7] A preview of the Marquis study has been published as "Ways of Organizing Projects," in *Innovation* (Issue Five), 1969, pp. 26–33.

☐ Thus, responsibility can be treated in a completely un-traditional manner. It is not abolished; rather, it is dispersed throughout an entire project without regard to interpersonal, departmental, or organizational boundaries. With this approach, areas of responsibility are not one man's or one organization's territory. Although many managers are reluctant to face the fact, a territory is established whenever we make a traditional assignment of responsibility. As an unfortunate consequence of the jurisdictional view of responsibility, the man or organization attempting to compensate for another's oversights or deficiencies is viewed not as a help-mate but rather as someone more akin to an imperialist launching an invasion.

☐ With the untraditional approach, responsibility is *dispersed* rather than concentrated and specifically assigned. The dispersed system may seem vague and disorganized compared to the *jurisdictional* approach, described in some detail in this chapter, but it can be a highly effective means of eliciting maximum individual initiative, especially if it is used with groups whose relationship is one of long-term interdependency—a characteristic of advanced technologies.

☐ Needless to say, the dispersed system requires a fairly long preparatory stage for a sense of responsibility to be shared by the group as a whole. Ideas and plans must be developed in discussions in which all relevant members of the various organizations are given ample opportunity to contribute and undertaken only when a consensus is obtained. Each member then shares responsibility equally, as part of a group which participates in a project that all deem vital. Each one makes whatever contribution he can—a contribution he sees as supported by those of all the others in the project group. Responsibility and commitment are deeply felt, but they are not anyone's assigned property.

☐ The Japanese approach to managing responsibility in organizational life is somewhat similar to that just described. Responsibility is dispersed via a lengthy process of agreement, internalization, and dedication, and finally comes to fruition as part and parcel of the group effort. It is certainly possible for Americans to disperse responsibility rather than concentrate and localize it, but we need to approach the problem differently. We recognize the long-term interdependencies existing among participants in advanced-technology programs, but, nevertheless, we give support to a tentative style of relationship among them, assembling competitors and striving to get them to do their best under the pressure of competition. We say to the participants in a project, "You are all in this together, but please prepare to be judged and to be responsible as individuals." Clearly, then, if we are to disperse responsibility, it will be simpler for us to impose the dispersion process from without.

☐ NASA's single-minded goal of a moon landing by 1970 served this function to some extent. Inspired by this objective, Apollo project members were able to overcome at least partially the difficulties involved in the jurisdictional view of responsibility. Successful project and program managers often achieve the same kind of effect on a less grandiose scale. Thus our ability to unite to achieve objectives we perceive as worthwhile serves to shield us from the worst consequences of our illogical treatment of the question of responsibility. Unfortunately, it is far from simple to continually devise magnificent unifying goals, and not every project has charisma. One cannot escape the conclusion that eventually we will have to make basic changes in our present approach to the administration of responsibility.

MANAGEMENT CONTROLS AND RESPONSIBILITIES

☐ A project or functional manager's interpretation and perception of his "responsibility" will be affected by the control systems that are used. In the daily course of events, managers have to use, and be responsive to the use by others of, a variety of control measures. Some are consistent with, and critical to, what we have called "dispersed" responsibility; others represent the more traditional concern with "jurisdictional" responsibility. For example, if heavy emphasis is placed on traditional incentives, a rather legalistic view of who deserves credit or blame is encouraged. The manager is induced (or seduced) to narrow or confine his efforts to "beat the system." In the real world of advanced-technology implementation both types of controls are necessary. However, the manager and the organization should be able to make the appropriate discriminations as to which to use for what!

Controls Emphasizing Jurisdictional Responsibility

☐ These are the control systems and techniques that receive the greatest emphasis in the engineering-management literature and in exhortations, both verbal and printed, to the technical manager. We shall not describe or analyze these in

any detail; our discussion is designed to illustrate the underlying organizational mechanisms.

□ In a sense these *jurisdictional* controls handle the very
high- and the very low-level relationships of the manager.
(The highly critical middle level is dealt with by the *dispersed* controls we shall discuss later.)

High-Level Controls

□ Like any large organization, the complex project and
program needs to convince both its own top management
and its outside sponsors that it is reasonably efficient in
moving toward achieving its major goals. At the simplest
level this might mean showing them what percent of a total
program is completed in a given fiscal year. If possible, it is
always useful to show that either the rate of completion or
the rate of accomplishment per dollar of expenditure is
improving.

□ The distinctive quality of these high-level measures is that
they are intended to reassure those who are not sufficiently
close to the scene to be able to see or evaluate any of the
detailed activities. If properly used, they may ward off in-
vestigatory activities and provide sponsors and top management with ammunition to counter skeptics and political
opponents. Inevitably, these measures have a public-
relations quality about them, and unfortunately a good deal
of internal effort may have to be expended accumulating
statistical information to support preestablished contentions.
Nevertheless, it would be unrealistic to conceive of any
large organization, public or private, in which higher echelons would *not* be sufficiently far removed to require some
efforts of this kind. Our business world has the advantage of
a slightly (but only slightly) less arbitrary system called *profit
accounting,* but its limitations in measuring managerial performance are also well known.

□ Recent developments in cost-benefit analysis have been
designed to improve the rationality of this type of payoff
measure. Rather than merely saying "more has been accomplished this year than last" (with "more" being defined in a
variety of ways), these newer tools seek to compare the
respective public benefits and goals of alternative uses of
funds.[8]

□ Thus high-level controls are not controls in the usual
management sense of the term. In complex endeavors
where very substantial expenditures are required to com-

[8] Cf. Chapter 2.

plete high-risk programs and where many years may pass before the results are in, it is necessary to provide some regular feedback to those whose dollars or reputations are involved. Hence they are shown measures that demonstrate but do not prove efficiency and that do not provide adequate bases for continuing supervision. It is not clear that either supervision or efficiency are appropriate concerns, however. Can Congress directly supervise, for example? And what is efficiency in basic research?

Low-Level Controls

□ By low-level controls we mean the checking procedures established to ensure that neither financial nor technical decisions are made without adequate review and that no necessary step has been omitted. Some typical rules might be:

All expenditures over $500 must be approved by the Comptroller's office.

When "off standard" temperature prevails for more than 5 minutes, written authorization from the Chief Engineer is required to continue processing procedures.

Storage of flammables within 50 feet of Building 209 requires permission by the Safety Officer.

Any substitution of materials must be approved by the subsystem engineer, the functional manager, and a representative of the Project Office.

Such regulations are "old hat" and may be useful in classical scientific management, but there can still be problems in their application. When a check with a control group or functionary must be made *before* some action is taken, and when the action is part of a work-flow sequence, the checking can be a serious interruption.[9]

□ Important decisions are often subject to "before-the-fact" review by a number of people. Thus in a technical program, a design decision by an engineer may be reviewed by his functional manager, a technical specialist in the project office, the project manager, and then the program office. Parallel-system managers may also be involved.

[9] In another context we have sought to clarify which types of checks should be made "before" and which "after." See Eliot Chapple and Leonard Sayles, *The Measure of Management,* New York, Macmillan, 1959, pp. 27–29.

☐ Such sign-offs are time consuming both for the project and for those who must review the technical details. When there are a great number of decisions to be made, there is a temptation to give some just a cursory glance, at best.

☐ Thus, there are two somewhat opposed difficulties here. Either the large number of people who must give their approval itself becomes a major burden and drain on the energies of those who should be doing and supervising the work, or the system is frequently ignored to the detriment of adequate reviews.

☐ Another problem with low-level jurisdictional controls is their tendency to influence perversely managerial decision-making.[10] Many engineering managers seem to have an intuitive feel for game theory, and they balance off possible costs and gains seeking the classical "minimax" whereby losses are minimized:

A circuit problem appears that can be solved by adding redundant circuitry. This guarantees the manager that he will not be embarrassed by his subsystem failing an upcoming endurance test. However, this redundancy increases the spacecraft weight over the original target level. Experience suggests that the total system's weight will increase during development projects as a result of many subsystem changes. The weight problem is likely to be dealt with at a later stage of the project, and no single manager will be blamed. Given a choice of seeking a time and dollar solution that is costly in time and dollars and that may penalize him heavily in the short run, he chooses a solution that will avoid those penalties (which also minimizes the risk of a test failure) in favor of a possible modest future penalty.

☐ The minimax propensity makes people tend to protect themselves from criticism, often at the expense of the larger system. The same tendency can be observed when managers have schedule and procurement trade-offs. As long as they know that jurisdictional controls will be emphasized by *their* managers, they act in such a way as to ward off major criticisms.

☐ A manager keeps his own and his subordinate's "skirts" clean by making sure that each control procedure is followed precisely. Then if a problem emerges it can be argued that "it is the other guy's fault" because everything required was done and there are the checks to prove it. As such,

---

[10] We are indebted to our former colleague, Professor R. R. Ritti, for some of these ideas. He has recently completed a study of engineering managers, *The Engineer in the Industrial Corporation,* New York, Columbia University Press, 1971.

many of these "low level" controls represent a kind of "closing the loop": making sure all authorizations and clearances have been received, budget levels maintained, design changes recorded, data banks updated, and so on.

Controls Emphasizing Dispersed Responsibility

Middle-Level Controls

☐ Middle-level controls are designed to guide managers to do things that contribute to overall systems effectiveness, not to paper "wins" and immediate payoffs. They concentrate on the organizational system and its potential to fulfill mission objectives. They are more concerned with keeping the total system going than having managers look good in terms of numerical ratings or scores. Such controls contribute to assessing the organizational effectiveness and performance of various contributors to the system and to predicting where breakdowns are likely.

☐ Much of traditional management literature dealing with delegation and controls stresses the autonomy that must be given (for motivational reasons) to subordinates. The superior *waits* to intervene (and to reward and punish) until the subordinate has failed or succeeded; otherwise he stays out of the process.[11] Obviously in very costly programs in which minor problems have widespread implications, failures must be prevented at all costs, including the risk of interfering with someone's designated responsibility and thereby relieving him of legal liability.

Penetrating the Other Organization

☐ Whether the work is being done by a contractor, within another functional group, by an experimenter, or in another part of the organization not immediately accessible to the project manager, there is the constant problem of predicting the likelihood of successful completion. In complex projects managers learn to expect the unexpected, that what looks

---

[11] Interestingly, even the subordinate cannot afford to wait for a technical process to go "out of limits" in these complex, interdependent endeavors. Thus in the launch-control procedure, there are numerous engineers whose job it is to call a halt to the countdown if the pressure or temperature they are watching goes beyond some precisely defined limit. But they cannot afford to wait until the limit is exceeded; they must seek to predict if it is *likely* to go out, particularly during the latter stages of the countdown. Obviously this takes more judgment and carries with it greater risk, responsibility, and personal stress than simply waiting for a clear signal of trouble.

good today may be in deep trouble tomorrow. While it is considered obvious advice to say that more attention should be paid to projects with greater technological uncertainty, it is not easy to ascertain these differences in advance:

The heart of the experiments package on one NASA spacecraft was a sophisticated measurement instrument. The project manager did not feel it was necessary to exercise close control over the contractor's production of this critical piece of hardware because the instrument was almost exactly the same as two earlier instruments produced by the same contractor for previous flights. Unfortunately, serious problems emerged during fabrication, causing major delays and cost overruns. It was later discovered that during the work on the two previous instruments, a particular supervisor had exercised unusual diligence to assure himself that certain very difficult and critical stages were performed with meticulous care, and several of the steps involving cleaning a surface prior to the application of a tricky bonding agent were repeated under his immediate observation. These "hand" operations involving visual judgments by an experienced craftsman were, of course, not incorporated into the specifications. Their contribution was not even known, and since the supervisor had been transferred to other work prior to the work on the third instrument, extra care was not taken.

☐ There are many such unpredictable failures, for no set of specifications ever incorporates all that must be known. Highly experienced computer manufacturers have experienced crises because they failed to adequately specify the characteristics of new families of transistors. These, it turned out, varied along dimensions other than those previously found critical in transistor manufacture. NASA once ran into difficulties because an air duct located near a loading dock occasionally brought fumes into a delicate assembly area. There had been no specifications for air-duct location in other related projects!

☐ Many managers have found that a better predictor of the amount of monitoring needed than the degree of technological uncertainty is the competence of the management, its adaptiveness and responsiveness to problems, and the degree to which the various contributing organizations are maintaining reasonably effective coordination and making reasonable trade-offs.

☐ Thus it becomes important to assess the capability of the organizations that are dealing with the various subsystems, their leadership, diligence, and competency. (Analogous to some U.S. anthropological research during World War II, this is an effort to assess culture at a distance: What are those people like, and how are they really performing?)

☐ The project manager, himself and through coordinators, seeks to build a network of contacts within the various organizations whose work is vital to the completion of his responsibilities. He seeks contacts that are sufficiently low-level to provide relatively firsthand, as distinct from highly filtered and refined, information. Many of these contacts will be "worked" daily during critical periods or during the early period when these relationships are being established.

☐ Information concerning schedule and budgets is obviously necessary, but data are also collected on the organization itself. The project manager wants to know how energetic and qualified the managers and their key technical people are (what specific background they have), how much priority they assign to his project, as opposed to their other work, how effectively they work together, and what kind of support they receive from upper management and service groups.

☐ There is sometimes a circularity in the monitoring process that can be self-defeating. When a manager is concerned about how the work of a subordinate or a contractor is progressing or when the participants are strangers to each other, he will tend to check on them more frequently. From the point of view of the man or group being checked upon, frequent checking indicates a lack of trust. It may also be a material handicap because of the time consumed in responding to requests for data and filling out reports. Also, when an individual suspects that information will be used against him, he tends to be circumspect about what he reveals. It is thus easy to move into a position where the person being controlled restrains the flow of information and the controller must keep increasing the pressure to extract valid progress reports, and a dangerous spiral of administrative costs and conflicts can ensue. Contrariwise, with credibility on both sides, the respondent is more candid, less time and effort are required to obtain information, and less information is requested.

☐ Interesting to observe is the extent to which even relatively high-level managers dealing with advanced technologies seek to gain a feel for the actual, raw technical data. They are not content to look at staff summaries or "exception" reports, and indeed there is a clear indication that this immersion in the technical detail is necessary to keep abreast and knowledgeable.[12] Some even insist on sampling all the correspondence concerning project progress and problems.

□ Very typical of this point of view are the following remarks:

There is just no substitute for having the technical sophistication and the willingness to go into the other guy's shop and look around. In R & D you've got to find out what he is *not* willing to tell you. The estimates, the test reports, and the progress reports tend to be too optimistic, and you'll go under every time if you take them at face value. The designers are always optimistic about future performance and the project people naturally cover up their problems so you've got to be their technical equal and get into the real data to know where you stand.

□ Rather than emphasizing regular reports, managers place greater importance on random organizational probes designed to identify coordination problems. Thus, each manager's manager concentrates on monitoring the interfaces which his subordinate must maintain. These include suppliers of components and subsystems, the next and preceding work-flow stage, test and control groups. It is in these linkages that trouble is likely to show itself first.

CONCLUSION

□ A recurring theme in our data is the inability to predict problems and crises, what we have called an absence of good "middle-level" controls. The very nature of these projects, even those that utilize a generally well-explored technology and meticulous testing procedures, is such that unanticipated obstacles tend to occur frequently. There are just so many variables, both technical and human, involved that one can be reasonably certain one or another combination will produce trouble.

□ Obviously, then, a control system is needed that predicts the capacity and competence of the organizations involved to *respond* adequately. Unfortunately, most high- and low-level controls try to measure accomplishment: how actual costs, schedules, and performances compare with the original estimates. This can be misleading, in part because such controls assume rigid plans, compartmentalized jurisdictions and responsibilities. ("Our engineers are mesmerized

[12] This also raises the obvious question of whether managers not technically sophisticated can properly serve in these posts.

by watching dollars when they should be watching technology and people.")

☐ As we have seen, project management requires enormous quantities of human energy to cope with the dynamic interfaces. Ever changing technical factors require assessments and adaptations in which human intervention plays a key role. People will only make this kind of effort, and it will only be usefully directed, if managers have a conception of responsibility that is broader than their organizational jurisdiction. Traditional job descriptions and incentives and controls cause a manager to look inward. Both he and his superior are concerned with what is inside their formally defined territories: the costs, the quality, the test results. To meet these internal criteria they are willing to, even urged to, erect barriers that impede trade-offs and creative improvisations and deter people from giving advance information. ("If the other department knows too soon that you aren't going to meet a schedule, they'll start pressuring you, and responding to this takes more precious time.")

☐ Measures of managerial performance must direct the attention of subordinate managers to the total system's requirements and to the breakdowns that threaten its performance. What starts out as neat, clean definitions of accountability actually serve to muddy the responsibilities which are external, interface responsibilities.

TECHNOLOGY AND SOCIAL ADMINISTRATION

FIFTEEN

The interdependencies of modern life are reflected in the growing emphasis on *systems.* The term is not to be escaped: systems management, urban systems, the systems approach. Most frequently, regrettably, the implicit or explicit meaning is simply technical relationships: airplanes and airports, distribution channels, and inventory. But most environmental and technical interrelationships also involve organizational interrelationships. To be sure, in the past organizations had relationships with one another. However, most were static or impersonal, defined by rather rigid legal agreements (setting forth mutual responsibilities) or governed by the invisible hand of the marketplace or the more visible hand of the government regulator. Only recently have we come to recognize that most of our contemporary "problem" areas require both the close collaboration of many institutions and rapid, dynamic mutual adaptation.

□ We easily observe this in the growing concern over health services, the court system, and many other areas of public and private investment. We have sought to begin the exploration of the human and managerial accommodations required by these complex systems with an intensive investigation of the U.S. space program. This "federal" organization has many of the hallmarks of these new, extensive systems. It is both public and private; its nonroutine work requires intensive collaboration among highly trained, proud, and normally "independent" professionals committed to diverse personal and institutional goals.

SUMMARY OF THE STRATEGIES AND TACTICS OF SYSTEMS MANAGEMENT

□ As in all development organizations the major managerial challenge is one of maintaining the regularity of a complex flow process, first during the planning stage as competing conceptualizations and goals are modified, then during the design and development stage as sponsors ally themselves with supporting contractors, and finally during the operational stage, in which still other organizations may be involved, and "users" take over.

☐ Distinctive managerial techniques are associated with the various interlinkages necessary to align diverse segments of this work flow. Project managers, a host of "intermediaries" and methods of monitoring, intervention, and persuasion abound. While it is easy to play the cynic and observe that the rather traditional strategies associated with economics and politics—the quest for power and profits, status and jurisdiction—are still much in evidence, there are also a number of new and more subtle organizational strategies designed to limit the impact of the centrifugal forces inherent in these large systems.

☐ A theoretical model of the large-scale system is far from easy to devise. So many specific elements at first appear to be crucial that one can become overwhelmed by the enormity of the task. However, from the standpoint of our research observations, the administration of large-scale systems seemed most appropriately characterized as the creation of a *pressure system* that functions to correct errors (the inevitably poor forecasts, plans, and budgets) and to prevent major distortions from arising. Management provides pressure in the right direction so that most of the time the system will be brought back to its original course. And management devises machinery that keeps the system operating in accord with procedures. It is not necessary to uncover all failures, but it is crucial to make *visible* the significant elements the system is not handling and digesting.

☐ A single predictable managerial strategy will not serve the needs of the large-scale system. The system will manifest oscillations which reflect the manager's need to meet diverse requirements, in part to gain the necessary support and positive response from its milieu: a multidimensional political, economic, and social arena. Inevitably the manager comes to employ a battery of polar, or contradictory, strategies which serve to cause oscillations in the system. These oscillations cannot be avoided, but keeping them under control is one of the primary functions of the manager. (See Figure 1, Chapter 13.)

☐ Thus the manager employs both dependency *and* redundancy, diffusion *and* integration, to name two mutually contradictory organization strategies. He allows professionals reasonable autonomy and forces close coordination. Specialists have to be committed to functional disciplines *and* interdisciplinary projects and teams. Scientists and their experiments must retain integrity and credibility at the same time they are learning about engineering and the required trade-offs. The manager uses high-level controls to assure his sponsors that the program is efficient and worthwhile, low-level controls to assure the technicians, and middle-level controls to guide his own interventions. He seeks to get each individual and group to accept responsibility; at the same time he seeks to reduce compartmentalized responsibilities.

☐ The administrator uses controls to get the system to the point where he can concentrate on forward direction of the mission or missions. Although he recognizes that he always will be working with a relatively unstable system, the controls he employs must be able to override the potentially detrimental effects of this built-in instability. Surprisingly, the top administrator must accomplish all this in order to proceed with the most important part of his work. The key part of his role involves taking the lead and showing those involved in the complex enterprise at hand how to get through it successfully, by integrating upward to the highest common denominator.

☐ While the top man does not want to confine people, this type of leadership for the achievement of excellence is hardly a passive process. For instance, we have commented on the multiple pressures surrounding his programs. To cope with these he must set benchmarks below which he will not permit the enterprise to operate and above which he will maneuver.

FUTURE STRUCTURES AND THEIR MANAGEMENT

☐ Our studies have pointed to various other factors that seem to make for program success. In our international research we found a good technical concept which immediately leads to expectations about the future and the kinds of commitments needed to be important. Then in forward planning, objectives can be set in the proper range, neither too specific nor too general. Structural design also contributes to success; especially essential are autonomy and freedom from continual dependency on political decisions. Another important aspect involves including, in the original design, plans for the implementation-user stage, thus providing for continuing cooperative relations among the partners. Success in terms of achieving eventual implementation is most apt to occur in programs that attend to these political-type uncertainties, and least apt to occur in those that focus only on technical and procedural uncertainties.

☐ Others have found that the probability of success is heightened if there is a clear and agreed sense of purpose, if objectives are limited to a specific task, and if the program is undertaken by a small, specialized agency. All these findings point to the same conclusion: The well-designed, predictable package, safe from surprise, is the most likely candidate for success.

☐ Unfortunately, these criteria for effectiveness conflict with the direction that the mission-oriented program is taking today. The days of the clearly specialized sponsoring agency are numbered. Objectives and the distribution of power and influence are becoming increasingly diffuse. The purely operational mission is becoming a luxury item. Operations are more and more mixed with regulatory functions. And to add further to the complexity, missions have become interrelated. Oceans, pollution, health, urban development, interact with one another. More complexity is added by the fact that in fields such as oceans and space purely national management appears to be politically unacceptable. In addition, users are demanding more and more of a voice in these programs. The criteria for success outlined above undoubtedly are valid, but fewer and fewer programs will be able to meet them.

☐ One might well ask what programs of the future—especially those of the "post-space" era that are moving into socio-technical areas such as environmental control—can learn from advanced-technology efforts such as NASA.

☐ NASA's most significant contribution is in the area of advanced systems design: getting an organizationally complex structure, involving a great variety of people doing a great variety of things in many separated locations, to do what you want, when you want it—and while the decision regarding the best route to your objective is still in the process of being made jointly by you and your collaborators.

☐ NASA continually demanded systemwide performance visibility and used a large battery of techniques to attain it—data banks, configuration management, endless performance-review meetings, and so on. It gave constant attention to the integration of widely separated efforts. It also nurtured an in-house capability that enabled it to know more about the total effort than any of the contracting parties. NASA was able to penetrate the total work system that it had created in an almost unprecedented manner—contractor monitoring became a fine art. The agency also struggled valiantly with the tricky question of providing incentives for excellence in R & D work. To retain its options in the face of the uncertainties it had to cope with, the agency employed a phased-project-planning system. Its massive engineering programs required a great deal of spontaneity, of political judgment and human wisdom. In fact, they taxed to the breaking point the managerial skills and conventional managerial wisdom derived from our more traditional industrial and bureaucratic pursuits. Even detractors must grant that this was an impressive effort.

☐ But compared to some of the socio-technical programs on the horizon, NASA had a simple life. NASA was a closed loop—it set its own schedule, designed its own hardware, and used the gear it designed. It was both sponsor and user. Space was no one's territory. The populace did not feel threatened by the program; on the whole the popular mood was supportive. NASA's actions had no element of the punitive or of sanctions: It was not taking away anything that previously existed; no property rights were violated.

☐ As one moves into the socio-technical area, this luxury disappears. The Department of Housing and Urban Development does not control housing. It encounters vested interests wherever it turns. An environmental-control agency will have complex relationships with industry, which will be a contractor, a user, and an element the agency is regulating! Missions in housing and environmental protection also have the flavor of construction and maintenance efforts, involving continuous upgrading and improvement. Many of these programs will have to deal with political complexities NASA never dreamed of—interfaces that are more readily identified than managed. Dramatic goals to mobilize public opinion and focus diverse professionals, such as landing on the moon, may be hard to come by. The day New York City gets fresh air may be of great significance to man on earth, but it does not have the same impact.

☐ As we noted at the outset, we are not saying that there are two types of large-scale systems: rational types such as AEC and space programs that brook no political nonsense and political types such as urban development which quickly become a morass of competitive and conflicting interests. All large development organizations constitute *political-business* systems.

☐ With that caveat expressed and understood, we would still insist that these large systems can be understood and managed. And indeed management and organizational skills will be many times more critical in these inherently unwieldy public-private systems than in more traditional organizations. What passed as inherited management principles, the rubrics of scientific management, and the primitive psychology of human relations will hardly suffice.

☐ As we have said many times before, our cultural proclivities toward optimism, delayed gratification, time and fiduciary responsibility—and awesome brute energy on the part of "driven" top managers—have saved many companies and government missions from the disasters to which their management "skills" entitled them. It is less likely that the future will be as beneficent.

☐ Regrettably management, as such, has little prestige among disciplines, but these challenges may change all that.[1] At least we hope they will. And surely NASA's managerial successes must be considered a big step forward in that direction. They proved that large, complex systems, both human *and* technical, can be managed.

[1] See Leonard Sayles, "Whatever Happened to Management or Why the Dull Stepchild? *Business Horizons,* vol. XIII, no. 2, April, 1970, pp. 25–34.

INDEX

71 72 73 74 7 6 5 4 3 2 1